S0-AFQ-594

FLORIDA STATE
UNIVERSITY LIBRARIES

APR · 4 1995'

TALLAHASSEE, FLORIDA

Moral Knowing in a
Hindu Sacred City

An Exploration of Mind,
Emotion, and Self

Moral Knowing in a
Hindu Sacred City

An Exploration of Mind,
Emotion, and Self

STEVEN M. PARISH

New York
Columbia University Press

DS
493.9
N4
P37
1994

Columbia University Press
New York   Chichester, West Sussex
Copyright (c) 1994 Columbia University Press
All rights reserved

Library of Congress Catalog-in-Publication Data

Parish, Steven M.
   Moral knowing in a Hindu sacred city : an exploration of mind,
emotion, and self / Steven M. Parish.
      p.   cm.
   Includes bibliographical references and index.
   ISBN 0-231-08438-2.—ISBN 0-231-08439-0 (pbk.)
   1. Newar (Nepalese people)—Psychology. 2. Moral development—
Nepal—Bhaktapur.   3. Newar (Nepalese people)—Social life and
customs.   4. Bhaktapur (Nepal)—Social life and customs.   I. Title.
DS493.9.N4P37   1994   94-366
155.8'495--dc20   CIP

Casebound editions of Columbia University Press books are
printed on permanent and durable acid-free paper.

Printed in the United States of America

c 10 9 8 7 6 5 4 3 2 1

p 10 9 8 7 6 5 4 3 2 1

To Alice Parish and
in memory of Lyle D. Parish

CONTENTS

ACKNOWLEDGMENTS

If it came down to a choice, I would rather know Newars than write books about them. Writing this book—a commitment of a number of years—reflects my enduring respect and affection for the people who welcomed me to Nepal, guided me, challenged me, patiently answered my questions, and nudged me in the right directions. It represents my effort to understand something of their cultural lives, and to let the world know about their culture.

In Nepal, the Research Division and Centre for Nepal and Asian Studies of Tribhuvan University gave essential support to my research. In the United States, the University of California, San Diego, the National Institute of Mental Health, and the National Science Foundation, provided research funds. Some of the ideas and perspectives incorporated in the book were first worked out in a year of writing supported by a Newcombe Fellowship.

I can name only a few of the many individuals who have helped me. Melford Spiro, Roy D'Andrade, and Aaron Cicourel provided crucial inspiration and guidance. I have Bob Levy to thank for introducing me to the Newars, for sharing his insights into their culture, and for much guidance and moral support over the years. I would also like to thank Edward Lee, Stan Stevens, F. G. Bailey, David Jordan, Gerald Berreman, Suburna Tuladhar, Barbara Brower, Don Pollock, Al Pach, Bruce Owens, Eugene Kumekawa,

Todd Lewis, Tom Barfield, Charles Lindholm, and Allan Hoben for acts of kindness and/or intellectual influences too varied to detail.

I want to thank three remarkable scholars, K. P. Malla, Ramapati Raj Sharma, and Gautum Vajracarya for their conviviality, practical assistance, and for many enjoyable and illuminating discussions about Newar culture. One of the pleasures of fieldwork was the opportunity to work with Krishna Rimal, whose energy and enthusiasm for ethnographic fieldwork in a complex urban setting greatly contributed to my understanding of Newar life. Rita Shakya conducted interviews with women and children for me, and has helped with translations. I have benefited from her many and complex insights into the moral and practical life of Newars.

Kedar Rajopadhyaya welcomed me to Bhaktapur, made me feel at home, and offered invaluable guidance and support. I am deeply grateful to him and to his family, and will never forget their kindness.

I wish to thank Dan Linger for many stimulating conversations in which he delivered the kind of intellectual provocations that shape a work in subtle but essential ways. Taft Chatham first posed the problem of "learning to see" in the Arizona desert many years ago, and sensitized me to the aesthetic qualities of cultural and religious life, which proved invaluable in a place that *is* a kind of work of religious art, among other things. Ernestine McHugh read the entire manuscript at an early stage, and reread some parts later. Her comments clarified my efforts and her encouragement sustained me in periods of doubt.

Finally, let me thank several anonymous reviewers for their intelligent and useful comments on the manuscript, and my editors at Columbia University Press, Gioia Stevens and Joan McQuary, for their help in guiding the book through the publication process.

Chapter 4 is based on an article published in *Ethos* 19, no. 3 (September 1991). Reprinted by permission of *Ethos*.

Moral Knowing in a
Hindu Sacred City

An Exploration of Mind,
Emotion, and Self

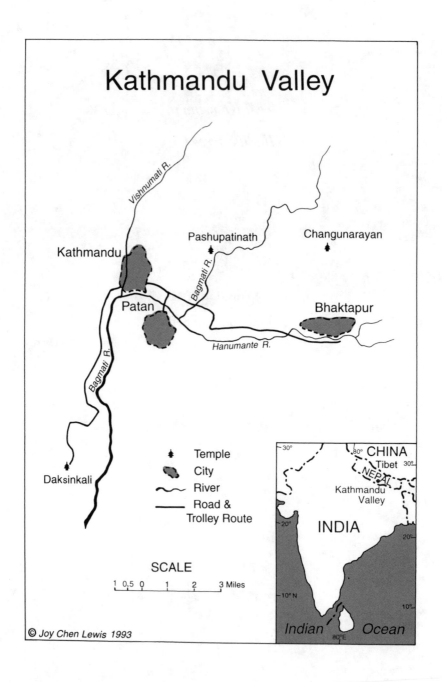

Kathmandu Valley

Vishnumati R.

Kathmandu

Pashupatinath

Changunarayan

Bagmati R.

Patan

Bhaktapur

Hanumante R.

Bagmati R.

Daksinkali

Temple
City
River
Road &
Trolley Route

SCALE

1 0.5 0   1   2   3 Miles

© Joy Chen Lewis 1993

30°

CHINA
Tibet 30°

NEPAL

Kathmandu
Valley

INDIA

20°

20°

10° N

10°

Indian 80°E Ocean

Introduction

This book explores the making of moral consciousness. In it, I examine the way people create themselves—as moral beings—by working through their relationship to cultural life.

This is an active process; and while it involves psychological development, it is ultimately a cultural process. The moral self, I maintain, develops out of a dialogue with culture. To understand this process of cultural development, I examine multiple, intertwined, unfolding discourses of world-fashioning and self-making among the Newar inhabitants of a Hindu sacred city in the Kathmandu Valley of Nepal, whose cultural life stands in radical contrast to Western culture.

This book is a study in cultural psychology.[1] Simply put, cultural psychology—an important emerging field—focuses on the way culture interacts with mind, self, and emotion. This book breaks new ground for cultural psychology by opening up inquiry into the cultural organization and development of the moral self and consciousness.[2]

As a work of cultural psychology by an anthropologist and ethnographer, this book challenges some of the central assumptions of the dominant tradition of research into moral development, as practiced by such seminal figures as Jean Piaget or Lawrence Kohlberg, and their many followers in academic psychology. This tradition has stressed the psychological underpinnings of moral consciousness, not the role of culture. Often, this research renders culture virtually invisible, and reduces moral life to a disembodied and *unlived* psychological system. In reality, it seems to me, the formation of moral consciousness is in crucial ways the result of a person's engagement with cultural meanings and practices — not simply the product of psychological development that takes place apart from culture, as this dominant tradition of research has assumed.

In this work, I hope to help restore some balance — not by attempting a formal refutation of Western moral theories, but by showing how culture-laden moral life and consciousness is. To do so, I will rely on some of the insights of contemporary culture theory, and will make use of an ethnographic approach to explore the way cultural life nurtures and produces moral consciousness. By showing how moral knowing grows out of cultural experience, this ethnographic project invites us to re-envision moral experience and development. We need to see how moral life is created and continuously regenerated in those self-defining and consciousness-creating dialogues with culture that form the core of any human identity.

I do not suggest we can or should replace psychological theories of moral development; I only propose that we need to displace them, to make room for cultural theories of moral consciousness. I do not doubt that what I view as a cultural process has psychological underpinnings. What I doubt is that the kind of conceptualizations found in Western psychology — itself partly a product of its culture — are enough to give us a full and dynamic understanding of moral life and consciousness. Whatever the psychological foundations of moral consciousness are, self and consciousness are always at some point pitched out into a cultural world, where they take cultural shape. Ultimately, in life, the moral self is a cultural self.[3]

Arguably, the dominance of the assumptions and methods of psychological research — predisposed to formalism and cognitivism, uninterested in the messy world of social life — has obscured the role of culture in the moral domain. If this dominant tradition reflects pervasive, powerful assumptions in Western culture, assumptions that may underpin the ways many Western thinkers define reality, then all the more reason to be wary, and to seek balance by developing cultural theories and ethnographic approaches.

Of course, if psychology has tended to eliminate culture as a factor shaping the development of human beings, anthropology has often excluded self from its discussions—as if experience, mind, and emotion had no place in cultural life. While this may represent a healthy rejection of some of the more questionable individualistic assumptions of much of Western thought, if taken too far I believe it ultimately distorts the reality of cultural life. These gaps—the place where "culture" has been erased from psychology, and "self" from cultural studies—make it difficult to understand the genesis of moral consciousness in the encounter of self and culture.

This, then, is a study of culture and self. More precisely, it explores the interface of culture and self within what Jurgen Habermas (1990) terms the "phenomenology of the moral," looking within the intricate "web of moral feelings and attitudes that is interwoven with the practice of everyday life" in a Hindu sacred city.

This choice of ethnographic setting—a Newar Hindu city in Nepal's Kathmandu Valley—requires us to enter the "phenomenology of the moral" of a radically different culture and society. By exploring the development and organization of moral consciousness in a non-Western society, I believe we can more clearly define the role of culture in the making of mind, self-understanding, and morality. Working exclusively in our own culture, we may mistake culture for nature, and view cultural constructions as natural developments. Ethnographic studies are important in part because they help break this habit of "naturalizing the cultural" (Ochs and Schiefflien 1984).

Thus, this book—although it presents rich material on a fascinating and important type of community—is intended as more than a contribution to the ethnography of South Asia and Nepal. It invites a rethinking of the organization and development of moral lives, selves, and consciousness everywhere.

The Setting—a Newar City

The town of Bhaktapur is the most traditional, and most Hindu, of three cities that came into being in the Kathmandu Valley before the creation of the modern nation-state of Nepal. Until 1769, it was a city-state, the walled capital of a small independent Hindu kingdom straddling ancient trade routes over the Himalayas to Tibet.

It was not north to Tibet, however, that Hindu Newars turned for cultural innovations, for inspirations about what life was meant to be, but south to India. The people of Bhaktapur—kings, priests, traders, scholars, artisans, farmers, untouchables—harvested the cultural developments of South Asia to create their own world.

Life in Bhaktapur today reflects this. Bhaktapur is a sacred Hindu city, and a Hindu moral community. As such, it has retained many of the most significant features of an important type of traditional Hindu community. In a decade or two, much of this will vanish forever. Some of the surface structure has already been rubbed off, and the deep structure is threatened.

Bhaktapur is still very much a place integrated by religion, by the evocative power and moral force of sacred symbols at play in human minds. The human world is poised in a religiously conceived universe; the city and self are both "known" in terms of religious symbols and meanings. Divinities protect the moral order of the city, and monitor the self. To build a house, or cook a meal, to give birth or die—to know who you are, and what life is about—are religious and moral acts. Almost every human action and role has a religious and moral context.

These juxtapositions and multiple frames for religion and morality are significant, I think. They express the coherence and pervasiveness of the religious and moral in Newar life. Elements of the Newar moral code are rendered almost holographically, redundantly, and recursively, so that one can recover meaningful chunks of the whole (the moral "code") from fragments of experience, pieces of ritual, stories, talk, children's games, ordinary and esoteric practices. Significant encounters with a range of moral values and concepts are thus inevitable and redundantly structured.

In a society where people are variously Hindus, Buddhists, high caste, untouchables, farmers, traders, craftsman, traditional and modern, male and female, there are many ways of knowing self and society. At the same time, however, there is a unifying ethos and world view, giving some coherence to this dynamic diversity— a problematic web of connecting threads of moral meaning which Newars, like anthropologists, seek to discover and trace. The world Newars have fashioned for themselves, the lives they live in this world, the social realities that form the hard surfaces and dangerous depths of these lives, the selves they imagine they are, all reflect or refract pervasive religious ideas and moral values. Thus,

Newar diversity is counterpoised by a striking, if problematic, unity.

This poses certain dilemmas for the ethnographer. My approach reflects the increasing recognition of diversity in contemporary ethnography and cultural theory—every culture contains multiple points of view, a range of different, often radically different, perspectives. Moreover, if we need to recognize the internal diversity of culture, we also need to recognize the internal dynamics of culture—"culture" often seems to be moving and shifting even as one attempts to "locate" it. This recognition in contemporary anthropology provides an important corrective to a tendency to depict other cultures as more unified and static than they are.

In light of this, I have incorporated the testimony of Newars of different castes and backgrounds, but I have also run up against the difficulties the project of representing the internal diversity and dynamics of cultural life entails. While I have not presented Newar culture as homogeneous, I have not been able to incorporate anything close to the full diversity of the culture into this work. No Buddhists speak here; few children; women testify less than men (since women were less willing to talk to me); there are Brahman and untouchable voices here, but not the full range of Brahman and untouchable voices. Like any anthropologist, I have selected a few voices, excluding others. Although unavoidable, I find this disquieting, not because there has been much recent academic talk about the problem, but because I wonder what those voices have to say.

I have also had to wrestle with the problem of how to incorporate diverse points of view without representing Newar culture as more divided and fragmented than (in my view) it actually is. While Newars have radically different perspectives on, and different life-worlds within, their society and culture, part of what Newars seek to experience and create, to construct and negotiate, as the subjects and agents of cultural lives, is precisely the unity of their culture. Their identities and voices are shaped by this, as well as by their diversity. Newar culture consists not just of disparate and disconnected voices, although there is much disconnection, but also of multiple voices trying to find each other, voices speaking out of diverse life-worlds, voices often subversive, seeking to define a separate reality, but just as often joining together in varied ways to attempt to define the common grounds of their lives.

Just as classical ethnography represented cultures as more uni-fied and static than they actually are, contemporary ethnography runs the risk of representing cultures as more fragmented than they are. While I endorse the rediscovery of the inner diversity of culture by contemporary anthropologists, I wonder whether the search for unity in traditional ethnography and the search for diversity in contemporary ethnography are not part of a larger Western discourse, like the classical oppositions of nature-culture and individualism-holism that have been central to Western reflec-tions on human existence and which seem to me ultimately inade-quate as the basis for interpretations of Newar life. In any event, we cannot deny Newars either their diversity or their unity. I have tried to let this work reflect both in some small way.

For description and interpretation of Newar culture, I refer the reader to the important work of Gerard Toffin (1984), and to the monumental study of Bhaktapur as a religious system and sym-bolic order by Robert Levy in collaboration with Kedar Raj Rajopadhyaya (1990).[4] With their ethnographic studies as a solid foundation, this work moves in new directions. It is the first per-son-centered study of the "inner world" of the Newars, of their minds, selves, and emotions. Most importantly, it attempts to shed some light on the mystery of how moral consciousness develops and takes shape in Newar Hindu culture.

Any choice of focus excludes much from consideration. I am keenly aware that cultural and psychological analysis can take us only so far in understanding a society and way of life. History, eco-nomics, and politics shape Newar life, too: war and conquest, pestilence and earthquakes, the stratagems and policies of Hindu states and kings, the location of trade routes and the fertility of the soil of the Kathmandu Valley have all contributed to making Newar culture and consciousness what it is. I will neglect much of this to pursue my focus.

I hope students of Newar social and religious life may be able to glean some insights from some of the material presented; but the book is a study of cultural psychology, not an investigation of social or religious institutions. I will describe certain aspects of Newar social life and religion, but only in relationship to my pri-mary focus.

One glaring omission requires explanation. I will not discuss the Newars' caste system, one of the most complex in South Asia. The

Newars' hierarchy of castes—with Brahmans at the apex, untouchables at the bottom, and a variety of castes in between— organizes much of life in Bhaktapur. Many of these castes have symbolic and religious roles, as well as economic and occupational ones. Caste life, however, poses certain critical problems for the Newar moral imagination. Since I examine these in other work (Parish n.d.), I will not consider them here. Rather, here I explore some of the fragile connections and constructed harmonies of Newar life from different points of view, but do not neglect the tensions of social and cultural life that generate much of Newar moral discourse. Both Brahmans and untouchables testify here, voicing moral visions that are similar in some important ways, and very different in others.

While, as a person-centered study, this is a first for the Newars, it is also one of a very few such studies in the literature on South Asia. I found inspiration in such rare and important books as Margaret Trawick's *Notes on Love in a Tamil Family* (1990) or Gananath Obeyesekere's *Medusa's Hair* (1981), although my focus is different. As far as I know, no other person-centered ethnography has focused on the dynamic interconnections of self, emotion, and relatedness as features of moral discourse in the context of a traditional Hindu city. Thus, I believe the material and interpretations presented here offer new and important insights into the minds and culture of the inhabitants of a Hindu city—and so into what it means to live and know Hinduism.

A Note on Organization and Method

While I hope anthropologists and specialists in South Asian culture will find something of value in this work, I also address it to a general educated and interdisciplinary audience. Thus, although this work has a highly technical base, I have tried to make it accessible to a range of readers. I have drawn on the insights and perspectives of linguistic theory, cognitive anthropology, psychological anthropology, developmental psychology, and moral philosophy, among other fields, but I have tried to incorporate the insights of these fields into the narrative flow of the ethnography. Also, I have tried to keep in mind the needs of readers who are not specialists, by consigning some discussion to endnotes, and by omitting other material a specialist reader might expect to find here.

I have two basic reasons for risking the justifiable annoyance of specialists. First, technical works in moral studies, like technical works in South Asian studies, can seem obscure and impenetrable to readers outside those fields. Such studies have their essential place. I believe, however, that interdisciplinary dialogues are required to achieve a deep understanding of the nature and varieties of human moral life, and I have tried to keep this potential audience in mind. Second, I wish to keep the focus on what Newars have to say. Engaging in the lengthy technical discussions many points deserve would distract from the account of Newar culture and self I am presenting.

This account is the product of fieldwork, of a kind of long conversation with Newars. Anthropologists are always engaged in conversations; the heart of our discipline is ethnography, which involves encounters and conversations with others— Newars, Tamils, Navahos, Javanese—who help us know what we know. In part, then, this work is a harvest of voices. It documents what some Newars say about some aspects of their cultural world and experience to an interlocutor from another culture. I have incorporated their testimony in the form of extensive quotes.

To preserve privacy, I have disguised identities and used pseudonyms. In quoting Newars, I have edited out some repetitions and many digressions for the sake of brevity and ease of reading. My questions to Newar subjects are in parentheses, while explanations, comments, clarifications, and bridges are in brackets. I have, of course, struggled to retain as much as possible of their meaning, although something is always lost or altered in transcription and translation.

As you will see, many Newars are highly articulate and reflective about their culture. Indeed, conversing about culture and values is a practice that many Newars are familiar with; they come to define interviews and conversations with the ethnographer in terms of their own interpretive practices and communicative forms (Briggs 1986). While I believe people everywhere have interpretive powers, and should be seen as society-interpreting, culture-interpreting, and self-interpreting agents, talking about what they know may not be a cultural practice, a communicative skill needed in their daily lives. Newars can often put what they know into words. Their testimony shows how they weave moral meaning into a personal world view, and use such meaning to relate themselves to tradition, to others, to social life.

Despite the limits of any interview methodology, I believe what Newars had to say in these person-centered, free-ranging, discovery oriented interviews reveals much about how they experience and evaluate cultural life. Naturally, I supplemented these person-centered "research conversations" with standard ethnographic interviewing and observation, which guided what I explored in my more in-depth interviews and provided necessary context.

Women as well as men were interviewed in the course of fieldwork, but my data, and my insights, into the lives and experience of women are more limited than I would like. This is partly because of local norms; the ability of a foreign, male, unmarried ethnographer to talk freely with Newar women was somewhat restricted. My interviews with women were mostly carried out with the help of an assistant, and this imposed some constraints. Moreover, there were female domestic spaces that I could not enter. At the same time, Newars—men and women—defined me in male terms, as having a "male self," and interacted with me in ways that tended to socialize me into male perspectives; for example, in the way they addressed jokes to me, or made them at my expense, mocking and teasing me, gender was often subtly defined. Insights into Newar life came along with this, but the gender emphasis in my interactions means there is a greater depth and thickness in my data on male understandings, lives, and selves. In my effort to understand my material, I have gone over much of it with Rita Shakya, a Kathmandu Newar. She also helped me conduct some interviews with women. Her insights into women's experience have helped provide some balance.

In chapter 1 I describe Bhaktapur and introduce key aspects of Newar life, covering much of the kind of material presented in the "setting" chapters of traditional ethnographies. This discussion will supply the reader (and especially the reader without any special knowledge of Nepal or India or anthropology) with the background needed to read later chapters. I hope the chapter will also, in a small way, bring Bhaktapur to life.

Chapter 2 juxtaposes an exploration of concepts of society and person with an exploration of key moral concepts, showing how they come together to fashion a moral order—but not precisely the same moral order, or world, for all Newars.

In chapter 3 I explore the way Newar concepts of the person and relatedness help shape empathy and moral responsiveness in the Newar family. I also present an alternative way of viewing the relationship of self and society in South Asian life, modifying the idea of "holism" that has been used to characterize South Asian culture. As often used, the construct of holism leaves no room for the study of the individual self, since it defines the person as encompassed in relationships in such a way that concepts of the individual have no cultural meaning or reality—only group life has value. While I, too, claim that social embeddedness is one of the key values of traditional South Asian life, I believe our use of the construct of holism needs to be modified to make room for the analysis of a cultural "self."

In chapter 4 I talk about Newar concepts of mind, self, and emotion, which constitute what I term "the sacred mind." The title is ironic; it blurs genres kept apart in Western thought. For Newars, however, the "inner world" has a religious essence; for them, mind, self, and emotion are embedded in a religious ethos. While I will be concerned with aspects of emotional experience in almost every chapter, here I focus on emotions the Newars view as central to moral existence, emotion that defines what it means to be a moral person for them. Just as cultures have "key symbols" (Ortner 1973), they also have "key emotions" that relate self to social and cultural life in crucial ways.

In chapter 5 I also concentrate on the cultural production of moral consciousness, but in the context of ritual rather than of ethnopsychology per se. The chapter suggests how certain life cycle rituals mediate the development of the moral self.

My postscript contains some reflections on the relationship of culture and moral consciousness.

Thinking moral thoughts, making moral judgments, knowing self and world in moral ways—as the chapters of this book strongly suggest, these are not merely a matter of passively absorbing culture or of psychological development alone, but rather a product of redundant organized engagement with cultural forms, which range from family structure, to key emotions and ethnopsychology, to mythology and ritual. This engagement is reflexively meaningful—it defines who people are, and what their lives mean—and dynamic. In some ways, these consciousness-creating dialogues with culture stand at the heart of self-making and wold-fashioning. They produce moral selves and moral worlds. What Newars are and what they know *as moral beings* is a result of the way they actively experience and fashion themselves as cultural beings.

Part One

A Hindu City and

Its Sacred and

Moral Order

CHAPTER ONE

Learning to See a Sacred City

At the end of summer, the children of Bhaktapur fly kites in the sky above the city. The winds are ideal, with the passing of summer's monsoon rains—the sky a perfect blue emptiness.

To fly their kites, the children and young men of the city climb onto the housetops, three or four stories above the streets. From there, they send dozens of kites, made of bright red, blue, and yellow paper, soaring into the sky. There the kites do battle, as each kite flyer strives to cut the strings of other kites.

When a kite is cut loose, it glides down toward the ground, and can meet one of several fates. Groups of shouting boys chase the dangling strings of loose kites through the streets. Sometimes they catch one before it wafts away over the houses, or lands on the roof of a house or the pagoda roof of a temple devoted to the Lord Shiva, or the Lord Vishnu, or the Goddess in one of her many forms. The winds may take some out of the city altogether, out into the fields, across the river, over the cremation grounds.

Tradition prescribes the season for flying kites. It can rain heavily during and after the harvest, when people want to dry their rice in the autumn sun. Newars say flying kites at this time of year tells the gods not to send more rain.

Nowadays, some children fly kites earlier in the year, before the autumn festival; doing so can be seen as a sin, of sorts, and some of the older people disapprove, saying these are truly children of the

Kali Yuga, the last age, the era of the cosmic cycle when virtue disappears.

Not every Newar thinks so, of course, and most are no doubt more urgently concerned about other matters. Still, the connection forged between flying kites and the Kali Yuga signifies something about the way Newars think and feel. It resonates with a way of knowing and relating to the world as they imagine it to be, a world of fragile, easily disordered, relationships among people, and between gods and human beings.

It thus represents one of the ways Newars have of conveying to themselves their sense of the rightful order of things. Kite-flying, like almost everything else, reflects this order, or should. This "should" gets us the grumbling about the children of the Kali Yuga, and is, I suspect, primarily felt; at root, it has to do with one of the "structures of feeling" of the Newar life-world.[1]

Such feeling is mediated by cultural beliefs, and can be justified in terms of beliefs, if one has to have a rationale for disapproving: you should fly kites only at certain times of the year, so that you will not disrupt the world's order and bring harm to the community by sending the wrong signal to the gods, bringing on the wrong kind of weather. The rains might stop too soon, during the growing season, when the growing rice needed water, and this would be a terrible thing. Yet I suspect that what matters most is not what they believe (about kite-flying, or equivalent matters) but what they feel about order-in-life. This sense of order is not to be ignored or mocked.

Thus, while I am not sure all Newars see kite-flying in moral and cosmic terms, I am convinced it represents a rather common way of feeling, a basic attitude in Newar culture. If this attitude does not find expression here, it will find expression elsewhere. What matters for Newars is the emotional affirmation of the sanctity of tradition, the felt perception of order in the pattern of life, the sense of an obligatory enacted pattern followed year after year by human generation after generation. When these kinds of feelings attach to it, kite-flying stands for the moral order itself—like many other things. Having acquired such symbolic meaning, flying kites at the proper time of year, or grumbling about children who do not, provides an opportunity for some to polish a sense of order and tradition, to work it still deeper into consciousness.

Other Newars will find other ways of expressing their sense of what must be, of the order of life and world.

I did not see any of this at first. We see what we know, making it hard for us to see what others see. We impose our concepts on their world, observing their world from within our own "horizon of expectations," as Karl Popper put it, only slowly breaking through to some approximation of their way of seeing, of knowing. As a naive observer in Bhaktapur, I saw children flying kites from rooftops, not children flying kites in harmony with the cosmos, not children flying kites in the Kali Yuga, not children flying kites at the time of year ordained for flying kites. I thought the winds were good, and that it was fun; these are true perceptions as far as they go (Newars fly, and fight, kites with great zest). Kite-flying was only an event for me, something people did, not a way of saying something about one's relationship to the world, not a signifying practice weaving moral meaning and emotion into a life-world— and so I was unable to make the synthetic, symbolic connection between the activity I saw and the sense of order it reflected.

I had to learn to see the city. Of course, I could see what was there—the houses, the temples, the people going about their business—but I could not see this world as Newars saw it. I could see what happened, the flow of events, but I could not see what others saw in it, what it was for them. As an outsider, an alien from a different cultural world, I did not see things in cultural terms; I was blind to much of the significance of what happened before my eyes. I saw a city, but not the city Newars lived in. They lived in a city invisible to me, a city built, not of bricks, but of meanings, a city known and experienced in ways I had no way of apprehending.

When I first arrived in Bhaktapur, the streets were a labyrinth, a new world; it was easy to get lost in them. Doing so was exhilarating. Wandering at random, following some small lane, perhaps no more than six or seven feet wide, I would suddenly come across a shrine, or people engaged in some ritual performance, offering flowers or making blood sacrifices to deities. I had no insight into the significance of any of this, although it made a deep impression on me.

There were many examples of this problem of sight without insight: on the street, I see a man. He walks purposefully by, carrying a goat's head in a basket—why? What does it mean? On

another day, early in the morning, a woman—one of my neighbors—places flowers on a stone standing on a street corner. In the
night, processions march by playing trumpets, beating on drums.
Early in the morning, a man walks briskly through the fog chanting
the names of gods; he pauses in front of the temple in front of the
house I rented, and turns in place three times. I did not know why,
even though I saw these were religious acts; but—what is a religious act? What meaning does it have?

I had to find out something about the meaning and context of
these acts. The man with the head of the goat has sacrificed to his
lineage god, and the parts of the goat-head will be divided among
senior members of the lineage; the stone is a god; the nighttime
processions were connected with specific cults and festivals.
Knowing this much helps, but poses other questions. What does it
mean to have a lineage god? What is the cultural and personal
meaning of divinity? How is any of this experienced? What consciousness accompanies and animates these concepts and practices?

Groping for meaning with which to see and understand, I
missed much that was meaningful, as I sought moorings. Gradual-
ly, with much help from Newar friends and teachers, I acquired a
certain sense of how Newars perceive their cultural world, and
began to grasp, in a limited way, something of their basic concepts
of reality. In a phrase Spiro (1984) adopts from Bertrand Russell,
I became "acquainted" with their world, with their ideas, with
some of their ways of seeing things.[2]

Glimpses of the City

If you approach Bhaktapur on foot from the south, from the modern highway that skirts Bhaktapur as it goes on to Tibet, you can
see clearly how the city sits on a hill above the river. It has a skyline of multistory houses, with the pagoda roofs of a tall five-story
temple rising above the roof line of the city's houses. In the foreground are fields of rice or wheat. You might see the smoke of a
funeral fire from a cremation ground on the banks of the river.
Beyond the city, one can see the snow-capped peaks of the
Himalayas.

If you were to stand there, in the fields on the edge of the city,
pausing to stare up at the skyline, outside the city but about to

enter it, you might well seek to orient yourself by asking, what kind of place is this? What kind of place, what kind of world, have Newars built for themselves in Bhaktapur, out of bricks and out of meanings?

For the most part Newars turn not outward, toward wilderness and mountains, but inward into the intricate and self-absorbing life of the city, to find meaning, splendor, images of transcendence. The Newars pull their psychological horizons in close to them, in close to the boundaries of the city, confronting nature just beyond the borders of their city. Within these horizons, they have exercised a rich imagination in art and ritual, in city festivals and social life, and created a vast, involuted cultural universe, weaving together religious symbolism and moral ideas from a variety of South Asian sources to imagine their world into vibrant, compelling existence. It is this, more than anything, that defines Bhaktapur.

A city—even a small, sacred city—poses special problems of method and interpretation. The traditional field sites of anthropologists have often been small in scale—a small mountain village, perhaps, or a cluster of grass huts surrounded by gardens in a clearing in the forest. Bhaktapur is large and complex by these standards. As I wandered through the maze of Bhaktapur's streets wondering what was going on behind the brick walls of the houses, I sometimes wished I had chosen to work in a smaller place, a place where almost everything was done in plain view, and where you could hear almost everything else through the thin grass walls of the huts. Bhaktapur does not have this kind of transparency. Perhaps to think any community really does is wishful thinking.

In Bhaktapur, it was frustrating to find that even simple tasks were hard to accomplish because of the relative complexity of the place. What I wanted to understand had a tendency to recede, to vanish around a corner, to disappear in the complexity of the city, only to reemerge elsewhere, with new questions attached. Almost nothing was transparent.

I could not even sit down on a log and make a proper sketch map of the community. Over time, I developed a "mental map" of the city, a map that was more detailed for the parts of the city I used most. Here we will have to make do with a similar mental map, a kite's eye view of the city as it was when I was there, given in narrative form.

First, the city covers a roughly elliptical area about a mile long and half a mile wide. Except for temples, most buildings are not free-standing, but joined in rows or quadrangles. Some 40,000 people live in Bhaktapur, so although the city is small in area, the population density is high. Excluding undeveloped open areas on its outskirts, Levy (1990: 58) estimates the population density for the built-up residential area of the city as some 117,000 people per square mile. As he notes, despite this concentration of people into a very small area, Bhaktapur does not appear crowded, except during festivals.[3]

Even more remarkable, there is open space in the city. There are three large open squares that either contain or are bounded by monumental temples. Smaller squares are found in the neighborhoods. There are no parks, no trees, no gardens or "green space" in public spaces inside the city. One of the major squares contains a palace complex, once home to the king of an independent city-state of Bhaktapur; the palace has courtyards, which house an important temple to the goddess Taleju, the protective goddess of the kings, and one of the most important goddesses for the entire city.[4] This is one of the symbolic centers of the city.

Since groups of several houses typically enclose open courtyards, the city has a porous texture, a loosely celled pattern. The side streets are narrow and winding, opening into temple squares, at times passing under houses, cutting through courtyards. These streets often cross at odd angles—there is nothing of the rectilinear, of right angles and crisscross grids about Bhaktapur. It does not have the blocks and straight lines of a modern city. If houses line streets in Western cities, streets in Bhaktapur are the spaces between buildings. They are footpaths and alleys—not anything like the assertive avenues or expansive boulevards that give linear direction and shape to a Paris or Los Angeles.

The main street runs roughly east and west, in a gently meandering course that takes it through two of the main temple squares, but bypasses the old royal palace square. Shops line the main street for much of its length, forming a bazaar. The city itself is an elongated, bent oval, longest on its east-west axis; some Newars compare its shape to the conch shell of the god Vishnu.

The houses of Bhaktapur are typically four stories tall, and are built of brick. The roofs of older houses are made of tile, but new tin-roofs are replacing these in many cases; the modern tin roofs glint sharply in the sun, in contrast to the muted red-brown tone of brick and tile. On the whole, the view is reminiscent of parts of some European and Mediterranean brick-built cities that originated before the industrial revolution—the kinds of cities and towns that are sometimes termed "organic" rather than "planned."

This explains the mazelike quality of Bhaktapur's streets. The city was not built to a master plan, the product of a planner's controlling vision, with a grid of streets expressing an overall design. The city grew into its present form, as an expression of the needs and self-images of a community. While shaped in some cases by royal will and priestly conception, Bhaktapur is not the city of an imperial state, or the product of modern bureaucratic rationality, where agents of the state could and would simply dictate urban form, as if they were simply drawing lines in the sand. Like the people of Bhaktapur today, the kings and priests of Bhaktapur past were content for the most part to act "as if" the actual space of Bhaktapur conformed to the ideal space of their religious conceptions. The city they imagined was a sacred, a moral, order.

During festivals, the city itself is involved in religious action, just as if it were a temple, a sacred space with a liturgy, shaped by symbolic forms. In fact, Newar urban space is sacred: not only is the city the setting for collective ritual and public worship, but urban space and form are structured and used in ways that help to evoke religious moods.

The City as Mandala

One means urban space is imagined as, and made, sacred is through the placement of systems of shrines (Gutschow and Kolver 1975), such as the shrines of the eight protective goddesses, the Astamatrka, that encircle Bhaktapur. Most of these shrines on the edge of the city are (or once were) open to the sky. Some of them have groves of trees around them; there are no trees inside the city, which is a maze of brick houses and brick streets, a built world. These goddess shrines mark, not just the edge of the city, but the edge of the moral order. Joined in a web of relationships to sacred sites inside the city, the goddess shrines on the edge of the city make Bhaktapur a mandala, a sacred circle, in touch with the divine at the center and protected by the goddesses against dangerous, chaotic, demonic forces outside the city, thus keeping humans safe from ghosts, diseases, earthquakes, invasions, and other calamities.

In these protective shrines on the city perimeter, the goddesses are worshiped in the form of natural stones. The shrines are attended by low-caste people, who keep portions of the offerings of food and money made to the goddesses. Inside the city, there is another set of shrines, one for each of the goddesses, called "godhouses." There, these Tantric goddesses are given form in metal and wood, and high-caste priests conduct rites for them, as they do for the great Hindu gods. These images are portable, and are brought out in palanquins to celebrate certain city festivals. The contrasting features of the two types of shrines—natural stone vs. metal statue, low-caste vs. high-caste attendants, fixed vs. portable images of the goddesses—mark a transition from natural to built environment, from "nature" culturally conceived to "culture" forming as a natural, but fragile, order. Hierarchy, centrality, and the fluid multiplicity of the sacred are symbolized by these differences, as is the difference between chaos and danger (outside the city) and a moral order (within the city).[5]

Other Boundaries

The city was walled in the medieval era, and these walls were used for defensive purposes, but they have long since vanished (Slusser 1982). Only the idea of Bhaktapur as a bounded order, set off from the outside, remains—and this "sense of separation," of "order" created within defended boundaries is quite important in Newar religion, as Robert Levy (1990) has shown. There is a gate at the Western entrance of the main street, but the town has spread beyond it.

Fertile fields surround the city. Rice is grown in the spring and summer, and wheat in the winter. These grains predominate in the encircling fields, but there are also patches devoted to tomatoes, potatoes, hot peppers, and other horticultural crops. The transition from city to field is fairly sharp; you know clearly when you are "in" the city, and when you are "outside" of it.[6]

To me, the fields outside the city always looked remarkably orderly and tranquil, gardenlike; I saw them as "nature" ordered and domesticated, unlike the mountains, deserts, and wilderness of my own culture's vision of raw, wild, pristine nature, untouched by human hands. For Newars, however, the fields are in some ways "wild" places. In their experience, "nature" is not totally under control; it can be unpredictable and chaotic. Here, outside the city, in the fields, Newars are directly dependent on the forces of nature, on weather, on the willingness of plants to grow, and on the fertility of the soil. The harvest, and life itself, depend on being able to control these forces, to bring order to nature. But their ability to do so is always uncertain; the unpredictable forces of nature always threaten to break loose and spin out of control. Too much or too little rain can fall; it can come at the wrong time of year; seed may not sprout; blight can spread through the growing plants; rot can set in; plants may be stunted; the harvest can be poor. This generates a sense of vulnerability, a fear of the disordering potential of nature, that is dealt with in various ways in the city's religion.

Irrigated rice agriculture supports Bhaktapur's economy. A caste system—one of the most complex in South Asia—organizes much of economic life. In addition to the farming castes, who make up the majority of the population, there are a variety of nonagricultural specialists: Brahmans, astrologers, merchants, Aryuvedic physicians, Tantric priests, shopkeepers, potters, untouchables, and others. Many of these groups have symbolic roles in the life of the city (Levy 1990). Ensembles of caste specialists are involved in the elaborate annual cycle of citywide festivals, and have roles in domestic and temple rites.

There is some tendency for different castes to cluster in different areas of the city, with higher castes more likely to be found closer to the old palace and other central locations, and lower castes found in more peripheral areas (Gutschow and Kolver 1975). The untouchable Pore, or sweeper, caste lives in a separate area conceived of as "outside the city."

The place where the untouchables live outside the city is near one of three cremations grounds for Bhaktapur, on the banks of the Hanumante River. The river flows past Bhaktapur on the south, running roughly east to west, so the city is to the "right" of the river as it flows past the city. The cremation ground is across the river, on the "left," making the river a boundary between the city and death.[7] Following traditional paths (Gutschow and Kolver 1975), funeral processions will come out of the city, down to the river, and (in this case) across a bridge to the burning grounds on the far side. The funeral procession proceeds in ways that echo processions that take a god to install it in a temple, and the corpse is "likened to the god and the afterworld to the temple" (Levy 1990: 679). The river is conceived of religiously as the sacred Ganges and receives the ashes of the dead, as they make their ultimate journey out of the city.

One of the older Newars I spoke with had vivid memories of the smoke from the funeral pyres of the dead during epidemics in his childhood. He had almost died, he told me, of cholera as a child. He talked of the disease as a kind of deity or demon who lived among the Pore untouchables—although this may have simply been a convenient metaphor—and feels he was saved by one of the goddesses of the city, who appeared to him in a dream vision. He acknowledged the fear and dread of death, but, looking back, also described a kind of "terrible beauty"—as W. B. Yeats said of another world of death—in the funeral processions, in the way women wailed in the streets on their way to the homes of the dead, clutching each other for support, and in the smoke of the cremation fires rising above the city.

Bhaktapur as a Hindu Sacred City

As all this suggests, looked at from one point of view Bhaktapur as a city is a religious system (Levy 1990). The city's Hinduism is complex and all-encompassing, and yet intimate—playing a role in organizing both the city as a whole and the minute details of life and death. Indeed, phrases from Clifford Geertz's (1973: 90) famous definition of religion work just as well to define Bhaktapur; the city is a community of symbols that shape selves, acting "to establish powerful, pervasive, and long-lasting moods and motivations" in its inhabitants "by formulating conceptions of a general order of existence"—which may be understood in different ways by different actors. With the help of symbolic forms and ritual enactments, certain religious concepts of reality and existence come to possess "such an aura of factuality that the moods and motivations seem uniquely realistic" to Bhaktapur's citizens, even when experienced through the prism of caste and class differences, by actors positioned in society in different ways.

Bhaktapur is thus one kind of religious city, a city of the sacred, a city constituted by the action of sacred symbols, a city known, experienced, and organized in terms of Hindu belief and practice. It is, even today, a city that achieves a fragile integration through ritual action and religious consciousness, rather than by having secular laws applied by an administrative bureaucracy—the political structure was, until recently, deeply embedded in religion. Bhaktapur is not a sacred city in the sense of being a major pilgrimage site, although pilgrims do come; nor is it an ecclesiastical city, the center of an institutionalized religion, despite the importance of city wide religious festivals (much of it emanating from, organized by, or associated with, the Taleju temple in the palace complex). Bhaktapur is sacred in the sense that religion permeates the texture of life, and organizes, frames, and illuminates the conditions of human existence for Newars.

Much of this remains. The persistence of some of the city's integrating religious and communal traditions may, in part, reflect the way Bhaktapur was long ignored by the wider society. In any event, when I was there, Bhaktapur was still very much a traditional Hindu city of a special kind, as Robert Levy has shown in his magnificent study (1990) of the religious life of the city. Levy's work provides one of the necessary answers to the question of what kind of place Bhaktapur is, of how it is "imagined."

In later chapters, I will explore some aspects of religion in terms of moral consciousness. Here I can offer only a few tantalizing glimpses of Bhaktapur as a sacred city, but I think they will give a sense of the way religion encompasses virtually all aspects of life there—including moral awareness. The debt I owe Robert Levy (1990) and his collaborator, Kedar Rajopadhyaya, will be evident.

The City of the Goddess

Let me begin in autumn, with myth coming to life in the city beneath the kites in the sky. At this time, Newars celebrate the festival of Mohani, one of the great sacred moments of the Newar religious year. The people of Bhaktapur enact a sacred myth within the city—in their temples, on their streets, in their homes, in

FIGURE 2 Bhagavati, the form of the Goddess worshiped in the festival of Mohani, stepping on the head of a water buffalo. Photo by Todd Lewis.

their hearts—and on the edge of the city. In this enactment, they join in a cosmic battle, and harvest the power of the sacred. They affirm the Goddess Devi—known by many names and worshiped in many forms, each possessing a specific identity and special meaning for Newars—as the power of life, and as the power of death acting to protect life.

The festival of Mohani celebrates the victory of Durga, the Warrior Goddess, or Bhagavati as she is also known in Bhaktapur, over Mahisasura, a Demon. In the myth that tells the story of her battle and victory, Bhagavati is born from the heat and light of the other gods, who had been unable to defeat the Demon. In fear and anger, they combined their energies, forming the Goddess, giving her their powers and weapons.

The Devi Mahatmya, an important religious text read in Bhaktapur before and during Mohani, describes the creation of the Goddess and the battle that ensues. The heat and light from the ordinary gods became "unified in one." Then the "matchless light born from the bodies of all gods . . . turned into a Woman enveloping the three worlds by her luster." Her body joins together parts of the bodies of other gods; she is an encompassing whole. "Her face was produced from the light of Shiva, her hair from that of

FIGURE 3 Statue of Bhagavati with eighteen arms driving a spear into the Demon Mahisasura.

Yama, her arms from the luster of Visnu, her breasts from that of the Moon . . . her thighs and legs from that of Varuna."⁸ The text goes on to tell of how, riding her vehicle, a lion, to battle, she slays the Demon, who has assumed the form of a water buffalo. The blood of the Demon's army flowed "like a mighty river in the field of battle."

Since myth, if fully experienced, suspends ordinary time and actuality, and identifies self with sacred beings and events, the Newars of Bhaktapur, in a sense, stand with Bhagavati on the battlefield, even become part of her, like the gods. Myth and ritual transport them to the field of battle. Identified with her, they slay the Demon with her, as they sacrifice water buffalo in the main temple of the city and elsewhere. They share in her victory. As a consequence of this victory (their victory, for they participated through ritual), the order and peace of the universe are restored, becoming suddenly palpably present, like silence after battle — "the sun shone with perfect brilliance; the sacred fire burnt in a tranquil manner; and the strange sounds that had filled the quarters of space also disappeared."⁹

In a Newar folk painting of Bhagavati I keep on my wall, she appears with a halo of orange flame around her. Her face and arms

FIGURE 4 Image of the Goddess on the Golden Gate, the entrance to the Taleju temple.

are painted red. She is depicted with eighteen arms, and one hand holds a sword above her head. She is making mystical gestures with the hands of two of her arms that she has raised in front of her. Another plunges a spear into the chest of a figure that is half-human, half-buffalo, representing Mahisasura, the Demon who took the form of a Buffalo during the war with the gods. Bhagavati is called the "Slayer of Mahisasura." Even as the spear plunges into him, he is attempting to draw a sword from a scabbard. A buffalo head lies near him, at Bhagavati's feet. Bhagavati's vehicle is a lion, and in the painting a lion stands with her, facing, and snarling at, the Demon. Bhagavati's face in the painting is calm.

The buffalo head lying at Bhagavati's feet reminds me of the buffalo heads I saw lying on the street after the sacrifices of Mohani. I imagine it does so for some Newars, too—the "rivers of blood" that flow in Bhaktapur's streets during Mohani commemorate the "mighty rivers" of blood she spills in battle, and I believe Newars are invited by their culture to implicitly identify with Bhagavati as they cut the throats of sacrificial buffalo. Sacred symbols are, in part, symbols of self. Myth and ritual and art resonate with

FIGURE 5 Goddess on the supporting strut of a temple. Photo by Todd Lewis.

each other, enriching and heightening the consciousness of religious belief and practice.

There is, of course, more to the rites of Mohani than animal sacrifice. At the beginning of Mohani—which lasts for ten days—sand or soil from riverbeds or streams thought to have special, sacred power is gathered and brought home. The soil is taken to a room designated for the worship of Bhagavati and spread out on the floor. Barley grains are planted in it; when they sprout, they will be worshiped. They are interpreted as representing Bhagavati's sword. Early in my stay, one of my informants spent quite a bit of energy getting me to see the barley shoots as swordlike—the image now seems natural.

A metal or clay pot, with an image of Bhagavati as the Demon-Slayer painted on it, is also brought to the room. Bhagavati is "present" in the room in the form of the pot, in which, as Newars say, she has been "established." She will be worshiped in this form. A painting on paper (such as the one just described), which will receive blood sacrifices, and other images and symbols of the Goddess may be brought in later. In some households, a sword will be kept in the room, continuing the warrior imagery.

The barley shoots seem to link two aspects of the Goddess. Interpreted as swords, they refer to the ultimate Goddess in her manifest form as Bhagavati the Warrior Goddess who spills rivers of blood—protecting the world with the power of death. This power is also symbolized by animal sacrifice.

The imagery of the sprouting barley grains, of the young shoots they become in the course of the festival, suggest the mystery of life and regeneration, of the fertility of soil and seed—deep, vital mysteries in a community linked as closely to soil and field as Bhaktapur. The young shoots, as symbols of fertility and regeneration, reveal the life-giving creative power of the Goddess in her ultimate form.

Levy (1990) sums up the meaning of Mohani by pointing out how the Goddess as creator of the universe and as the giver of life "presides over the earth and grain and is represented in the plants themselves as they develop." Yet the Goddess who makes life possible "is a warrior goddess," the slayer of Mahisasura, "the bloody warrior goddess of the Devi Mahatmya." In this fusion, a nexus of meanings—relating to organic growth and death, power and nurturance, the chaos of force and the order of life—is created, in which "the success of the agricultural cycle, the generative powers of earth, seed, and weather are . . . allied with the forces of the warrior, *kṣatra*, in the battle against the forces of disorder" (1990: 560).

An important aspect of this festival is the fact that its rites are performed in every household, and also in the Tantric temples and, most importantly, in the Taleju temple (Levy 1990: 561). I will return to this point later, after describing more of the religious life of the city.

During Mohani, the people of Bhaktapur visit each of the protective goddess shrines around the edge of the city, and the one in the center; they go to one each day, clockwise around the city, until they return a second time to the shrine visited on the first day. Men go in musical groups, with drums and cymbals, women take offerings, at night children carry paper lanterns on poles. The press of people is impressive, each person eager to make an offering at the shrines.

The city takes on a special life at this time. There is a sense of release from the ordinary, and the dominant religious attitude seems to be a determination to engage and draw on the power of the sacred. For in the Newar view of things, life requires the sacred; it must be brought into an essential relationship to life. Gods and goddesses protect the human moral order, protect people from danger, and can release people from suffering. The autumn festival is a time for renewing and deepening contact with the sacred: the people of the city immerse themselves in religious action, seeking the blessings and protection of the gods and goddesses — and join with them in the victory over the forces of disorder.

The most visible sign of this is the sacrifice of large numbers of animals. Some sacrifices are secret, but others occur in public, in the streets and squares of the city, where attentive crowds of children and adults gather to watch the animals be killed. In one set of sacrifices, sponsored by the state, soldiers chop off the heads of goats and water buffalo with a single stroke of a large, heavy *khukuri*, the curved knife of Nepal. The headless bodies are then dragged in a circle around the sacrificial area, leaving a trail of blood; sand is thrown on the blood to soak it up. I have seen old Newar men try to rush in past the line of police guarding the event, to gather up the blood-soaked sand in their hands; the police, exasperated by this, strike at them with their sticks. The old men

FIGURE 6 Preparation for animal sacrifice to a bus adorned with flowers and ribbons. Such sacrifices are made to a variety of potentially dangerous objects, such as knives and guns, as well as to cars, motorcycles, and trucks. Newars sometimes explain this practive by saying that Bhagavati/Durga is "hungry for blood" and might "possess" dangerous objects such as cars, causing accidents that injure or kill people to satisfy her hunger if blood sacrifices are not made. By sacrificing, people gain her protection from accidents throughout the year.

FIGURE 7, 8, 9 The throat of the animal is slit and blood spatters on the bus and on the tools in front of the bus. Note the facial expressions of the children.

seemed not to mind too much, as long as they got their handful of sand.

In the sacrifices Newars perform for themselves, the throats of goats and water buffalo are slit; the animal is held so that its blood, pumped by its still beating heart, spurts on whatever is being worshipped or consecrated; the animal dies, and is dropped to the ground, where more blood seeps out, forming dark red pools on the street.[10] Crowds of onlookers gather to observe these sacrifices here and there in the squares and byways of the city, then break up and scatter when the rite is finished. As they move away, you can see the severed heads of goats lying a little apart from their bodies in puddles of blood, lying still and blind on the brick pavement. There is something mysterious and disturbing about this to an outsider — and perhaps to Newars as well.

The felt response to what the eyes encounter is part of the scene; it shapes the experience, fusing sensibility to perception. Cultural and personal meanings influence this. One Newar told me that he once felt distressed, nauseated, at seeing animals killed at a temple, so he left without worshiping. He said the god caused him to feel and do this, because he did not believe strongly enough. The scene of animals being sacrificed is filled with meaning of this sort for him, as it is for some other Newars.

We might interpret this person's unease at viewing sacrifices as expressing an identification with the victim. This is not necessarily an unconscious meaning. Some Newars will tell you that, when young, they thought that they too might have their throats slit; they felt afraid and thought killing the animals was wrong. Adults may encourage, or prompt, children to identify themselves with the animals being sacrificed. I observed adults teasing children by threatening to sacrifice them, making a show of hiding a knife from the child; the children responded with fear, running away, and the adults laughed. The empathic identification with the victim of sacrifice is overcome by the time Newars grow up — perhaps replaced, or supplemented by, identifications with the person with the power to kill, perhaps even with the deities to whom animals are sacrificed.

I do not know if these are valid interpretations; they suggest, though, how complex the cultural psychology that mediates the felt response to a cultural scene may be. What I observed disturbed me in some ways, but it did not evoke quite the same emotions and feelings, or play on the same meanings and motives in my "inner world," as it did for Newars. We saw, and felt, different scenes—even when we observed the same event. While I "felt" the scene of blood and death, I did not grasp the religious significance of sacrifice in the way Newars did, nor could I bring the same personal meanings to it. I had never seen these events as a child, or felt fear when an adult threatened, teasingly, to sacrifice me.

I still cannot see a Newar city the way Newars see it. But I learned something. I cannot see blood-soaked sand as worth risking a blow from a policeman's stick, but I can appreciate that something of the essence or power of deities can be retrieved with whatever has been offered to them, and that they will protect the moral order of the city. I can see how people might identify with them, and with the animals sacrificed to them.

If the autumn festival is a time of religious emotion and dramatic rites, it is also a time for conviviality and kinship, for the pleasures of feasting and company. The animals sacrificed are cooked and eaten at the feasts, and people drink the liquor made by the women of their household. Warmth and amity, as much as religious mystery and danger, are part of the season.

Other Aspects of Religious Life

Encounters with religion cannot be avoided in Bhaktapur, even when festivals are not filling the streets with religious drama. The built environment, the public art and architecture of the city, embody religious concepts, presenting them to the eye.

Not only do ensembles of shrines sacralize public squares and the city as a whole, urban space embodies a cosmology and a sacred geography, expressed in the architecture of temples and houses and in the rituals, festivals, and celebrations that make use of urban space, which are enacted in and for the city, in and for neighborhoods, in and for individuals and society.

Myth becomes art in Bhaktapur, transforming the utilitarian into symbolic expressions of the sacred world. Old Newar water taps, for example, often are not simply utilitarian fixtures, but sculpture, myth-in-stone; in some, the water emerges from the head of a *makara*, a water creature, carved in stone; beneath the water spout itself there is often an image of Bhagirath, a king who, according to Hindu mythology, meditated for ages for the boon of having the Lord Shiva bring the personified river Ganges to earth. Many of these fountains still function, and women go there carrying brass pots to get water for their households.

On their way home, balancing their water pots on their hips, these women may pass by temples that pick up and transform mythic and religious themes in their art and architecture. Newar temples house images of divinities, of course, but they are also adorned with carvings; they fill visual space with sacred images, making them public and inescapable. For example the struts that help give integrity to pagoda-style temples often have beautiful, elongated carvings of gods or goddesses on them, with their multiple arms. Below these, on some temples, are smaller erotic carvings. I would sometimes see groups of children, male or female, walking arm-in-arm around the temple that stood in front of where I lived, looking up at the carvings—but at the erotic or the divine ones? They would run away when I went out to try to ask them.

The statues and carvings do not move, but one can also encounter divinity in motion in Bhaktapur. The gods and goddesses are represented in dance—they spin and pirouette beneath the temple eaves, dancing myth. A troupe of masked ritual dancers, the Navadurga, dance dangerous gods and goddesses in the public squares of the city. Their dance is considered a *yantra*, a pattern that has power. The sequence of dance performances in twenty-one locations in Bhaktapur each year weave a larger protective pattern, a more inclusive yantra, for the city as a whole (Levy 1990: 565). In each locale they visit, the Navadurga perform a dance drama in several episodes, which "protects" that area.[11]

In one episode, which you might stumble across during the day, attracted by the uproar that attends it, children mock one of the masked god-figures, making an undulating kind of noise by clapping a hand over the mouth, while waving the other hand at the god. The god chases the children, who run away down the streets. Later, in the interval of the performance, one can see people touch the masks, and then themselves, as if to transfer something— power? blessings? grace? This gesture is respectful, simple, serious, in contrast to the mockery, which involves a kind of playful risk-taking (for to be caught is mildly inauspicious, since it could cause illness, which is why the god should be placated with the offering of a coin), but is enjoyed as a performance. Newars are not totally somber about religion. In the streets of Bhaktapur, the divine can offer comic relief, before assuming a more dangerous face.

Even this playful episode has a "moral" message. The playful violation of hierarchy (for the gods should be honored) and risks assumed (for the gods have the power to punish violently) speak to the issue of violating hierarchy, one of the key organizing principles of Newar society (Levy 1990: 573).

The Navadurga accept blood sacrifices, and thus belong to the category of "dangerous" Tantric deities. According to myth, they originally lived in the forest outside of the city, and caught and drank the blood of travelers, before being brought under control by Tantric religious specialists—and are always in danger of spinning out of control, of harming people.[12] As Levy (1990) suggests, it may be their dangerous qualities that make them good protectors of the moral order from external threats, and also make them potent guardians of the moral order against threats to that order from within society. These fierce, amoral divinities portray what a person's fate will be if he violates moral norms or subverts the moral solidarity of the group. The blood sacrifices offered these dangerous, amoral guardians and protectors of the moral order are palpable symbols of what a dangerous divinity might do, if unleashed (1990: 285).

Each year, the caste association of Navadurga dancers fattens, and then slaughters, a buffalo they have made drunk. The sacrifice echoes Bhagavati's victory over Maishasura. The Navadurga get part of their "power" from drinking the blood of the buffalo.

What struck me most about a performance I saw, where the Navadurga drink the blood of the buffalo, was the projection of a feeling of wildness brought under tenuous control: the masked figures would surge toward the place where the blood was, in a chaotic mass, entwined with each other, would be blocked and pushed back by the Tantric priests, and then would surge forward with even more powerful movements—driven by their desire to drink blood. I found it an impressive performance, done at night, in a scene of fitful lights and shadows, with the dancers pushing into the crowd, causing confusion—where to stand? Where could one avoid the press, be safe? Where are the boundaries in the scene, the borders behind which you can be secure? The chaotic performance challenged one's equilibrium. The Navadurga surged over and through implicit bounds — and I found myself experiencing them as dangerous. I think the Newar audience, men, women, children, found it a powerful performance as well. After it was over, we offered some coins, and were given a multicolored sacred thread to wear, marking us as having encountered the Navadurga in the night of the Tantric city.

The Navadurga dances are only one ritual cycle in Bhaktapur. During festivals, the inhabitants of Newar settlements worship and make offerings to important deities; in the Newar cities, these affairs are elaborate, involving visits to temples dispersed within the city and to the shrines of the protective goddesses on the city's edge. In one of these festivals, the most important god of the city and his consort are brought out of their temples, placed in chariots — temples on wheels more than forty feet tall — which are then pulled through the streets. Lesser deities are brought out into the streets and squares in palanquins. People enjoy themselves — some get drunk, some perform devotions, some watch the scene, while others paint red powder on bystanders — and one could suppose that the gods and goddesses enjoyed themselves as well, being borne in a circuit of an area of the city by devout and drunken men, through a pressing throng of people, accepting offerings, being adorned with flowers, having (symbolic) sex. All this is done with (what seemed to me) joy and devout seriousness.

As a Hindu community, the central act of worship in Bhaktapur is *puja*. In brief, this involves making offerings of water, foods, flowers, coins, and other items to divinities. Typically, these offerings are made to objects or symbols — a statue, an abstract design, a stone. However, these are not mere tokens of absent powers, lifeless representation of the divinities; rather, they possess the life and being of the deity. From the point of view of the worshiper, the god or goddess is a living presence; the deity is in the image

Worship typically requires a preliminary purification or separation of self from the ordinary. This may be achieved minimally by such acts as taking off one's shoes to approach the image of the deity, or it may involve bathing and fasting, paring nails and cutting hair. As part of worship, people may circumambulate shrines and light lamps to the deities; they will pray, show respect and reverence, and ritually bring themselves into the presence of the deity.

Worship may be done in a brief, abbreviated way—a quick prayer, a ritual nod to godhood—reduced to hardly more than a passing gesture. It may be done in an elaborate, time-consuming manner, requiring deep concentration, coordinated group effort directed by religious specialists, and great expense.

Offerings to divinities are retrieved; the items retrieved are *prasad*. Worshipers consume prasad to receive the god's "blessings." They scatter flower petals on the crowns of their heads, or tuck whole flowers behind their ears; they may receive a mark on their foreheads showing they have worshiped and will eat a portion of the food that has been offered to the deity.

Acts of worship, from the simplest to the most complex, honor a god or goddess, and forge a connection between worshiper and divinity. As Fuller (1992: 57) says, puja "can also create a unity between deity and worshiper that dissolves the differences between them." Short of this unity, divinity and worshiper are brought closer together. In practice, there is a kind of intimacy involved in worship, an element of empathy. Quite often, the worshiper seeks to evoke a protective attitude in the deity, by building up a relationship of mutual responsiveness. Thus, a ritual empathy that speaks to the needs, nature, and pleasures of the deity is as much a part of this relationship as ritual deference that acknowledges power and divinity—worshipers seek to please the gods and goddesses, and to make them feel for humans.

Thus, hierarchy and empathy come together in worship, forming a nexus that I think resonates with the structures of feeling of Hindu Newar family life: the worshiper anticipates and responds to the deity's desires and needs; bathes, clothes, adorns, feeds, cares for the deity; shows respect, expresses reverence for the deity, does homage "from the heart." The worshiper wishes to experience the deity's presence, and to draw to self or to some segment of the human community something of the deity's grace, power, blessing, or aspect. At the same time, a deity (*dya:*) is a superior and powerful being, and often in practice the worshiper, hoping for the help and protection of a god or goddess, wants the deity to know and be moved by the plight or intentions of the self.

Puja, or the promise to perform a puja, can draw the deity's attention.

Of Sacred Beings and Their Moral Relevance

"God" or "divinity," as these glimpses suggest, exists for Newars in a variety of forms. The divine is male, and female, and neither. It can be nurturing—but also terrifying and destructive. Sacred beings may be moral, or beyond human morality.

What Newars "know" as divinity, and the ways they experience it as sacred, varies as they employ different concepts of god in different contexts and encounter divinity symbolized in radically different ways. Some of these forms are all-encompassing, absorbing the divine into a single image or being that is ultimately "unknowable" from a human point of view; other forms of god are not as remote from human experience, possessing instead an individual and concrete character or aspect that can be known, loved, or feared.

When Newars need help, for example, they may call on "god" as Bhagavan. Doing so, they relate themselves to divinity conceived of as an all-encompassing principle—"god" in the widest, most total, sense. They condense divinity into a singularity, implicitly making it one, a single, unified being that is all that is divine.

While a Newar woman praying for help may not care much about the finer points of theology—she simply wants a solution to her problem—she might, in a more speculative, philosophical mood, define Bhagavan (or Shiva, or the Goddess) as the godhead, as the divine creative principle that generates all the other gods and goddesses of the Hindu pantheon.[13] Conceived of in this way, Bhagavan is aware of the human individuals who pray for help, and may help them, but is a rather remote and abstract entity. Bhagavan is not a "person"—and cannot be experienced as a palpable presence made tangible in symbols and myths. "God" as an all-encompassing principle lacks the personality, the individuality, that particular Hindu gods like Shiva or Vishnu have for Newars.

If Bhagavan is abstract, Shiva and Vishnu are concrete. Not formless, but embodied in living forms, they take on a specific, compelling identity in the religious imagination of Newars. They have faces much like human faces—if you are willing to overlook the third eye in the forehead and, sometimes, fangs protruding from the mouth. They have bodies much like human bodies, if you overlook the fact that, in some of their forms, they have a few extra arms; but even these represent merely a multiplication of human features. They have gender and are sexual beings, know love and experience passion. Like humans, Shiva and Vishnu are actors in events and have social relationships; they experience desires and emotions; they get into and out of trouble. At times they are portrayed as having limits and facing challenges, and as having lives that engage and involve them—not as all-knowing and all-powerful beings entirely detached from life as humans know it. Their powers and abilities are more than human, but not absolute. Thus, in contrast to more abstract ways of imagining divinity, Shiva and Vishnu are—in some ways and in some contexts—conceived of as very much like living, social, persons.[14] These resonances with the experiences and conditions of personhood are part of what makes them meaningful for Newars.

For example, in one set of myths well-known to Hindu Newars, Shiva gets into trouble because he "doesn't care" (as one Newar put it) about the consequences of his actions. In these myths, Shiva has great power, but poor judgment. In some, he gives power to demons—such as the power to destroy anything they touch, even Shiva—as a boon because they have pleased him with their worship. The demon who has received the "power of Shiva" then begins to misuse it, threatening even Shiva himself. Shiva runs away, and Vishnu must find a way to trick the demon (using flattery or deception) to restore the order that Shiva, in his insouciant way, has upset.

This illustrates some of the meanings Shiva and Vishnu have for Newars. Shiva generates problems that the more integrated Vishnu must resolve for the sake of the moral order and human community (Levy 1990: 211). Vishnu represents the moral order; Shiva symbolizes aspects of the human problematic of dealing with that moral order. His characteristic behaviors and proclivities—his indifference to social norms (seen both in his disruptive sexuality, his seductions and licentious liaisons, and in its opposite, his ascetic withdrawal from social engagements proper to Hindu life), his tendency to act on whims, his self-absorption—are traits any community might find disturbing and difficult to deal with (Levy 1990: 211; O'Flaherty 1973), especially one in which the social order demands as much of the social actor as Bhaktapur's does. People can, I think, identify with Shiva; they know, in some sense, what responsible social life costs them. They are not free to be careless, to act on whims, to be self-absorbed, to express all of their sexual desires. They are not free to ignore burdensome social obligations. They have had to give up much of what they could be to meet the demands of social life—and this surrendered potential exerts a kind of wistful fascination.

Even this interest in the vanished possibilities of self must be held in check and subverted within consciousness, since it might lead to efforts to reclaim the potential that has been surrendered to the moral order. Mythology allows the actor to know, and to deny, aspects of the nonmoral self, thus shaping a moral self that can be projected into the business of living. Thus, while Newars often feel their responsibilities are heavy burdens, they also affirm them, as necessary and moral, and affirm themselves as moral agents. Doing so, Newars may identify with Vishnu, as the sacred symbol of moral agency. They must act in relationship to themselves and others as Vishnu does in relation to Shiva; Vishnu, with his greater "social" intelligence and ties to the social order, helps ground and center Shiva, getting him out of trouble and cleaning up his messes, redirecting his energies toward the social world. In particular local usages, Vishnu and Shiva are, in some sense, symbols of self and society. Shiva represents and resonates with the socially denied desires of the self; Vishnu represents, not only the social order, but the use of rational intelligence to preserve it. He embodies the sharpening of judgment, the ability to focus and act decisively, needed to preserve the social order (qualities also needed reflexively—if self has some of the qualities of Shiva—to maintain self-control). The mythology of Shiva and Vishnu in Bhaktapur is, then—among other things, and in terms of the specific local emphases given meanings and themes selectively taken and transformed from the vast corpus of South Asian mythology—one of many mythologies of self.

Vishnu has various other meanings relating to the moral order. Vishnu is the witness of people's moral lives, and keeps track of the good and the bad they have done. In this role, Vishnu may intercede with Lord Yama, the God of Death, when people are being judged after they have died. For many Hindu Newars, the key to salvation is moral action and spiritual practice; anxiety about the ultimate fate of self, and hope for salvation, are channeled into worship of Vishnu. The dying person must pray to Vishnu, meditate on Vishnu, and try to make their last word Vishnu's name.[15] In some accounts I collected, Newars claimed that people's sins will be dissipated if, with their life's last breath, they call on Vishnu. More generally, however, Vishnu offers salvation to moral persons: to those who have been good social persons, who have fulfilled their social obligations, and who have not violated the moral law, the dharma. In other contexts, Vishnu is the aspect of divinity that dwells in the heart of every human being.

Shiva is more complex and ambiguous. If Vishnu, in some sense, tends to represent the way the divine enters the human world, and sustains the human moral order, Shiva is, as Robert Levy (1990: 212) has proposed, more of a "bridge to the world beyond the city, and beyond all cities." Some of Shiva's traditional, mythological meanings invite a transcendence of the social and moral world — they celebrate life outside of the social, the life of the yogi, the life of a person who has renounced the ordinary world of marriage, family, and social obligation to become a completely spiritual, god-focused being. For the most part, Newars do not pursue this potential spiritual path very far; while I lived there, at least, few Bhaktapur Newars seemed to desire to cut themselves off from the social world, its obligations, limits, and pleasures. Renouncing the world is symbolically enacted, and then itself renounced, in some rites of passage.

Newars have other — more disturbing — ways of representing the way out of the city, and out of the social order. As Levy (1990: 212) further notes, if Shiva is a *bridge* to the world outside the city, it is the Goddess who for Newars represents "the world outside the city and its order." As Shiva passes into this "radically *extrasocial* world" beyond the city, Shiva is transformed, and, "overtly in Tantric imagery, becomes a corpse."

Ordinary and Dangerous Divinities

Vishnu and Shiva are examples of what Robert Levy (1990: 207) calls "ordinary gods," in contrast to certain other Newar divinities, who are "dangerous gods." The distinction is based on local thought and practice. "Ordinary" divinities are attended by Brahman priests; "dangerous" gods are attended by their own special priests. Blood sacrifices and offerings of alcoholic spirits are made to the dangerous Tantric deities, but never to the ordinary Hindu gods. While the most important of the ordinary gods are male, female goddesses are most important within the group of dangerous divinities. Describing their iconography, Levy writes that the goddesses are sometimes depicted as "garlanded with necklaces of human heads or skulls, and carrying a human skull cup for drinking blood in one of their many hands" (p. 207), sometimes "with cloaks of flayed animals or human skins over their shoulders" (p. 227). They may also be represented "as exaggeratedly erotic forms with the faces of beautiful young women" (p. 207), as "full-breasted figures of an almost hallucinatory sexual desirability" (p. 228); but this erotic beauty does not imply safety, since the beautiful forms "bear the same murderous weapons as the frankly horrible forms" in their multiple arms, and "they, too, demand blood sacrifice" (p. 228).

Although it may not be strongly stressed at a particular moment, and each of the major goddesses have specific meanings for Newars, the various dangerous goddesses of Bhaktapur in some sense all ultimately emanate from the Goddess Devi, the all-encompassing form of such divinities. This form of the Goddess is, in South Asian tradition, often identified as the creative principle; she generates the world, conceived of as a delusion or set of illusions. In this aspect, Devi is seen as creating, sustaining, and destroying the world; she generates the other gods, including Shiva and Vishnu.

More important in Bhaktapur is Devi manifest and embodied as Bhagavati the Warrior Goddess, whose victory is celebrated in the autumn festival. This if the what Levy calls the "full" or "maximal" manifest form of the Goddess—not the Goddess as principle, but as an actor, a mover and shaker of worlds, striding across the universe, doing battle, taking life.

As the "maximal" manifest form of the Goddess, Bhagavati can generate and command an even more violent and terrifying form, the goddess Kali, who will kill and devour the enemies of the gods (Levy 1990: 251). In Bhaktapur, this goddess is one of the Navadurga, and is called Mahakali. "Flesh-devouring, blood-drinking, intoxicated, cadaverous," as Levy describes her, Mahakali embodies the Goddess in her most fierce and frightening form. In the dance dramas of the Navadurga, the god Seto Bhairav mocks and shows disrespect to Mahakali (by shaking his head in an insulting manner, and by keeping his head covered in her presence). Enraged, she seizes his shawl, and refuses to give it back to him. Seto Bhairav wants it back, and attempts to appease her. He makes a gesture of respect and reverence, but this does not work. He then asks the human audience of this event to give him coins, and makes an offering of these, hoping they will please her. She takes the coins but does not give back his shawl. Finally, Seto Bhairav offers a live cock to Mahakali. She refuses at first. She turns and takes it suddenly, angrily; she throws the shawl in Seto Bhairav's face. She bites off the cock's head and as its blood spurts from its neck, she drinks it.

Later in the day comes the episode where the god Seto Bhairav chases boys and young men through the street. The theme of showing disrespect is repeated here; the boys mock the god, who angrily pursues them up and down the streets. His chasing of the boys is called "going fishing"—this deity is a fisher of men, too, but he does not offer them redemption. Instead, the boys who are chased, like Seto Bhairav when he shows disrespect to Mahakali, are flirting with destruction—the cock Mahakali kills is a substitute for Seto Bhairav. The episode dramatizes not what happens to a person who violates social convention, and disrupts relationships among people, but what happens to a person who disrupts the hierarchical relationship of humans and dangerous gods, a relationship that makes the survival of the moral order possible (Levy 1990: 571–575).

Taleju

Taleju, the lineage goddess of the Newar kings who once ruled Bhaktapur before the conquest of Newar cities—who is thus the political goddess of Bhaktapur—is closely associated with Bhagavati. During Mohani, Taleju becomes identified with Bhagavati in a ritual enactment of Bhagavati's victory over Mahisasura. On the eighth day of Mohani, an intoxicated water buffalo—it has been given alcohol to drink—is run through the streets to the Taleju temple, symbolizing Mahisasura. Twenty-four other water buffalo, one for each of the twenty-four traditional neighborhoods of the

FIGURE 10   Statue of a Newar king facing the entrance of the Taleju temple, honoring the Goddess.

city, are also brought to the temple, representing the armies of Mahisasura.

In a courtyard of the Taleju temple, the throats of the buffalo are cut, beginning with the one representing Mahisasura. Blood is sprayed on an image of Taleju; the head of the animal is then cut off. The other animals are sacrificed. In this bloody reenactment of the victory of Bhagavati, the long-departed king of Bhaktapur plays a vital part through his surrogates, the priests of the Taleju temple. The king participates in the victory, and his special goddess is the Great Goddess, the power that makes life, the harvest, and the moral order, possible.

If Taleju becomes Bhagavati during Mohani, she also makes an appearance as a human girl. Legend says Taleju used to appear to the Malla kings in her full divine form. One day, however, the king displeased her. There are several versions of what he did: one explanation says she did not like the way he looked at her, as if he wanted to know her secrets; another says he failed to keep something secret; yet another suggests the king had sexual thoughts about the goddess. In any event, Taleju, angry, vows she will never return again. The king begs her not to do this; finally, Taleju relents, saying she will never return in her divine form, but will return as an untouchable girl. The Brahman priests find this unacceptable, however, since it would pollute the temple. Instead, Taleju returns as a young Buddhist girl—as the Kumari, the living child-goddess. She serves as an oracle. During Mohani, the Kumari is worshiped, and her behavior watched for omens and signs.[16]

Taleju is the "older sister" of the Navadurga (as one Navadurga dancer put it). She gives them power during Mohani, supplementing the power they get from drinking the blood of the water buffalo—again representing Mahisasura—that they have sacrificed in secrecy at the edge of the city.

Moral Meanings of the Dangerous Deities

Even more than Shiva, the dangerous deities represent and deal with problematic aspects of the relationship of "person" to moral order. They do not, however, deal with *relatively* "moral" aspects of this issue—the problem of being a properly social and moral person—but with the *radically* "nonmoral" aspects of self and person. While Shiva drifts away from the social order into self-absorption or becomes so involved in meditation that he pays no attention to social obligations, he is still a relatively moral figure: he embodies cultural values. More than that, he expresses the contradictions of the Hindu moral system, as he shifts from one set of Hindu values to another, from social engagement to ascetic withdrawal. For Newars, he poses the problem of commitment to social life vs. self-absorption. Even his eroticism has a place in social life, although his seductions and licentiousness violate norms. Although he represents conflicting values, and the problem of committing self to the moral order, Shiva is essentially a moral figure, and even his lapses and violations are, in some sense, failures of a potentially moral self, who can be saved by others—by his friend Vishnu or his wife, Parvati—and these failures are relevant to, and grounded in, the moral system. Shiva is careless, and pulled in different directions, but is not radically nonmoral, a being with no grounding in the moral system at all.

In contrast, the dangerous divinities of Bhaktapur often represent the "person" or "self" radically decentered from the moral order; the dangerous gods are not grounded in moral life. They do not embody moral values, or contradictions in the moral system, or the problem of being moral. They have not lapsed from morality, and cannot be restored to a moral state. In fact, they have no identity in the moral order at all. They have no moral nature. Quite the contrary—they are by nature nonmoral. Although they protect the human moral order, they have no being, no essential reality, in it, and no commitment to it. They are creatures of power, not moral beings.

As Levy says, the dangerous gods have some of the characteristics of persons—they have names, they have humanlike forms, even if these are strange and disturbing; they speak and experience emotions. If, however, as Levy (1990: 284) suggests, logic and morality in some basic sense define the essence of what it is to be "true persons," then the dangerous deities are something other than persons, or persons only in partial, and strange, ways, for they are not bound to logic or morality. They are, as he says, "radically peculiar and unacceptable persons . . . persons in flux," "related to the forces and forms of `nature' outside the city, wild and dangerous but at the same time vital." Levy says they are also related to "psychological modes" such as dreams and insanity, and to "passions and impulses" such as cannibalism, that are "beyond what are acceptable even to a tolerant view of what a person is or should be" (Levy 1990: 284). Killing and eating people comes naturally to them. It has no ethical significance for them.

What can we make of these contradictions? What do they tell us about Newar experience and the construction of the Newar moral world? How do these sacred but nonmoral beings help generate human moral meaning or behavior? and how do they mediate the relationship of individuals to the moral order? These are interlocking questions; they may have interlocking answers. I can only offer some speculative ones.

As nonmoral beings at the edge of the moral order, we could conceive of the dangerous divinities as showing people, powerfully, their vulnerability and dependence on beings stronger than they are. Inflation of self, a disruptive assertion of self, hubris in any shape and form, defiance of the hierarchical order of reality, is averted, because the most obvious reality of the world is that others are more powerful than self, and are perfectly willing to destroy you, if you do not act properly. This kind of fear can be a motive for monitoring self to find and prune out disruptive desires.

As sacred but nonmoral beings, the dangerous deities represent and evoke the nonmoral in a threatening relationship to the moral domain of human life. The concrete and dramatic way they make the nonmoral palpable and tangible as a threat to the moral may have implications for the way people know and evaluate self and the moral order. As radically nonmoral beings, the dangerous deities pose the problem of the status of the *ongoing relationship* of moral and nonmoral, making the dissolution of the moral order (and moral self) into nonmoral chaos seem possible. This threat energizes action—conformity to ward it off, and ritual efforts to stabilize the relationship of the moral and nonmoral, of order and chaos. The dangerous deities, creatures of power controlled through the use of power, are captured and deployed to protect the moral order. They embody the threat, and constitute a response to it. The principle is—meet force with force; power only respects power. The moral order depends on a religion of power organized in a very different way from the ethical religion embodied by Vishnu and the other ordinary gods.

Furthermore, as noted above, for Newars the dangerous deities are the agents of the destruction of those who fail to follow moral norms. They have the power of life and death. Although themselves nonmoral, they destroy those who violate the moral order.

How do they mediate the relationship of the individual to the moral order? We can speculate about the psychological significance of the dangerous deities, about how they may shape a sense of self, or perceptions of others, in ways that might help determine the relationship of the individual to moral order. If people contemplate self, others, and the world in terms of all that the dangerous deities represent—and this is the kind of thing that minds often do, outside of conscious awareness—they might find parallels in themselves, in others, in life. If they did find echoes of the nature of the dangerous deities in themselves, others, or elsewhere, I think they might possibly experience a profound fear of self and other, an abiding uncertainty about the stability, safety, and reality of self, other, and life. Taking this speculation one step farther, I can imagine how this fear might shape orientation to the moral order. It is, after all, really the fear that the boundaries of self will collapse, and all that you believe you are, and think you must be, will dissolve. This loss of self may be only prelude; perhaps you will become what you fear most in yourself. Or perhaps someone else will be transformed into a dangerous creature of the nonmoral—some loved one, a relative, a parent—because of something self has done, or failed to do. (A child might feel this fear keenly. When Newars teasingly threaten to cut the throats of young children watching animal sacrifices, the children often cry in what I imagine to be terror.)

Perhaps it is life itself that has no logic, no moral foundations, no reality. Hinduism, with its concepts of maya, of illusion, might prepare a person for this view of things. Or perhaps the experience of Hinduism and Hindu social life prepares a person for the philosophical concepts. In any event, I believe individuals who, even unconsciously, question reality and self in this way will seek to reground or recenter themselves in the moral system, to hold fast to morality, out of their fear of the void within, or the chaos in others.

The possibility that the imagery of the dangerous deities constitutes an imagery of the nonmoral self—either as a projection of what people deny in themselves, as in classical psychological anthropology, or as a way of generating and defining the self, or both—is intriguing. I think it would warrant exploration in future studies; in the balance of this work I will mostly be concerned with the "self" in various moral contexts.

The Imagined City

As these glimpses of the religious life of the city suggest, Bhaktapur is a place known, experienced, and organized in terms of symbols. As a cultural world, the city has been conjured into existence, and been given form and coherence, through symbols. The most important of these symbols belong to the religious sphere, and they define reality for Newars. Over the centuries, Newars have worked out, and elaborated certain of the imaginative possibilities of human life, creating a self-image and a world-image out of a rich synthesis of South Asian and Himalayan cultural material; they now keep these images of themselves and the world enshrined in traditions, in their communities of memory, and in rituals and religious festivals. This offers an encompassing worldview.

While the symbols that constitute Bhaktapur are of many kinds, and work on many levels, Robert Levy (1990) points out the special significance and elaboration of what he calls "marked symbolism." A symbol, of course, "stands for" something—any object or event that "has meaning" can be considered a symbol in some general sense—but a symbol can "stand for" something in a number of different ways. There are different genres of symbols, and they have different uses and implications. "Marked" symbols announce their significance in special ways, calling attention to themselves, making themselves stand out. The masks of the Navadurga, for example, are marked symbols. They have special iconographic features—some have three eyes and fangs—thus announcing that they are not "ordinary." The special treatment and honor shown the masks also marks them off (for example, people make gestures of respect to them; they are kept in special places; they are cremated at the end of the ritual cycle). Furthermore, the dramatic ritual dances performed by Newars wearing these masks, and the animal sacrifices they perform as part of these rites, also dramatically call attention to their special, heightened significance, involving as they do such unusual and violent acts as drinking the blood of a chicken that has just been decapitated, or tearing out the beating heart of a pig. Moreover, since myth is danced in these rites, and dance, as a special performance genre, moves beyond the ordinary, it can be seen that the framing and marking of the rites as having special significance is done redundantly on several levels, helping to ensure that people become engaged with the symbolism, and receptive to it. The masks, the rites, the sacrifices are all examples of marked symbolism.

"Marked" symbols, Levy (1990: 27) suggests, stand in sharp contrast to the "embedded" symbols that structure everyday, mundane life. Marked symbols mean what they mean in ways sharply different from the way embedded symbols mean what they mean. Embedded symbols are the kind of symbols that organize a person's "common sense," their ordinary sense of reality. When people perceive the world in terms of embedded symbols, they are typically not aware of using symbolic meaning to define and construct objects and events, of attaching meaning to them—they take what they know and perceive as part of reality, as derived from the events and objects or from their perception of them. Since people are for the most part not aware of actively attaching meaning to many culturally perceived objects and events, these are experienced as possessing an obvious and unquestionable "natural" meaning. Embedded symbolism tends to make things seem natural and necessary—the disgust a high-caste Newar may feel toward an untouchable is based on the construction of the untouchable as "impure." High-caste Newars are not typically aware that the untouchable is a symbolic figure, defined in terms of cultural meanings; they experience the untouchable as "impure," without any consciousness that this experience is symbolically mediated.

Marked symbols, in contrast, provoke and challenge consciousness and, if experienced in certain ways in certain contexts, have the power to detach receptive persons from commonsense moorings, and to generate in them an extraordinary sense of reality, making them "know" and "see" the world in certain special, consciousness-shaping, ways. Marked symbols, and the sense of reality they shape, are of central importance in Bhaktapur; their pervasive presence, their structuring significance in a variety of contexts, constituted one of the reasons I experienced Bhaktapur as fascinating but opaque. Marked symbols made Bhaktapur strange to me.

What made Bhaktapur strange to me may also make it "strange" to Newars in a very different sense. Levy argues for this interpretation, maintaining that the people of Bhaktapur have constructed, and live in, two worlds at once, one a world of "self-serving common sense" and the other "the strange world of marked symbols." In the first world, such things as the caste hierarchy, and concepts of purity and impurity, "make sense," seem necessary and natural. In the second realm, the gods live, and dance through the city. "Bhaktapur," Levy concludes,

> places most of its marked symbols in the religious sphere, which is the realm of the gods, a bounded domain of a still larger Hindu religious universe, a great mind in which gods along with all living, sentient things participate, out of which they are generated, whose immutable moral laws they are subject to, and whose ultimate nature they can come to glimpse.

The city itself is a kind of symbol of this Hindu universe, evoking religious consciousness in manifold ways. Levy goes on to define what I take to be an essential aspect of the nature of Bhaktapur, of the way it is imagined:

> Other complex civilizations whose citizens shared the "symbol hunger" of Bhaktapur's citizens have elaborated realms of marked symbols, but came to place them elsewhere. Thus, in the West, secular drama, literature and art, are marked as extraordinary—by setting, cadence, presentation, and other devices—but have come to represent a class of communications that is in some sense "imaginary," "*only* symbolic," not to be taken literally. Until its contemporary transformations most of Bhaktapur's extraordinary statements have not called themselves imaginary, but as belonging to another sort of reality, the reality of the god's divine sphere. In a different bounding than the Western one, both Bhaktapur's everyday reality and the reality of the gods can be seen as imaginary, as *maya* [illusion], when grasped by the highest intuitions of religious awareness. But, for the most part, gods and Bhaktapurians are content to remain in their divine illusions and by putting the imagination of the extraordinary in a religious subsphere to give it and its representations the strongest possible position in the life of the community and its citizen's minds. (1990: 605)

What Newars know and see is shaped by marked religious symbols that "make the city strange" to them. In many ways, their encounter with these symbols transform Newars. The symbols provoke consciousness, proposing new ways of interpreting reality and catalyzing special kinds of religious and moral "knowing." In making the city strange, these sacred symbols require and generate "faith"—they provoke suspensions of disbelief and of ordinary knowing, and thus make it possible for Newars to participate in the sacred, transporting them into myth. These symbols invite fascination and engagement, articulate self to myth models, and sustain a religious vision for the city, the cosmos, and the self.[17]

Glimpses of Social Life in the City.

A walk through Bhaktapur, pointing out how basic social units inhabit the physical and the imagined city, suggests how the city is a kind of self-image for Newars, reflecting who they are and how they live their lives.

The Setting

Urban Villages   A Newar city is an cluster of urban villages. Traditionally, Bhaktapur consisted of twenty-four such villages, or wards, called *twa:*, inhabited by an average of 1,600 people (Gutschow and Kolver 1975; Levy 1990), each containing a public square and a shrine to the elephant-headed Hindu god Ganesh. Most of the people of a twa: know each other; this familiarity forms the basis for social judgment and control. As we will see in chapter 2, the twa: is also conceived of as a community that unites for the common good.

The Streets   In most areas of the city, houses form continuous rows along the streets. The Newari word for neighbor translates literally as "right-left," taking meaning from the way neighboring houses always stand on the right and left of your own. There are no front yards—the houses abut and "wall in" the streets. A curb or stoop of stone runs along the edges of the street, at the base of houses, preventing water from running into houses during the monsoon, when torrents of water rush down the streets. During better weather, people often sit on this curb, to chat and gossip. During festivals, when deities are brought along the streets in processions, women and children stand on this shelf of stone to get a better view. At all times of year, people sit at windows and watch what goes on in the street. Some traditional windows are designed so that you can look out through a lattice work without being seen from the outside, while others let you be seen; people converse back and forth between window and street.

Some back streets are so narrow that overhanging eaves shut out much of the sunlight. Walking in the shade of these streets, I would sometimes feel slightly oppressed by the gloom, closed in, and look up reflexively at the sliver of sunlight and sky above. Then, turning a corner, the street might open into a sunny square, where children play, shouting in the sun, and women wash clothes.

The spaces underneath the eaves of many houses are used for storage. Farmers hang some of their tools there (their wooden implements, not metal ones). The bamboo poles used by builders to construct scaffolding may be stored there as well. This space frequently serves as a larder: ears of drying corn, sheaves of herbs,

FIGURE 11 An image of the elephant-headed god Ganesh, associated with beginnings and success. A shrine to Ganesh is found in each *twa:*

braided strands of garlic, bundles of hot peppers are hung suspended from the eaves. Some people keep parrots there, or songbirds in bamboo cages (birds valued for their colors as well as their songs). A lamp to light for the gods may hang from the eaves as well.

In winter, in some of the narrower, darker streets, a white mold grows frostlike on the bricks. The damp and cold invades the unheated houses, especially the lower floors. People get chilled and cold, and go outside to find a place to sit in the sun. They congregate in the open squares or in the wider streets where the sun penetrates. There is a humorous anecdote Newars tell to of illustrate the value finding a spot to sit in the sun. It tells of a boy who had found a place to sit in the warm sunlight. A second larger boy came along, and stood so that his shadow fell over the first boy. This provoked the first boy to say that depriving him of the sunlight was equal to the "five great sins," and that for doing so the bigger boy should, that very day, die vomiting blood.

During the harvest, farmers use the city's squares and its wider streets to dry and winnow grain. They have to guard their rice and wheat from the cows that roam freely through the city and sleep under the eaves of the temples in the main squares; cows are not so sacred that people will not beat them to run them off if they are eating up the rice a family needs to dry and store. Hot peppers are another important crop for Bhaktapur's farmers and when they harvest these the city blossoms a bright red, as the hot peppers are put out to dry in the streets, in the squares, and on the rooftops.

Many of the people on the streets wear traditional clothing, and this marks their place on the social scale. Women of the farming caste, for example, wear distinctive black and red saris. Many men also still wear more traditional clothes — baggy draw string pants, a black vest over a long-sleeved shirt — but others, younger ones especially, wear Western-style clothing. Men and women alike may wear shawls around their shoulders and over their heads during colder weather.

The Courtyard   The courtyard, enclosed by the adjoining houses of a number of families, often and ideally related to one another, is an important feature of Newar life. It is considered to be public space, in the sense that people pass through it to get to the entrance of any house they might want to visit in the chowk, but a courtyard "belongs" in another sense to the people living in

FIGURE 12   Bhaktapur's Royal Square. The large building on the right with two lions in front is part of the old palace complex, from the time when Bhaktapur was an independent kingdom. In the background is a pagoda-style temple.

the houses that encircle it, whose windows look down into it, and who use it the most.

One of my informants, Ganesh Lal, a middle-aged farmer with white hair and mustache, lives on one such courtyard. Forty families sharing Ganesh Lal's surname (making them members of the same thar),[18] including most of the households of his core kin group, and two families that are not of the same thar, live on this courtyard and on three lanes leading into it. Thirty families — more than 250 people — live on the courtyard proper. In addition to belonging to the same thar, the families of Ganesh Lal's group are also united by having the right to be initiated into the service of the goddess Taleju in the Taleju temple in the royal palace complex. For the older generation, this service is central to their identity.

In the center of the courtyard is a well, and next to it a water tap. The courtyard is used a variety of ways. I would often see old ladies and babies asleep in the sun. Courtyards, like the small squares in each ward of the city, are used for agricultural processing — grain is dried and winnowed, vegetables sorted, and there is

FIGURE 13 A Buddhist procession stops at the Golden Gate, the entrance to the temple of the Hindu goddess Taleju within the palace compound.

a rice mill in one of the buildings. On a platform a deity is displayed during one of the annual festivals.

The House Ganesh Lal's house stands on the west side of the courtyard. The entrance is low, and has a door that can be shut and locked; it will be barred from within at night. Here at the door, space begins to be defended, and one customarily announces oneself, by calling out the name of the person one wants to see or, more politely and interrogatively, one calls out, "Who is up there?" This suggests the social dimension of the Newar house, marking the boundary between public space and domestic space. The house has a symbolic architecture, with the lower floors associated with outsiders, dirt, impurity, and death, while the upper parts are intensely domestic, intimate, private spaces—separate, pure, and sacred.

The ground floor of a Newar house is called the *celi*, often used for storage, or to keep animals. In many Newar groups, this is the place where a terminally ill person is taken to die; it is associated with death. I was told dying persons should be close to the earth,

FIGURE 14   Bhaktapur's main bazaar.

their "mother."[19] This floor is the least "defended" space of the
house and, if the door is not shut, one can ordinarily enter here to
call up the stairwell. Higher floors are more private. Early in my
stay in Bhaktapur, I once started up the stairs of the house of a
high-caste friend, calling out as I went—I was not used to yelling
loudly in Newari, and I wanted to make sure I was heard in the
upper recesses of the house, so I climbed to the second-floor land-
ing. The Newars call this floor the *mata(n)*. As I peered up the
stairs, the female head of the household came down with her hands
in front of her, open palms toward me—a clear stop signal. She
feared I might keep coming up. As a foreigner, and a non-Hindu,
I was not only an outsider, but impure and alien.

She seated me in a room on the second floor, the mata(n), where
guests are generally received. This is a social space, appropriate for
friendly conversation and a cup of tea with friends and guests, a
middle ground between the public world of strangers and polluted
castes, and the intimate inner space of family life.

People may sleep on any floor above the ground floor, but most
commonly on the second and third floors. Often there are no separate sleeping areas, no "bedrooms" associated with privacy and
the separation of a personal self from the flow of domestic life

FIGURE 15   One of the narrow
streets of the city.

often found in American culture. Indeed, Newars often have an
aversion to sleeping alone.

Ganesh Lal's house is very narrow, not more than ten to twelve
feet wide. Since the stairway runs through this, even less space is
usable. The reason for the narrowness of the house became apparent the first time I visited. He called out asking for matches, which
were handed in from the next house through the window: this is
his brother's house. The window itself was once the window for a
single house, with wider rooms; when the joint family divided they
partitioned the house vertically, and each brother got half a window. Dividing houses in this way gives each family access to the
ground floor and to the roof tops and sunlight. Partitioning the
house vertically rather than horizontally maintains the symbolic
structure as well; each family continues to have access to the higher floors that are more pure and private.

The top floor—generally the fourth story—contains the
kitchen, or hearth; this part of the house must be kept ritually pure.
Cooking may be done with wood, dung, or kerosene. The smoke
blackens the roof, and billows out through the roof tiles.

Rooftops   The top floor of a Newar house generally opens into a

FIGURE 16   Newar houses with elaborate wooden windows.

rooftop porch. People use this area in a variety of ways: to hang out clothes to dry, to sort and dry crops, to greet the sun-god with a ritual gesture. In the winter, people sometimes bathe out here, in the relative warmth of the sun. Some grow flowers in pots on their porches, to be used as offerings to the gods and goddesses. Resting their elbows on low brick walls enclosing the porch, Newars may look over the rooftop world, or down into the streets, watching the flow of people below, listening to the sounds of the street, the voices of the city. At any given moment, they might hear the murmur of conversations, one voice calling a person's name, another voice chanting the names of gods, voices raised in argument, women wailing in grief, or the sounds of children at play. Often, the music of processions and devotional groups fill the streets, and people step out onto their porches to watch.

The People

Hearth and Household   The "ideal" Newar household group consists of a man and his wife, their sons, along with their sons' wives, unmarried daughters, and the sons' children—a patrilineal extended family.[20] This unit shares a cooking area—as Newars say, it is "one hearth." From that hearth comes the food that the family shares—the domestic group "eats from the same rice pot."

The act of sharing food even more than dwelling in the same house defines a family. To identify the family with cooking and sharing food is to say something about relatedness, about how lives are joined together. It asserts you are "at one" with those who eat what you eat, who eat with you, from the same rice pot and hearth, from the same common store of food. For Newars, the purity of the hearth, of the food, and of the store of food, are important, and people are morally responsible for maintaining this purity. Cultural theories amplify the meaning of food as a medium of relatedness; through food, a person can incorporate something of the other into self, and contribute something of self to the other—eating together, people blend their natures or essences, making themselves alike, forging a bond.

But some people may not want to blend in this way; high-caste Newars will not share food with lower caste Newars. Those who eat together do not eat with many others, and this provides one way of generating a social identification with kin and caste.

The Domestic Cult Religious practice also provides one of the organizing centers of family life, and marks the boundaries of family and lineage. Each family and lineage segment worships deities of the male family line (the patriline, the *kul*) in a closed cult, typically maintaining a shrine room on one of the upper floors of the house. Outsiders are excluded; they are barred from entering the shrine room or seeing the household gods and goddesses, and they should not be told the name of the family deity. Secrets such as these create outsiders—and unify the family unit internally. The boundary of the domestic group is stressed in this self-image of the family, even more than in the image of the common hearth.

The Lineage When I had been in Bhaktapur awhile, I noticed small groups moving through the streets—some marching proudly, some straggling along—carrying the equipment Newars use to perform puja. I followed them out of the city, where I saw them sacrificing goats to small stones in a field. Each procession represented a group of related households—called a *phuki*—and were engaged in performing rites for a kind of lineage deity called the *digu dya:*. The phuki is a patrilineal unit, organized on the basis of male ties; the core of a phuki is a group of brothers, living in separate households, and their sons and grandsons. Women are included as unmarried daughters "of the phuki" or as wives who have married "into" the phuki. The phuki is generally the largest kin unit that acts in concert, as a united group, as in this ceremony (Nepali 1965: 253).

The phuki traditionally had a central role in making sure that members of the phuki married within their own caste (or higher). When a phuki member marries a woman of lower caste (as long as she is not from an "impure" or "untouchable" caste), he remains a phuki member. His children, however, becomes *mathya* — they are excluded from the lineage, denied the rights and privileges of membership in the group, including cooperation in important rituals and worship. The following account, by a high-caste man, suggests some of this, and also shows that while a phuki may no longer be able to enforce these rules, it can still make life hard for those who marry into other castes, and for their families.

> **My son married a woman who was excluded from our kin group and our caste [because she came from a caste of slightly lower status]. But my son liked her very much. [The dilemma was that] the woman my son marries becomes my daughter-in-law, but she is excluded from our group — and yet, I, too, love her very much. Since I feel this great love [*maya*] for her, I make her part of my family. I bring her into my caste. My phuki does not like this. So my phuki and I separated, because I brought this daughter-in-law in. Because of this, I also become illegitimate for them, an excluded man . . . the other phuki members despised me, and they forced me out. I don't like them either, and so we separated. We have become distant. Not distant [as blood relatives], but distant all the same. I see the people of my phuki, and I feel pain. I had no fault in the matter, I was not to blame, I did nothing wrong, but despite this fact, they cast me out. I get angry when I see them.**

Notice how he has invoked the concept of love (maya) to define relatedness and commitment. Love justifies the marriage of his son with a woman of another caste, in the face of opposition by the lineage group, who feel that the marriage violates traditional norms and breaches the integrity of their caste.

The passage suggest how the phuki acts to uphold values and norms. It is a key reference group for constructing a life and for evaluating actions, and as a social unit exerts pressure on individuals to conform. When some phuki member violates a norm, pressures mount to increase social distance. The distancing may be subtle or overt. For example, it may take the form of gossip and evaluations which are carefully kept from the person, out of fear of open hostility. At the other extreme, a transgressor may be ostracized. Newars believe the enmity of phuki members, once established, may persist for a long time, even for generations. As a Newar proverb puts it, "a snake without poison, a person without enmity"—by proclaiming a contradiction in terms, the saying asserts one Newar theory of human nature.

Some Actors

Shiva Bhakta's City

If Bhaktapur is a sacred city, it is also a bazaar, an urban emporium, filled with shops along the main street. One of the men you might see in the bazaar early in the morning, or visiting a tea shop in the afternoon, is Shiva Bhakta, who lives in a large house in one of the central neighborhoods of the city. When he goes out on to the streets, he meets people of equal and lower status; he is high caste, a Chathariya. Only the Brahmans are higher in status, at least in theory. His caste—by which I mean what Newars would call his *jat*—is one of a group of castes forming the traditional elite of Bhaktapur. Dressed finely in traditional and Indian rather than Westernized fashions, almost always wearing a formal black hat, Shiva sees in Bhaktapur the familiar sights of the city he grew up in—where places resonate with decades of memory. A successful businessman, he is proud that his family have been important merchants for generations, and were once connected with the court of the old kings of Bhaktapur. I think a certain confident, almost possessive, familiarity informs his perceptions of his city. He has, I believe, what Robert Coles, writing of the American elite, has termed a sense of "entitlement"—an "emotional expression," not just of money and power, but of caste status and family history.

Energetic and competent, Shiva Bhakta describes himself as *calak* — meaning vocal, articulate, clever. He is a man of words and means.

Mahila's City

Mahila knows and experiences the city in very different ways — as an untouchable. Mahila is a member of the Pore caste, the Sweepers who are employed by the city to clean the streets, and by private householders to clean their courtyards or latrines. When he sets out to work in the morning, he crosses a symbolic boundary; his home is conceived of as "outside the city." When Mahila sees people in the street, he sees the same people I have described — farmer women in red and black saris, Brahmans, merchants, and others. But I see Newars as an outsider, and Mahila sees Newars as high-caste people.

Mahila is ambivalent about his place in society; he is resigned, he accepts, he even affirms, the caste system — but he also rejects it. He resents his stigmatized status, but recognizes that his survival and family's well-being depends on his relations with upper status people.

What do they see? They see a middle-aged man dressed in dirty, ragged clothes, carrying the tools of his trade, smoking cigarettes when he can afford them, outwardly diffident and respectful. They see an untouchable, a sweeper — a person who is "dirty" and "impure" because of what he does, but even more so because of who he is. In caste ideology, his impurity is a matter of essence, not just occupation. As an untouchable, Mahila not only cleans up the dirt, garbage, and feces that accumulates in the city, he signifies the caste order, making it tangible. Untouchables have a special, psychosymbolic value as the "other" that defines the "self" of high-caste Newars. In addition to being removers of impurities, the Pore are linked to the inauspicious planet Rahu, responsible for eclipses and much human misfortune. High-caste Newars see untouchables as living a special hell on earth, and say untouchables must have committed grave sins in previous lives to warrant the suffering and degradation of their present circumstances.

High-caste people exclude lower-caste people from much of

their everyday life; they will not share food with Mahila, allow
him to enter the tea shops and restaurants where they gather to
socialize, or permit him to enter the upper stories of their houses. Traditionally, housing, too, symbolized status. Mahila sees
that higher-caste Newars have houses of four stories, with tile
roofs. His house is only two stories, and has a thatch roof. In the
past, untouchables were forbidden to have multistoried homes
with tile roofs, and many untouchable houses are still two stories
and have thatch roofs. Looking at Mahila's house in the sweeper
quarter, where I see another Newar house, smaller, more modest
than some, run down as many others were, Mahila sees a house
that he does not want to live in. He wants a better house. He
hopes for a better life. With one breath, he says "caste is finished," and with the next, points out how dependent he is on it—
if he wants to eat.

Ganesh Lal's City

Ganesh Lal helps make the music of the streets. Early most morn-
ings and some evenings, he gets together with others to play devotional hymns. His music group plays in a *phalca*, a kind of public
porch or arcade found along streets and in public squares. Ganesh
plays a type of drum, an important instrument; learning to play
required a religious initiation and doing devotions to Nasa dya:,
god of music and expressiveness.

Life in Bhaktapur has, for him, the rhythm of ritual work at
the Taleju temple (where he serves in a capacity reserved for
members of his caste and thar) and of the festival cycle. He plays
his drum in religious processions that may take him in a circuit
around the city, or out to the shrines that encircle the city.
Ganesh finds much meaning in this; it is part of his social and
personal identity, something that he does, but also something that
his group does, integrating him and his group into the religious
life of the city.

As a farmer by caste—a Jyapu—life for him has the rhythms
of the seasons, too, of the cycles of planting and harvest, of the
growth and care of plants, and of other agricultural work. He
walks barefooted on the streets out of the city to his fields, brings
grain and hot peppers back to courtyard and street to dry, and

places his hopes for a good harvest in the city's religious obser-
vances.

Ganesh Lal, more than Mahila or Shiva Bhakta, is a devout
man. Religion is central to his personal and social identity, and he
has a strong sense of being dependent on the gods and goddesses—for good weather, a good harvest, good health. For Ganesh
Lal, even more than the others, Bhaktapur is a religious community. If Shiva Bhakta is a man of words and means, Ganesh is "shy,"
and a self-described "have-not." What he asserts and possesses is
an essential relationship to dharma, the moral and religious order,
as a farmer and servant of the goddess Taleju.

Durga Maya's City

Durga Maya, a middle-aged woman with bad teeth, goes to fetch
water from a public tap each morning. She greets other women
there: "Have you eaten?" she asks. "Have you finished worshiping?" She may talk and joke with the other women for a while
before she hauls the water back home in a brass pot balanced on
her hip. The women of a household get water for the household
each day, carrying it up the stairs to the hearth floor for storage in
large clay pots.

On the way home, Durga is careful not to touch a dog or crow,
or be touched by an impure person—this would pollute the water,
and waste her effort. When she gets the water back to her house,
she carries it up the stairs to the hearth room, exclaiming loudly to
announce her presence, as she labors up the flights of stairs, for no
one should stand in the stairwell above the water as she brings it
up; this would pollute it, rendering it unfit for use.

Durga Maya is diffident in public. Her family is poor, and she
works for others. Her relationship with her patrons is more than
an economic exchange; it has political and moral aspects. As
patrons, they help her and her family in a variety of ways: to find
work, to meet crises, to take advantage of opportunities, or to deal
with the governmental bureaucracy. As a client and as a woman (in
a culture that "officially" stresses the authority of men), she
accepts orders and shows deference to others, rarely taking the ini-
tiative, except in routine tasks, which she performs diligently and
calmly. While she is not low caste, her patrons are of higher caste

standing, and she carefully bows to them when she meets them. Caste distance and separation are maintained, but the relationship of patron and client ideally involves a kind of "hierarchical nurturing"—patrons "care for" or "look out for" clients who show respect and provide support and services.

Devi Maya's City

Devi Maya is a vigorous, dignified woman in her seventies, only slightly slowed down by age. In contrast to Durga, "Grandmother" Devi is an authoritative and self-confident woman; she calmly receives the deference of women like Durga. She is a Brahman, and the female head of a large household, with seven living children. Her daughters are married, and live with their husband's families, but they visit her frequently, bringing their children, and sometimes their husbands, with them. Her sons, also married, live with her in a large, old house. Her husband died several years ago; like most Brahmans of his generation, he was a priest. Devi is in many ways the key figure in her household. Not only does she have the culturally recognized and respected role of female head or "leader" (naki(n)) of the extended family household, she is respected for her own competence, knowledge, and sagacity. Every day she sits with her sons as they eat, and offers her counsel on family business and neighborhood affairs. With them, and through them, she exerts influence within her neighborhood and even in other parts of the city, among more traditional, religious Newars, who consult her and show her respect. Her children and grandchildren also come to her for support and guidance. Appreciating her own importance, she worries about what her family will do without her.

Krishna Bahadur's City

Krishna Bahadur, a thin, intelligent man of the Gatha caste, is a leader of the Navadurga ritual dance troupe, and has danced in the streets of Bhaktapur as the fierce god Bhairav and as the dangerous goddess Mahakali. Krishna Bahadur's vision of the city is shaped by his role in this troupe of ritual dancers—he knows when and where the troupe must perform, what must be done in each performance, how the Navadurga came to Bhaktapur, and what happens when gods or goddesses walk the streets. As a ritual leader of the Navadurga, he has the power to seal off normally public areas of the city for the performance of secret rites. For him, the city is a complex, fascinating, sacred drama danced by gods and goddesses for audiences of devotees; he sees the city in terms of ritual secrets and sacred power that both threaten and protect. Much of his social identity and sense of self grows out of his role in this ritual drama. I found Krishna alternately dreamy and gentle, moody and preoccupied, tender with his family, intense about his religious life.

While he recognizes that his "low" caste is stigmatized, and challenges this, he wants his son to dance in the Navadurga troupe, and is committed emotionally and intellectually to being part of the Navadurga. The ritual role is some compensation for stigmatized status.

Without being devout in the way Ganesh Lal is—perhaps because he taps religious power in his own right as a dancer and ritual leader—Krishna Bahadur often speaks of gods and goddesses as real presences, as beings one can encounter. For Krishna, the spiritual power (*shakti*) of the gods and goddesses, a power that passes through his hands, is as real, or more real, than anything else.

End Note

I do not see Bhaktapur as Newars do. It is not just that I am inescapably shaped by my own culture; my experience of Bhaktapur is also shaped by the way I was part of—and yet not part of—its cultural and social life. As an outsider, I run the risk of thinking of Newar culture as something Newars "have," not something they "live." Of course Newars do "have" culture—and much more than enters my account—but they live cultural lives.[21]

When Newars walk the streets of Bhaktapur, they see the city in terms of a vast body of slowly acquired cultural meanings, and through the prism of their own lives. Some of this must be very subtle, and much of it will escape the kind of cultural analysis practiced by anthropologists. Much of the significance, many of the meaningful nuances of life, may grow out of experiences in Newar families and religious practice that I have no way of internalizing, of making part of myself. I can decipher and appreciate much. Still, I also miss much. I had not always lived in Bhaktapur and would not always live there. I had no place in Bhaktapur, except through my self-appointed role as anthropologist. I did not have to live there. I could—go home. They were home. This makes a difference.

If my grasp of cultural life in Bhaktapur is shaped by such factors, however, so is the way different Newars engage and experience cultural life—they do not all have the same relationship with their society and culture. Different Newars live different lives, often radically different lives—as different as Brahman and untouchable. They know and experience their total "culture" in different ways. They see their lives and world in different ways. They take what exists for them as part of their shared cultural tradition and reinterpret it for themselves in the context of their lives and place in society.

Thus, Bhaktapur is not one but many cities—a plurality of *imagined* cities within a single urban space. Bhaktapur as a cultural world is distributed among many minds, each with a point of view, and is a different city within each mind.[22] Thus, ultimately, Bhaktapur must be described not from one point of view, but from many shifting and relative points of view. For as one shifts point of view, the city changes.

As a cultural world, Bhaktapur is largely invisible to the outsider. True, you can stand in its streets, even cross the threshold into some of the houses, observe what happens and watch what people do—but the real city is unseen by the uncultured eye. Even to Newars, however, who live their lives there, Bhaktapur is not totally transparent. Since the city is constituted from a variety of points of view, its reality is composed of diverse voices, high- and low-caste, rich and poor, male and female, child and adult, Hindu and Buddhist—in all their individuality, in all their power to impose different meanings, cultural and personal, on the city. Some of these "imagined cities" are opaque to each other: the Brahman may not be able to "see" the untouchable's city, modern youth may not be able to "see" the city of their parents and grandparents. Viewing life in terms of what they know, feel, and experience as Brahman or untouchable, as rich or poor, as young or old, Newars cannot easily grasp the meanings that life in Bhaktapur has for others, whose social positions and life experiences are different. Or they may see it only obscurely.

This book is just one telling of life in Bhaktapur; many others are possible. To some extent, the different versions of reality and visions of life that make up the total city overlap and interbleed, each into the other; there is a core of shared sacred symbols and religious meanings, of moral values, of political and economic structure, of social relations. While this cultural core affects virtually every one in Bhaktapur, shaping and constraining what they know and do, it does not yield one point of view. It would be wrong to privilege one vision, one version of Newar culture, making it canonical, thereby denying reality to others. Newar culture cannot be reduced to a single, dominant conception of reality. Indeed, what is shared—sacred symbols, the religious ethos, the caste system, principles of family organization—far from foreclosing diversity, generates the range of points of view we find, and spurs men and women to create many versions of "reality" as vehicles for their own socially and culturally embedded lives. Newars may experience even what they share—key symbols and social institutions—in radically different ways.

CHAPTER TWO

Society, Person, and Moral Order

One evening I went to a Newar feast at the shrine of the goddess Mahakali, outside the city on a hill with trees. This feast was a celebration, thanking the goddess for the good fortune of a family; goats were sacrificed, and many of the friends of the family were invited.

At traditional feasts, Newars eat sitting in rows or lines; the eldest or most senior person, in terms of the deference that must be shown him, sits at the head of the line. Young boys sit farthest away, at the end of the line. Brahman guests sit above other castes. All men except the host eat before all women; the host and his wife eat last of all. I sat, not in the main line but somewhat apart, with two others. Although the guests were explicitly ranked, the hierarchical symbolics of the order of seating did not prevent people from conversing with each other, in a lively and animated way, frequently laughing at jokes told in loud, cheerful tones. The local liquor being drunk lent something to the spirit of things. Symbolically, there was a mixed message: people were eating together, which suggests solidarity; but they were ranked by where they sat, expressing a hierarchical order. What struck me most of all was the conviviality, the evident pleasure and care taken in being social. In time, I came to see celebrations such as this as expressions of a vision of life; for Newars, the person, society, and the universe are sacred and moral.

I want now to explore certain aspects of Newar concepts of the person, of society, and of ultimate reality, and show not only how such concepts help constitute a moral order—surely an essential task—but also how these are reworked by social actors, as they seek to relate these concepts to their own lives and experience. Thus, concepts that are shared by all Newars—concepts that stand at the heart of the Newar moral order—do not necessarily have the same meaning for all Newars.

There are a number of reasons for this, but I think two are especially important. First, social experience makes a difference; key cultural concepts may acquire different meanings for persons positioned in society in different ways. Brahmans and untouchables, for example, are likely to formulate the meaning of the culture they share in radically different ways; basic elements of the Hindu tradition take on different meaning for them because they live different lives within the caste system.

A second reason has to do with human agency, with the capacity to reflect and act on culture. The capacity for reflection, for re-relating self to culture, and culture to self, surely contributes to the development of different meanings for shared cultural concepts or symbols; the dominant concepts of a culture may be resisted by reflective individuals, who may construct alternate ways of knowing self, society, and world, using any one of a number of modes of thought—by teasing out the implications of cultural concepts, by working through contradictions in culture, by juxtaposing and synthesizing different cultural perspectives, by reframing one set of cultural experiences or propositions in terms of another, or by narrating a new context for reevaluating the cultural construction of person, society, and world. Every culture, I take it, contains these dynamic possibilities within itself, since culture is the historical product of human thought and action.[1]

We can always use culture to reformulate culture, making it relevant to our experience in new ways, as the conditions of life demand. We are the agents as well as the subjects of culture. While a moral order is the product of a cultural tradition, people do not have an absolutely passive relationship to this tradition. True, they receive culture, and are shaped by it, and they come to know themselves within the framework of shared meanings that constitutes a moral order; but they also make and remake culture, and they can find new meaning for, and new ways of relating themselves to, pre-existing culture. They possess the capacity to reinvent themselves within culture and to reimagine the moral order.

Life-in-Society

"I think society is a god."

—a Newar Brahman

We can begin with the pleasures—and pressures—of life-in-society. The very idea of "society" (*samaj*) has conscious moral value for Newars; it invokes a sense of obligation. This may be experienced as a burden. At the same time, relatedness is experienced as a human need and a source of happiness; it is what people desire. Newar cultural concepts of "society," of the organized nature and significance of social life help constitute and focus moral discourse, making society an object of commitment, and shaping the experience of relatedness. This produces some ambivalence; even while Newars celebrate social life as central to their lives, they often seek to evade some of the demands of "society."

Newars often define "society" in contrast to the family or hearth group, the core of patrilineal kin. "Society" consists of those with the power to judge and sanction the family and its members. It thus includes kin outside of the immediate family, and a range of nonkin—friends, neighbors, the people of the city.

As Newars conceive of it, society ideally objectifies and embodies *dharma*, the moral order of the world. Dharma is most perfectly expressed in religious rites, but the conduct of everyday life should reflect it as well—dharma must be put into action in society. Within this framework, in which the basic connection of dharma and society is taken for granted, the idea of samaj in Newar moral discourse tends to be reified and treated as a concrete moral agency. "Society" judges individuals; people fear "society," even while they recognize its necessity and enjoy its pleasures.

Deifying Society

Let us first probe a serious thinker's serious reflections on the nature of society and morality. When I ask the Brahman Dharma

Raj why people do good, even when not threatened with punishment for doing wrong, he gave a reply that discloses something fundamental about the way Newars see "society."

> This is [the result of] society. I think society is a god. So society provides for punishment.
> (How is society a god?)
> It is a feeling [*bhabana*], a god-feeling. If I do not respect society, I am like an animal. So society is not like the god Vishnu, a god with arms, it is not like that, only a god. We have to respect society. Whatever you respect, that is a god. If this is so, then I will be moral [*naitik*]. If I do not respect society, then I will not be moral. To be immoral is a great sin. People have to be moral in this life. . . . This is an absolute truth. [He pauses.] But there can be different accounts of what is moral.

Notice how Dharma Raj frames his answer to implicate society; he then asserts that society is a god, and contradicts the supposition of the question, asserting that society would punish people. Intrigued by the idea of society as a god, I ask about it, and Dharma Raj then launches into his reflections: even when not faced with immediate punishment people are moral because they "respect" society. In Dharma Raj's thought, society is godlike because "whatever you respect, that is a god." Such respect, he says, is what makes people moral. People act morally not just because they fear punishment (although society will punish them, and they do fear this) but because they respect society.

Dharma Raj is a sophisticated thinker, and his views here bear a certain discernible family resemblance to Emile Durkheim's venerable theory of society and religion. Both thinkers deify society; Dharma Raj does consciously and deliberately what Durkheim said people do unconsciously—personify and represent society to the imagination in the form of a sacred being or symbol. Up to a point Dharma Raj would probably agree with Durkheim's (1915) argument that "society has all that is necessary to arouse the sensation of the divine in minds, merely by the power that it has over them"—like a god, society is a superior agency, and people are dependent on it—but he might not permit any simple closure for this idea. There is another side to his position: society is a god; it arouses respect and inspires moral sentiments (the classical

Durkhemian chord); but he will go on to assert that human agency and individual moral consciousness make a difference. People make society—and their capacity to do so is also godlike.

As a sophisticated thinker, Dharma Raj also recognizes the problem of moral relativism, of alternative constructions of truth and morality. He reflects on how you might know "truth" and recognize a "real" society—one worthy of respect, and of being deified. In his vision, society is a god, but society-as-god is a human moral construction.

> **A true thing must be moral. [We] ought not to do what is immoral. In order to be moral I must respect society. When I follow society, however, I must look to real society. If everyone here is bad, and if they keep on being bad, then society will be bad. To make society good is my work, your work, it is everyone's obligation. We should not make society bad. If we make society good, then I will be good, and everyone will be good. If society is hurt, then everyone will be hurt.**

In his discussion, Dharma Raj began by speaking of society as a god external to the self. Society-as-god must be respected; this will generate moral behavior. Now he has added another dimension to his discussion: he views a "good" society—one that should be respected as a god—as a human creation. It is not external to them, but the expression of their collective will and action. Dharma Raj apparently sees moral consciousness as the product of two objective realities: the power of society to shape people, and the power of people to shape society. For him, both powers are god-like.

I would not say Dharma Raj's views are shared by all Newars— there are few things all Newars agree on. However, he is not alone in his vision of a moral order, either among Newars or within the Hindu tradition. Kirin Narayan (1989: 227–228) quotes an Indian religious storyteller, Swamiji, who also envisions society-as-god. Swamiji spoke to her of god, Bhagavan, "as a morality monitoring force collectively projected within social relations." Swamiji, she writes, "sees Bhagavan as a system of rules that help people live together harmoniously, yet as a human creation based on inspiration from the divine Inner Self." Like me, Narayan was struck by the resonances with Durkheim. Equally striking, and more significant perhaps, are the parallels between the views of Narayan's

Swamiji and Dharma Raj's vision; the convergence suggests that "deifying society" is indeed an idea that many reflective Hindus find "good to think."

Even if unusually reflective and articulate, I think that Dharma Raj's meditation on society discloses a basic sentiment about society, and powerfully expresses fundamental Newar intuitions about social life.

Note, for example, how conformity is ethicized in his account. One argument Dharma Raj makes is that conformity leads to being moral; this argument presupposes that society is "good." Conformity is thus not an ideal for its own sake, but a means to an end—the collective good.

This argument poses a problem. If it is good or necessary to conform to society, what makes society good to conform to? If society creates the moral code, or if society reflects a moral code inherent in people's being or nature, then perhaps morality is simply relative—different societies and different social actors will have radically different moralities, either because they live in different societies or because their moral codes are inherent in their substance, in "what they are." Everyone is a thief in a country of thieves, as another Brahman told me. That is, the moral code that applies to them is inherent in the "being" or "substance" of their country—it is their "nature" to be thieves.

Dharma Raj rejects this moral relativism. He has a way to avoid it. He claims people should respect society, not because they draw their being or nature from society, but because society is a moral order. How is society moral? Not because objective moral codes are immanent in persons or society, but because persons act to make society moral. For Dharma Raj, the morality of society is made, not merely acquired as a member of society, and not simply derived from natural substance. There is a kind of paradoxical loop here, a willingness to juxtapose diverse and apparently contradictory perspectives to generate a fuller and more robust view of the nature of a moral order. Even if the moral order of society reflects the natural and sacred order, society makes people what they are. Even if society makes people what they are, people make society. Ethical human action makes society moral; but if people make society moral, society makes them moral. People should conform to a code that they both create (as agents) and inherit (as natural beings and as members of society). People make society into god. God-as-society is the collectivity, the people as a community of moral agents.

With this vision, Dharma Raj both displays and contradicts or transcends what has been identified as one of the key constructs of Hindu culture: the idea that people's moral codes are inseparable from their "nature," their biomoral substance, which they inherit at birth as members of particular social units and categories (castes, families, sexes) (Inden and Nicholas 1977). In this cultural construction of moral reality, what people do (or should do) is determined by what they are—as material bodies, as persons composed of substances, processes, and entities that are both moral and physical in nature. What people are also determines their place in society, since their "nature" fits them for certain social roles and enjoins certain patterns of behavior that fit them into the social order in defined ways; society expresses the ordered relations of different "natural kinds" of persons. In Dharma Raj's world, however, people *also* make themselves and society, and then live in the world they have made.

For although Dharma Raj's cultural metaphysics may assert as "fact" the belief that natural substance and moral code, physical and moral nature, are "mutually translatable" (as McKim Marriott phrases it), he elects here to privilege action, making it a higher order "reality"—thus validating human agency and the power to make culture, society, and self.[2] In other interviews, he suggested that the source of the capacity "to make society good" exists beyond gods and society, in the transcendent dharma. This reestablishes an "objective" order for the morality of society. He recognized that this, too, is open to interpretation. For Dharma Raj, the moral order is viewed as both objective and subjective, as both a reflection of the natural and sacred order of the universe and as the creative product of collective human will and action.

This does not resolve the basic ethical problem, but it shifts the locus of the argument, and enlarges the cultural "space" for reflective thought. What is "good" cannot just be inferred from the way society is. The good, the true, and the real must have some other grounds than the status quo; the moral order must be maintained and regenerated through the actions of a community. Dharma Raj's discourse is a spiraling, open-ended dialogue of diverse concepts and shifting perspectives, not a simple application of a single dominant premise. He constructs his interpretive discourse to gives himself access to the other side of every limiting premise, crossing almost seamlessly through opposing visions of society, self, and reality, raising different perspectives on the moral order, making it possible to "know" society and the person in radically disjunctive ways—taking society first as objective and natural, then as human construction, defining the person from one angle as a natural kind, from another as self-made. His discourse reflects the internal diversity of his culture, and the dynamics of his own interpretive work.

I believe his discourse also reflects the needs of practice, of lived life—as opposed to pure metaphysical or cultural speculation, although there is a philosophical quality to his arguments. I believe his intent, however, is not to advance a metaphysical system, but to probe the underpinnings of the practical politics of morality in Newar society. If this is his goal, he must leave room for collective action, for a responsiveness to moral suasion, to appeals to join in group efforts.

Experience and Society

Newars find meaning for society, as we have just seen, in moral analysis, in reflective thought. But there are pre-reflective modes of knowing society, too, and these also shape the meaning of social life. Newars not only argue that people are social, in the rhetoric they use to persuade themselves that they live in a certain kind of moral world; they experience themselves as social, and reflect on this experience in ways that affect their moral discourse. Their experience—of emotions, of commitments, of attachment—anchor the reflective, analytical thoughts of someone like Dharma Raj, and shape a crucial sense of identity for many Newars.

Dharma Raj speaks of such experience in the following passage, as he seeks to define what "being social" means: "People are social. Although I go to live in the city of Kathmandu, I love my home, Bhaktapur. Since I am a shaped in this way, shaped by my Newar turn of mind,[3] I am a person of this community, this Bhaktapur . . . It is in Bhaktapur that I must die—I must not die anywhere else." The "person" is defined here in terms of a bond with place. Dharma Raj identifies himself with the city, and expresses this in terms of an emotion, love, and an imperative, to die in the city.

FIGURE 17   Musical groups on a festival day.

Emotions express connections with kin, caste, and city. As an example of the social nature of Newars, Govinda Raj, another Brahman, cites the annual round of festivals; these are times of celebration, of conviviality, that are viewed as essential to being a Newar. "Newars," he says, "must gather for festivals" in the twa:, the neighborhoods of Newar cities.

During festivals, we must go forth in religious processions. We must carry the palanquins of the gods and goddesses in these processions. We must play devotional music [to the gods]. People must gather to sing hymns in each twa:. All of this will happen as long as Newars live together in the twa:. Otherwise it won't work. So it is necessary [to live together].

If a Newar cannot be here for our festivals, if he has to be outside, then he will be sad. If a Newar of Bhaktapur is somewhere else, but is able to return for the autumn festival of Mohani, he will be happy. If he stays away, if he does not come, then he will desire to be there—inside himself he will imagine the festival, he will remember everything—"My mother, my father, the God

FIGURE 18 A musical group on its way to one of the Goddess shrines that encircle the city during a festival. These men are farmers. Drums—of which Newars have many kinds—are important instruments.

and the Goddess, the feasts, the worship." He will be filled with memories of this, of these people. Sometimes he might cry, might cry. . . .

If at all possible, he will not stay away. He will return—to be near his brothers, to be near the people of his twa: and his court-yard, to be near his affines and his sisters. He will return home for the puja to brothers. The older brothers need the younger. The sisters need the brothers. Brothers need sisters.

I have cut Govinda off; he goes on to specify how each family member needs every other: the younger brothers need the older sisters, and so on, until he exhausts all the possibilities. He then sums up: "They are necessary."

Mutuality, reciprocity, and interdependency are central Newar values. Emotion relates self to these values. Note how Govinda frames his assertions about the structure and necessity of interdependence in terms of psychological experience; he stresses the

FIGURE 19 A Buddhist procession in largely Hindu Bhaktapur, passing by a house with the elaborate wooden windows found in many old Newar houses. In the right foreground is a structure known as a *phalca*, a typical feature of Newar neighborhoods, used here as a platform to observe the procession.

emotion associated with relatedness. Invoking emotion in this way, like the actual experience of such emotion, expresses commitments to persons, groups, places, and events. Thus, a person is linked to his "home," his family and community, by feelings: being away is haunted by memories that provoke sadness, bringing people to tears.

"The People Are a God"

In society, Newars assert, people must help each other. Govinda gives this example:

> Suppose a person is making a courtyard. . . . I must help them. Others must help. Even if the help is not really needed, they will help. Help must be offered when someone dies, too. This help is not just voluntary, it is a duty [*kartabya*]. It is dharma [said with

emphasis]. It is necessary that we do this. In this way, we give help to each other. But if we are alone—there is no help for those who are alone. We must have the help of others in order to live.

At the time, I thought it was odd that Govinda immediately followed up this assertion that Newars need the help of others in order to live by pointing out once again that Newars needs others in order to die. "When a person dies," he said, "they must be taken to the cremation grounds. Everyone is needed."[4] I was thinking, I suppose, of death as an individual phenomena, as a biological process—the individual body dies. This is not the way Newars view death. For them, death is also an event within the web of interdependency.

Death, for Newars, is a social process. Cooperation—in life as in death—has the status of a moral imperative. Kin, the members of a special group, the death society (*si-guthi*), and representatives from a number of different castes take part, helping with the process of dying, the preparation of the corpse, the cremation, and the death rites. The help given the dead and their survivors becomes a general symbol of interdependency as a fundamental principle of life: no one can be cremated properly without help; no one can obtain salvation without the help of kin and community.

Should a person reject the obligation to participate in community affairs, he risks community disapproval. A person should not do "whatever he likes," but should conform to public morality and respect the will of the community, or face enmity and isolation.

Living in a twa:, people should not do whatever they like. Rather, they should obey the rules. They should not do whatever they like, and they should conform to the rules—these are two sides of the same thing. While living in society, we must respect society's rules. The rules of society must be followed, meaning a person must go along with the desires of the people of the twa:. The desires of the twa: are good desires. If I harmonize with everyone to make the twa: good, then we will be raised up [will have *unnati*, prosperity, dignity, be elevated].

(The desires of others, the ideas of others must be followed?)

Yes, they must be followed. Good ideas must be followed. You must not just do what you want.

(Otherwise?)

If a person does things that are not to the liking of the twa:, then suffering (dukha) will come to that person.

(What kind of dukha?)

He could get sick. He would need help then. But people won't help. The twa: gives help to those who are liked—will help them when they suffer. Or this person might have to go frequently to Kathmandu. There would be no one at home. A thief might steal [from his home].

(Some people need help. They have needs. But nowadays there are many rich people who don't need help. So will they respect the ideas of others?)

In regard to that, think about the fact that Newars have to do religious work (dharma). For example, suppose there is a great god or goddess in this part of the city. We plan to worship this deity in order to ask for forgiveness—but we need money to do this. Or suppose a water supply is needed. To build a water tap, or to do a puja—everyone is agreed [on the need for this] and they all work as one. Since a lot of money is needed, they go to a wealthy merchant. They tell him—this twa: is about to undertake an important project, and we need money. Now if this person does not respect the wishes of the people of the twa:, he may not give them any money. There is no obligation. He can refuse. But even though there is no obligation, he will have offended the people of the twa:. And because they are offended, the people of the twa: may say, "This merchant, he has a lot of money, yet he refuses to give any for this work of dharma—he does not contribute to this public work." In the future, this person may need the people of the twa:—or maybe he will never need them. But money is not everything. Money and the heart are separate. The people of the twa: will despise him. Their resentment will be a great curse for him.

So it is better to be someone who is well-liked. And things happen. Even though he is rich, he could die. If he dies, he must be taken to the burning grounds. To carry him to the place of death, a *guthi* is needed. The twa: is needed. But they won't care. He did whatever he liked, without respecting the wishes of the people. . . .

He has money, and he commits a sin *(pap)* by not respecting the will of the people of the twa:. This is a Hindu samskara [idea, turn of mind, attitude]. If here all the people are—here where all the people are, is the god Vishnu/Narayana. So if you do not respect all the people, you are guilty of not respecting Narayana. The people are a god. The people, meaning Narayana.

Society (samaj) is here equated with the neighborhood, the twa:. The twa: is spoken of as a moral community; it undertakes collective projects for the good of all that require sacrifices by all, but especially by those with the greatest means. In return, the community provides help when needed. Individuals who fail to do what is expected of them, and thus sever the bonds of communal reciprocity, not only risk isolation, they arouse enmity. This criticism of social disengagement is ethicized by portraying the community as forming a divinity. The people, constituted as a community, are a god, a form of the god Vishnu, a deity who is an ethical activist, a preserver of the moral order. Since the will of the community is the will of a god who sustains the moral order, an offense against the community is, at least metaphorically, a sin, an offense against god.

Caste and the Limits of Solidarity

If the face-to-face mutuality of the family, kin, and twa: is one nucleus of social sentiment, solidarity with one's caste is another. A Brahman put it this way: "Long ago, Bhaktapur became a kingdom. We Brahmans settled here. In the same way, Butchers came to live here, outside [the area inhabited by Brahmans]. When a Newar builds a house there, he becomes like a Butcher." Notice, not only the spatial separation of castes—Brahmans live "here," in the heart of the city, Butchers live "outside"—but also how the Butcher caste is not even considered Newar in this passage, although they would be in other contexts. Following is a highly simplified overview of the most important levels of the Hindu Newar caste hierarchy in Bhaktapur.

1. Brahmans.
2. Chathar. Consists of 31 thars. Members of the Chathar like Shiva Bhakta are called *Chathariya*.
3. Pancthar. Consists of 35 thars. Members are called *Panchthariya*.
   (Note: The Brahmans, Chathar, and Pancthar are the traditional "high castes" in Bhaktapur.)
4. Jyapu (farmer) and craft groups. This level contains several ranked subdivisions, many of which contain many thars.

5. Borderline "impure" groups. Several ranked groups. This level includes the Gatha, the Navadurga performers, and the Nau, the Barbers.
6. Impure groups. Includes the Butchers and Jugis.
7. Untouchables. Includes the Pore. (Source: Levy 1990)

The Brahman goes on to say that a high-caste person who lives in a low-caste area would "have no honor" in the eyes of his own caste. Yet despite the fact that they have degraded themselves by living in a low-caste area, "they will try to stay with their own, in their own caste (jat)." Sensing, perhaps, that this was not clear to me, the Brahman endeavors to explain. "If a person is not with his own kind (caste, jat), if he lives someplace else, he won't have society (samaj)." Realizing he must now explain what he means by "society," he goes on:

To have society means—if one person is next to another, that is literally society, but we Newars think and feel that this is not really what it means to be social. When I live with people of my own kind (jat, caste), that is really society. It may not be so important at other times, but in order to have a *guthi* or in order to worship the lineage deity, in order to celebrate the festival of Mohani, you like to be with your own gods, you want to observe your own rules, and you wish to be with your lineage brothers. Sometimes your own people fight. But even though they fight, they love each other.

What he is saying, in essence, is that while economic and symbolic interdependency is possible in the caste hierarchy, moral and emotional solidarity with other castes is not possible. It is stigmatizing to even live among them, and one can only feel alien among them; you feel at home only with "your own" gods, rules, and kind. Note how caste and kinship apparently merge in his mind—he begins his discussion speaking of the separateness and honor of Brahmans, but ends by speaking of the love of "lineage brothers."

"Like a God"

If society is like a god, and "the people," as a community of agents, are a god for Newars, so is the human person, both as self and as other. Newars envision the individual, as well as the community, as godlike. This is true in several different senses. As an actor in the social world, a person may be "like a god" (as Newars put it), embodying some of the qualities of a sacred being. They may deserve the same kind of ritual respect and deference shown to a deity. Just as one bows to a god, one can bow to a person, or to the god within the person. Moreover, if a person is "like a god" in this social sense, a person is also truly a god, in an metaphysical sense, according to some religious perspectives available to Newars. The person is ultimately one with the godhead. The human world is illusory.

Let me briefly discuss the implication of the idea that a person is "like a god," since I believe this is a key concept in Newar social and ritual life. Note that what we have here is a comparison, not an identification—a person is not a god, but "like a god." This maintains the distinction between true gods and human beings, and between the human moral order and the sphere of action of the deities. I doubt that Newar moral consciousness would allow much free passage between the two. Not all Newar gods are moral, after all, nor are they subject to human concepts of right and wrong. Some are dangerous (remember that the protective goddesses of the city used to eat human beings) and must be controlled magically and ritually. Unrestrained, these dangerous gods may behave in ways that clash with the human moral order, acting on their desires without regard for the consequences, seeking self-fulfillment without moral concern for others. This is feared, not celebrated. Identification with this proclivity would threaten the human moral order. Thus, when Newar say a person is "like a god," they are not giving them social permission to act out destructive desires (although they may use the simile to excuse some mild antisocial behavior by some persons).

What they do with the simile "like a god" is create a kind of analogue to divine honor within human society. It forges a connection with the ritual system and within religious consciousness that permits the ritual validation of persons who are worthy of reverence because they possess some special social, moral, or spiritual quality. Such persons, if not "worshiped" precisely in the way deities are, at least become the recipients of ritual acts and offerings that are in some respects analogous to such worship. The godlike qualities of persons are associated mostly with social roles and transitions; individuals are "worshiped" as "like gods" or "goddesses" in domestic rites that celebrate who they are, or who they are becoming, as social persons, as they pass through the life cycle. For example, Newar girls, in one female rite of passage, are "like goddesses," and are ritually married to a god. Newars will tell you this is so the girl can never become a widow, and so will not suffer the often harsh fate of a widow; but it is also one of many occasions on which Newars declare and celebrate the sacredness of the person.

Such rituals leave little room for doubt about the moral value of persons—for if a person is declared to be like a god, and ritually treated as like a god, they are, in a potentially profound social and psychological sense, just that—*like a god*. They are identified with sacred beings who deserve homage. Since they are typically honored as social beings who do or embody dharma, they are further identified with dharma, that is, with the moral and religious order that provides the ultimate foundation for life. Moreover, this sense of the sacredness of self and other (and I think sacredness is not too strong a phrase) is continually reinforced, since everyone has the opportunity to be honored by others in this fashion, and to show respect to them; these mutual acknowledgments of worth help people sustain and nurture their vital relationships.

Children, in general, are said to be "like gods," and this comparison acknowledges their relative freedom from obligations and constraints, a result of their inability to conform to the moral code. Since children are "like gods," their many minor transgressions are supposed to be forgiven (if not necessarily allowed to pass without comment), and they are not stigmatized in the way an adult would be, since gods are beyond human morality.

Older persons, too, are "like gods." Their survival to a ripe old age is celebrated in a ritual called *budha janko*. Asked why the aged are "like gods," people give various answers: some said because they are full of experience and wisdom, and some said because the old are close to death. As with children who cannot be held responsible for their acts, older persons, too, may be excused by attributing to them a divine freedom from human morality.

The adult is sacred within the web of social relationships: brothers are worshiped by sisters, in the rite of *kija puja*, along with the gods, who are asked to protect the brother and give him a long life. The duties of husbands and wives toward each other are forms of dharma, and so fuse the sacred and the moral. Husbands are like gods; the wife "worships" the husband as godlike, performing many ritual acts of worship that are also performed on or for images of the Hindu deities.

I did not hear it said that wives are "like gods," although they have a dharma to follow as wives; this may reveal the patriarchal bias of this patrilineal culture, where the dominant, "official," ideology asserts the subordination of women to men. Women may be likened to Parvati, Shiva's wife. Parvati is a humanlike figure compared to the dangerous Tantric goddesses, and her mythology in Nepal conveys an idealized vision of the role of a woman. As Lynn Bennett has put it for other Nepalese groups, the Goddess in her gentle aspect, and especially as Parvati, embodies the "pure and faithful wife" and "selfless, nurturing mother"—constituting "an impossibly perfect model, embodying the contradictory values of Hinduism as they affect women" (1983: 273). Women may identify with the humanity of this divinity; as Bennett remarks, Parvati represents "Hindu women's own idealized perceptions of themselves and the problems they face" in Hindu society.[5] As mothers, Newar women are worshiped as "like gods" by their children, and given gifts of fruit and flowers on ritual occasions (Levy 1990: 433).

If people are "like gods" for many purposes, there are also ways in which they are more directly connected and identified with sacred beings and realities, and so, from certain perspectives, possess divinity. As I will show in later chapters, in Newar culture the body, mind, and self are not cut off from the sacred; they are permeable and receptive to it. Sacred forces and energies may be animated within the body or self in meditation or worship. Newars say a god—generally identified as a form of Vishnu—dwells in the "heart" of each person.

Indeed, each and every person is, from the point of view of one set of metaphysical ideas Newars possess, a projection of the godhead or ultimate soul, and can be reabsorbed into it. Dharma Raj, with his bent for reversals, gave a twist to this identification of human beings with divinity, suggesting that perhaps every god and goddess is a projection of the self. Worshiping the gods and goddesses, he said, is like looking in a mirror. We see ourselves.

FIGURE 20   Statue of Vishnu—guardian of the moral order and the
divinity who "dwells in the heart"—in his cosmic form at Changu Narayan.

The Scrutiny of Society

The way persons are godlike, and intimately connected to the
sacred, does not exempt them from the scrutiny of society, or make
them immune to social pressure. Concern for the opinion of others
is a key factor in Newar evaluations of behavior and in behavior
choice. Most Newars are keenly aware of the scrutiny of society, and
are highly sensitive to disapproval. While conformity is not, perhaps, a value in itself, powerful pressures to conform do flow from
the way Newars conceive of society as a moral agency. The Newar
concept of samaj has built into it the expectation that others will confer about and evaluate a person's behavior; "society" grants relatively little in the way of legitimate privacy and personal freedom.

For example, a Newar woman reported that when she would
come home at an early evening hour that her parents considered
late, they would scold her by saying "It is not proper for a daugh-
ter-child to be out late at night. What will society (samaj) say?"

Such statements are common; and society does say much about behavior considered irregular, making it the subject of gossip. "Society" in this mother's reproach of her daughter includes patrilineal and affinal kin, neighbors, members of the twa:, and friends—the major concrete reference groups outside the immediate family. *Ijjat,* which can be glossed variously as "prestige, social esteem, honor, reputation, worth or value in the estimation of others, or social standing" is a major concern "in front of" these groups.

At times, people seek to shield themselves from the scrutiny of society. I once asked high-caste Shiva Bhakta what he would do if his son married a woman of lower caste. He admitted this was a possibility; in the modern setting sons may earn their own money and so might defy their fathers. He went on to say that the main thing is to see that caste (jat) is not lost by an inter-caste marriage. If a husband eats food prepared by a woman of lower status, he risks losing his caste standing. If, however, a man marries a woman from a caste that is somewhat lower than his own (but not untouchable), and does not eat food cooked by her, then he will not lose his caste standing.[6]

> Even if [my son] married a woman of a lower caste, our own caste is not lost. This is the main thing. If a man in his house eats boiled rice [that the woman has prepared] then he will become low caste. But what this man can say outside is—"I don't eat the rice my woman makes. I make and eat my own rice." It is enough to say "I don't let the woman in the kitchen." It is easy to eat inside, in private. Inside where no one can see him, he can eat rice cooked by his woman, and if he does so, it is enough to say "I don't eat what she cooks." This kind of society (samaj), this is Newar society.

He does not go as far as to openly endorse such behavior, claiming rather that he is tradition minded—"I am still an old one"—but neither does he stress that it is behavior deserving moral condemnation. He presents it simply as what many would do in this situation. In his discussion with me, at least, he treated it as a solution to the problem of managing impressions so as to seem to be conforming to social norms. He maintained this was a common practice. So did others, who also noted that it was a transparent tactic; few would be taken in by it. The success of this tactic would depend on the sympathy and support granted the person attempting such a deception.

There is in fact a range of reactions to offenses against norms. Some Newars are severe in their judgment of violations, as indicated by the complete ostracism inter-caste couples often face. They ethicize the breach, defining it as deeply wrong. Others, as Shiva indicated, view some kinds of violations as a problem in managing impressions and securing support, maintaining that breaches of conventions do not matter as long as others do not know about them.

Often, the line between a sense of duty and a concern with social opinion is blurred. One high-caste Newar spoke of a number of things as "dharma" and "duty" which a person "must do"; but added that one would lose "prestige" (ijjat) if one failed to do so. He said that if people did not do dharma, things could go wrong, and a person would feel bad or nervous; then he might die. And then: "society will say, they did not do their traditional work, their dharma. So Ram died." Thus, Newars do dharma as a duty, but also out of fear of social opinion. Of course, some Newars might deny this is a distinction that makes a difference—since society is a god—but in their more pragmatic moments most Newars seem to distinguish these motives and evaluate them differently.

Newars both assert moral norms, and talk about circumventing them. People "talk up" the moral (society is good, one must follow the dharma) and so assert a moral basis for social life, and yet talk of ways to get around moral norms (for example, deny in public what you do in private), and use hedges such as "it depends on the situation." Such "deethicizing" discourse seems as important within the moral system as affirmations of values. In general, traditional Newars do not challenge the ethical status of the central institutions (family, religion) of the traditional moral system, with the partial exception of the caste order. Rather, they find ways not to do exactly what moral norms require them to do, but without directly challenging the values those norms express. The discourse and actions that disguise or reframe the moral character of violations create an ambiguity that allows people to act in violation of principles they uphold (E. McHugh, personal communication). The way that Newars speak of circumventing norms does not necessarily discredit the moral principles that are the grounds for those norms. Public exposure of violations could, however, discredit the violator. These principles thus retain a certain power,

even as people sometimes seek to get around them for various purposes and with various justifications, some moral and some not.

The Sacred Order

"To do what you must do, that is dharma."

A Newar Brahman, asked to give me a brief definition of dharma,
laughed and replied he could only give examples; he said doctors
must treat patients, birds must feed their young, and Newars worship. This is dharma. He went on to say, more abstractly, that
dharma is duty, is religion, is tradition, and that it depends on the
situation. He emphasized that it is both social and religious,
embodied in ethical acts, in conformity to tradition, in social reciprocity and solidarity, and in devotion to the deities. A failure to do
dharma would, he indicated, produce both social disapproval on
the part of others, and feelings of anxiety, regret or remorse on the
part of the person who failed to perform his "duty."[7]

Dharma does not have a single meaning; it is a mutable, open-tex-
tured concept, used flexibly in a variety of contexts. The core sense,
the abstract kernel of the concept, invoked each time the concept is
used, seems to be something like "duty" or "principle of right order,"
where these are understood to have a foundation in objective reality—that is, obligation and moral standards exist independently of
human actions, conventions, and agreements. Dharma is "what you
must do" because that is the way the world is, and because you are
who you are—a Hindu householder, or a bird, or a physician.

This empty, abstract notion of objective obligation is then filled
in with specifics: dharma begins as an abstract concept, but as it is
defined by social actors soon becomes a symbol of all that is important and necessary in life. "What you must do" is maintain traditions or perform rituals; society embodies the objective principle of
right order (dharma) in the form of a caste hierarchy, or a web of
reciprocity. Taking care of the young is a duty incumbent on living
beings; Newars must nurture their children with rituals as well as
food and love. Dharma is religion; Newars must worship their own
gods and goddesses. In this fashion, each particular precept and
concrete practice is imbued with the force of an objective moral
reality that 1) is necessary and natural; 2) defines what is good for
persons and society; and 3) orders life into patterns that, if fol-

lowed, support and protect individuals and the community. To fail to conform to these patterns is to risk self-destruction, or even the destruction of the moral order itself.

In a sense, then, the term *dharma* denotes the entire domain of the moral, as Newars understand it. This domain is characterized not only by specific ideas about what is right and wrong (you must not steal, and you should respect parents, priests, and those who have more wisdom than you do), but also by general conceptions of the good (what the ends of life are), procedural ideas (how to show respect), reality-defining concepts that set the stage for moral action (the workings of purity and impurity), and concepts of the person that endow self and other with significance for each other. Let us now see what some Newars do with the concept of dharma, how they define and use it.

Dharma Defined by Three Newars

Dharma Raj's Dharma Dharma Raj sees dharma in a way consistent with his role in society, with the scope of his learning as a Brahman priest. When I ask him, What is dharma? he places it beyond the ordinary world we perceive with our senses. He locates and characterizes it through paradox, beyond and within the human world simultaneously.

> **Dharma is not red, it is not green. It is not anything. Dharma has no form [*rup*]. Dharma is good works. Bad acts, these are transgressions against the dharma—only good acts are dharma. Although formless, if dharma has a form, it is the form of the god. Dharma exists in the god's form. Dharma also exists in the form of acts. When it takes the form of a deity, dharma is the god Vishnu, the Great God Shiva, the god Ganesh. In the form of acts, dharma is known through transgressions. It exists in this way. It is good works.**

Notice the negative assertions—here dharma is stripped of concrete qualities. It is not red, not green.[8] Dharma is abstract, formless. Yet it takes the form of ethical acts, and is embodied by the great gods. While he does not say so here, for him dharma is also the rituals he performs, which connect people to the gods, and in the stories he tells, which have moral points.

Shiva Bhakta's Dharma Shiva Bhakta, our high-caste Chathariya informant, answers in less abstract terms.

> We have kept dharma from long ago. If we worship the gods and goddesses, that is dharma. Those of long long ago, the ancestors, our great great grandfathers, they kept it . . . It is a very old matter. What it is, if you do puja to the gods, it is dharma. Doing *sraddha* [the rites for the dead] is said to be dharma. To give charity is dharma. . . . The things of dharma are what our mother, our father, and others, did. This came down [to us], and is said to be family custom [*kulacar*; from *kul*, family line, patriline, and *acar*, conduct].
>
> The things that have been done, and kept as customs from the distant past, this kind of thing is called kulacar. Because it is from the kul we must do so. If we do not, it is a sin.

Shiva Bhakta's response is perhaps a more usual one: dharma is an abstract domain, but what concerns people are concrete practices that can be enacted and interpreted as dharma. What is brought into focus are the complex elements that constitute tradition and obligation. The appeal to tradition as a moral obligation is common. But the Brahman's comment indicates the manifold nature of the Newar concept of dharma; it is at once religious, as dharma is manifest in the form of deities; ethical, since it is realized in "good" acts; and social, since it is the basis for relationships. Shiva Bhakta's statement suggests the way in which the definition of "good acts" is incorporated into received tradition. The concepts of kul and dharma raise tradition from the factual to the moral. The things of the past are not understood simply as events that happened, as historical practices, "quaint," "old-fashioned," and outdated, but as duties one is obliged to follow. To fail to do so is a "sin." A Newar conforms to tradition for a variety of reasons, such as fear of the disapproval of others, but a positive ethical justification can also be inferred from remarks such as the above, voiced by many high-caste and Brahman Newars: tradition links the moral actor to the transcendent moral order. It is partly through conformity to tradition that the "formless" universal dharma is embodied in concrete acts within families, lineages, and castes.

Shiva Bhakta views himself as linked to tradition. He knows he must conform to the traditions received from his patrilineal predecessors, his parents and ancestors; his commitment to tradition shapes his acts. Dharma is what one must do. This imperative flows from the realm of kinship. It is *kuldharma*, the dharma of family and kin. This links here-and-now social behavior with a sense of "ultimate values" through the links provided by the successive generations of the kul. A person inherits duties, and a moral career consists in large part in fulfilling these duties, which are a kind of debt. For Newars, one can speculate, harm to tradition is tantamount to harm to persons, to the family line—which includes the dead and those yet to be born.[9]

Low-caste Newars sometimes speak of dharma in different terms. They focus attention not on ritualized links with the transcendent, but on concrete needs.

Mahila's Dharma   Mahila, the untouchable sweeper, defines dharma in terms of solidarity and reputation.

> Dharma means whatever work we are given, to go to be with our friends, if they have some problem, or if they have gotten sick, if we help them, this is dharma. It is good. . . . If we follow dharma, if we do our work and follow our ways, then our sons will be good, our daughters too will be good. If I steal and deceive, then my sons and daughters will be called a thief's sons, a thief's daughters. This is bad. If I do dharma and good work then [people will say] "that man's son is very good. He is one who does great dharma deeds."

Notice how what self does sustains and regenerates morality for and in others whose lives are joined together in relationships. Asked what if he did not do dharma, Mahila says

> And then people will say "What a wicked man [*beiman*, wicked, dishonest]. He does not do dharma." They will say, "That man, he is a bad, dishonest person who does nothing, that's what he is." And then Bhagavan in heaven will know, and will say,"you are not one who does dharma." When we die, there will be no salvation for us.

Mahila takes his characterization of the person who does not follow dharma further when I ask what happens to such people:

They are oppressive and violent people, they are selfish—selfish people don't do dharma. [He gives an example in first person.] I am strong. While I am young, I am strong. But when I am old, no one will care. [While I am young and strong] I won't go anywhere, I won't go to anyone's place to do the work of my [lineage] brothers. If someone calls me, I won't have time. The person who says "I won't come," he is a bad person. He does not do dharma. While he is young he will bring trouble to everyone. And then when he is old and weak, when he is old with a bent back, we will not care for him. . . . They are violent people. Violent, meaning careless and arbitrary. They don't listen to anyone.

(What do they do?)

Later they will have problems. You won't go, and I won't go, and no one else will go to help them out. When that happens to one of that kind, when he gets sick, and lies curled up in a ball [in pain or misery] in the street, smoking cigarettes—like that. Because when he was strong, he did not help anyone. He said whatever he liked to everyone. This is bad. And so I won't go, I will refuse to help him. All of us, you too, will say—no. I will too. The person who has not done dharma, who did not care, who rebuked us, will be homeless, will have no place to go . . . He had no dharma. He spoke violently to us, and so his turn finally came. When he was strong, he said whatever he wanted. When he is old, there is no one to turn to. No friends. He is alone.

The naked importance of reciprocity and solidarity is evident here. Dharma is going to people to help them and share in their work. The person who fails to cooperate or who abuses others will find that his actions have logical social consequences. He will end up isolated, with no one to help him when he needs it. His "turn" will come; he will be abandoned; thus justice will be done. Mahila brings into view a justice scenario based on the logic of reciprocity.

The heightened consciousness of misery we see in this untouchable's account may be a critical factor in the subordination of the low castes. Low-caste men and women fear that they might be reduced to such a state of misery if they offend or threaten the high castes. If reciprocity is essential within their own kin groups and caste, access to work through the "moral economy" of the caste system is just as crucial; often, low castes workers need to maintain vertical economic ties with high caste patrons more than those patrons need them. Within castes also, when solidarity and reciprocity are important, dharma may be seen in pragmatic, not ritual or transcendent, terms.

In meaning construction, "blends" of the pragmatic and the ritual-transcendent senses of dharma naturally occur. None of this is intrinsic to the concept, however, and the meaning of dharma is not dictated by "culture"—if by culture we mean a disembodied system of ideas—but constructed in terms of concrete cultural experience and practice.[10]

Dharma has multiple meanings; it is a "space for" meaning construction. As the testimony of these three Newars—a Brahman, a high-caste merchant, and an untouchable—shows, moral meaning construction is shaped by the way actors are positioned in the social system. Thus, the scope and meaning of moral concepts vary as different social actors express different concerns, activating different meanings for cultural concepts, reflecting their experience of society and life.

This does not mean that the idea of dharma has no meaning apart from what actors confer on it from time to time—dharma is not a totally empty concept. Rather, actors draw on the concept of dharma when they want to frame their discourse in ways the idea of dharma makes possible. Invoking dharma as the frame of their discourse gives what they say or do a special moral emphasis and ethical significance. Being considered dharma gives words or deeds the sense of being deeply ordered and necessary to life. Meaning is built on this abstract "base." It is formulated as part of an intentional discourse, integrated into an intention to communicate something, brought in touch with life, as we saw in the above testimony. This is done by invoking or "profiling" a set of images or conceptual objects against the "base."[11] Actors' judgments or intuitions about what merits being focused in this way vary in ways related to their life experiences and life situations—differently "positioned subjects" construct the meaning of shared cultural symbols and key words in different ways. They profile different experiences and goals against the same "base."

Take the case of Ganesh Lal. As a farmer, he does not construct the meaning of dharma in the way a Newar Brahman, a high-caste householder, or an untouchable does. He constructs its meaning as a farmer, seeing dharma as the propitiation of gods and goddesses through offerings and sacrifices. He said that to leave the dharma was to become an atheist, and suggested that this would bring an intolerable uncertainty into the world, which he views as a natural, a moral and a sacred order, all at once. If there were no deities, farmers could not rely on them to provide rain and ample harvests. If there were no deities to make it rain, how would farmers survive? For him, survival depends on the existence of deities.

Ganesh Lal is a devout man, deeply involved in temple work and in devotional music, but one day when I asked him what heaven and hell were like, he burst out laughing (a rare thing, for he did not laugh much) and responded by asking how would he know, not having died yet. He is more concerned with survival than salvation. When it came to the rains, he believes, or believes he has to believe, in the gods and goddesses, and defines dharma in terms of belief and faith in these deities; but speculations about an afterlife were not the most central part of his faith. For him, dharma is for the rains; it is the religious order that makes the rains come when needed, ensuring a good harvest. Implied by what Ganesh "profiles" against dharma is the fear of suffering, of hunger.

When the rains do not come, I was told, farmers sometimes curse the gods, shaking their fists at the sky.

Dharma is a different moral object for different actors in Newar society. This diversity of meaning reflects their varied positions within society. Actors construct the meaning of dharma in ways that express the moral centers of different life-worlds. These life-worlds are embedded in society, and draw on a shared culture, yet are culturally different. This refraction of meaning is a central cultural process. The "unity" of Newar culture is refracted through the prism of social structure; what is shared metamorphoses into differences. The differences make a difference, constituting life-worlds—the worlds of socially positioned subjects within a larger society and culture.

The notion of worlds within culture may seem paradoxical, as if what is "inside" culture is bigger than culture itself. In a sense, I think this is true: the cultural experience of actors is richer and more complex than the cultural ideas that makes that experience possible. Dharma is an abstract idea, a concept that frames Newar moral thought, experience, and action. It can be understood in abstract terms. It can be treated as a value that people learn— internalize—and enact. Yet look at how Newars represent what dharma means to them. They *formulate a world* to constitute the meaning of dharma. The meaning of the concept of dharma is in the world formulated *around the lives they live*. Different Newar actors *project different worlds* around the base concept of dharma. In doing so, they generate radically different meanings for this key moral and religious concept.[12]

The production of diversity out of unity may reflect the necessary relationship of actors to culture, a relationship obscured in culture theory that implicitly assumes actors are themselves constructions of culture, and nothing more, with minds and selves that "reflect" culture. Actors so conceived receive meaning from culture, because meaning is "in culture." In my view, however, meaning is not located solely in culture, but in a shifting zone of interpretation where culture and actors are linked in interpretive action, in a dialogue, if you will, that is ongoing and open-ended. Actors construct meanings for symbols, for concepts. Cultural concepts and symbols do not interpret themselves; they do not "contain" their own meaning (Reddy 1979; Linger n.d.). Cultural concepts have no power to unilaterally program social actors to think, feel, and act in certain ways; actors must do more than passively internalize culture if culture is to shape their lives and understandings in the significant way it does.

In my view, actors interpret cultural concepts in terms of their total cultural experience, and activate other cultural models, scripts, schema, and scenarios in order to actively and dynamically construct the meaning of key cultural concepts — such as dharma. Lacking any fixed, final meaning, dharma is subject to processes of meaning construction. As the transcript of the words of Shiva and Mahila suggest, meaning construction is a socially mediated process. Meaning is generated in terms of actual social experience, not derived from cultural tradition without the mediation of experience. Actors' interpretations of any key cultural concept is likely to be driven and shaped by their social experience and by other cultural concepts available to them in the form, often, of cultural models (Holland and Quinn 1987). Furthermore, these interpretations will typically be formulated in terms of both cultural and universal processes of meaning construction, as the above passages of transcript illustrate.

Although they share a society and a culture, Shiva, Dharma, and Mahila live in different life-worlds. Can we say that they live in different moral worlds? In at least one sense, I think we can. The "worlds" they formulate to give meaning to dharma are different; they enjoin different kinds of commitments, reflect different kinds of imperatives, and evoke different emotions. What Shiva and Mahila "must do" differs, and the emotions implied and evoked by their discourses differ in parallel. Shiva's sense of continuity and tradition and Mahila's vision of solidarity on the edge of desperation embody dharma in different life-worlds, and these life-worlds are moral worlds for Shiva and Mahila.

At the same time, these worlds do not exist in isolation from each other, and they do derive from a shared society and tradition. Just as we would not today congeal culture into some mechanically abstracted, timeless, motionless, canonical version, we should not view these life-worlds as static. They too change and develop over time, and may recombine and reconstitute themselves in terms of ongoing experience of, and dialogue with, the larger culture and society.

Now let us return to a point made by Dharma Raj. Bad acts, he said, are violations of dharma. Dharma constitutes the possibility of transgressions.

Transgressions

"In this world we live in," Krishna Bahadur told me, "we must not sin." With his usual quiet passion, he listed acts that count as sin and as dharma. "We must not steal, we must not go with other's women. We must do dharma. We must be devoted to our mother and father. And we must from our soul respect, think of, and revere God. And then a person will be worthy. If he is good now, then later, when he dies, he will be saved." Here we can see that dharma and "sin," or moral error, are opposites.

The word I have translated—misleadingly—as "sin" is *pap*.[13] The translation is misleading because Western concepts of sin and Newar concepts of transgression have different connotations and import; after all, they originate in, and resonate evocatively with, different moral and religious traditions, and have meaning in different moral orders. I will also gloss the Newar word (which is derived from Sanskrit) as breach, error, and transgression.

In general, pap are deviations from dharma, violations of dharma. For Newars, a sense of "sin" or "moral error" is a significant aspect of life. They are not, as far as I can tell, overwhelmed or unduly depressed by it, but it touches them in a number of ways. Consider Krishna's words here; he is a gentle man, but you sense something of an inner struggle in his words and tone (at least I do); he is telling me about the way it is, but you can imagine how he urges himself to be good, exhorts himself not to sin.

Only some of their deviations are of real concern to Newars, though perhaps there is a mild pervasive anxiety about "sins," since there are so many things a Newar ought and ought not to do. In some ways, serious "sins"—the major offenses a Newar might term *Mahapap*—are not of great concern to most individuals. They are important for the legal system, and are highly threatening in principle and in fantasy, but such "great sins" are encountered only in rare and extreme crises. This does not mean they lack cultural significance. The proscription on killing cows, which carried a penalty of imprisonment of up to twelve years in the old state legal code (Höfer 1979: 204), is consistent with the cultural meaning of cows in Hindu thought. But the proscription is symbolic of sacred values and worldview, not a matter of practical behavior choice. Newars do not report that they have to struggle to restrain impulses to slaughter sacred cows. The problem in behavior choice does not arise. The intent to commit the more serious breaches are not acted on, either because such impulses never arise, or are controlled before they become motives for behavior. Such transgressions are enormities; they are outside the scale of ordinary life. They are represented culturally, but are for most Newars virtually unthinkable as actual acts. Yet they clearly carry the basic justice scenario of the moral system—as acts contrary to dharma, they expose individuals and the community to risks. The danger is proportionate to the enormity of the transgression. By knowing about such evils, people develop a sense of the central significance of order, and are made aware of the possibility of chaos.

Minor sins, on the other hand, affect ordinary Newars in ordinary circumstances. But although they are part of daily life—perhaps even, in the Newar view of things, unavoidable—these too are arguably not a central concern for most Newars, since there are ways to undo or mitigate their consequences. Although a sin may bring misery to the person who commits it, if not in the present life then in future lives, there are alternative explanations for suffering that do not see present misfortunes as caused by past actions.

If dharma is what you must do, then sin is what you must not do. When I ask Krishna Bahadur to tell me what a sin is, he gives almost the same answer that Mahila offered: "A sin is an act that you should not do." Krishna explains:

> **Your mother and father gave life to you. Here there is this order to things. In Kathmandu and Bhaktapur, we must do the death rites for our parents. If we do these *sraddha*, then we will be fulfilled in this life. Because of our mothers and fathers, we can all do dharma. If you do not do dharma, then your son's life will not be fulfilled.**

Where Mahila offered improper sexual relations within a lineage and the destruction of another person's property as examples of "what you should not do," Krishna mentions the failure to perform rituals and emphasizes the positive duty of religious tradition. He places sin and dharma in the context of receiving life from parents, and of transmitting the opportunity to do dharma to successors (his son). There is an implied debt. Both note that actions have emotional and relational consequences: if you sin, you have an "uneasy heart." If you fail to do dharma, your son may suffer for it. An ethic of relatedness is asserted here. Acts of dharma (the death rites) connect generations, parents and children, while sin threatens to break the bonds of interwoven duty and love, of mutual commitment.

Newars often report that sin results from ignorance, from a lack of understanding. "Why do people sin?" I ask, and am told, "They don't know" (a Chathariya).

In ideal, theoretical terms this may be extended to include other causes of sin, such as greed (*lobh*). People sin because they are greedy; they are greedy because their understanding is deficient. Many Newars are acquainted with intellectual traditions which explains all sin as caused by ignorance. However, making a mistake, through ignorance, which counts as a sin is not viewed as the same as the ignorance underlying greed. In ordinary life, greed is more reprehensible than a mistake. But both are sins. Different verb forms may be used to specify the difference. For example, informants say that using the verb *juigu*, "to happen," suggests an unintended (and so less reprehensible) sin. When pap is used with the verb *yaegu*, "to do," a greater degree of responsibility is asserted.

Since Newars view ritual as playing a vital generative role in the development of moral "understanding," children are not held fully responsible for their actions until their "intellect," "intelligence," or "understanding" (*buddhi*) has been captured or catalyzed by the action of the proper rituals. In contrast, adults are expected to have understanding and knowledge, and thus are responsible for their actions and transgressions. Whether they act out of ignorance or misunderstanding, what they do may be counted as sin (pap).

Mahila explains about adults and children:

> When a person is a child, there are no sins. We are adults, our word is true. We know everything. We understand all. This thing [pointing to a table in the room] does not understand. So for this reason—because we are men, we know how to converse—for this reason, we should not do wrong. So there are many sins [for us].
>
> (You think that children do not commit sins?)
>
> They do not—yet. Only when we become adult do we sin. Children really don't know.

The rules of the system apply because the individual has joined in as a fully capable agent, fully able to converse with others and exercise understanding (buddhi).

Consequences of Transgressions

Transgressions have consequences either in this life or after death; as Newars often put it, they bear "fruit." After death, a person who has sinned may suffer in hell, or may be reborn in circumstances that ensure suffering commensurate with the "sins" of previous lives.

Though they do not always make explicit use of it, Newars have a clear enough idea of what is generally termed karma, a complex concept used throughout South and Southeast Asia (Keyes and Daniel 1983).[14] Karma provides "a theory of causation that supplies reasons for human fortune, good or bad" (Babb 1983: 167); it is associated with the idea of a cycle of rebirths. For Newars, the moral career of a person is stretched out over a series of lives; what people did in past lives shapes their fate in this life. Deeds done now may rebound on the doer in the future. Krishna Bahadur, the Navadurga dancer, put it into these words, which reflect "official" moral doctrine, but also resonate with the fear of loss of identity and relationship prevalent in Newar experience:

> In this, our life, one day we are born, and one day we will die. In the future, it will be hard to be born again [as a human being]. We may have to wander for ten million lives doing dharma. Only then will we again see the face of god, see once more the faces of people, see the face of the world once more.
>
> Now, if we do dharma, we don't have to be reborn. If we don't do dharma, if we commit sin, then we may be reborn as animals or as insects. People are highest—among living beings, the highest are people. We people have buddhi ["intellect," "understanding"]. Other living beings do not have as much.

Here "understanding" defines what makes people human, what makes them responsible moral agents.

When asked what happens if a person commits a sin, Ganesh Lal, the farmer, responded "If we commit sin, then when we die, we will be reborn in circumstances we deserve because of our transgressions. We will be reborn in a place of poverty. We will have to suffer greatly."

A high-caste Newar comments on this statement:

> This is not a very good theory, if you think about it. It shows that they must have committed some sin, since they are poor, and they suffer. Because of their karma, they deserve it. If people think like that, others won't try to help them. And it creates a fear in people.
>
> (What kind of fear?)
>
> Fear that—that they will be born in poverty, and will suffer in the next life.
>
> (But that is in the next life.)
>
> Some people believe you don't have to wait until the next life. You can experience this in the same life, in your old age, as well.

(I don't understand the nature of the fear.)
It is easy to say someone else is suffering because of his karma, but when you are suffering you don't want to think like that.
(But you do think like that?)
In their minds, they think like that.
(And when you think like that—)
You feel anxiety.

One context in which Newars spontaneously draw on the classical concepts of karma and rebirth is as an explanation of poverty and untouchability. Mahila's caste, the Pore (Sweepers) is subject to a life of misery because—higher caste Newars sometimes say—they were sinners in previous lives. Mahila denies this. Conversely, high-caste Newars may claim that their present status is the result of lifetimes of accumulated merit.

If rebirth into a earthly state of suffering is one possible consequences of transgressions, a cycle of existence spent in heaven or hell is another. I asked Mahila, "What do you think happens when you commit sins?"

If we commit sins, then later when we die—it is said we go to heaven or hell when we die. One who has committed many sins will be sent to hell. If you have done dharma, you will go to heaven. The Lord of Dharma does this. So you should not commit sins.
(What is hell like?)
Hell is our shit. Heaven is our home. You will go to stay in hell if you commit sins. A man who does dharma stays in a house, he lives very well.
(What happens when a sinner reaches hell?)
Until his sins have been discharged, he will have to stay there.

Note that sins may be discharged. Hell is not suffered for an eternity. Like the concept of karma, the concepts of heaven and hell presuppose an "ethicized" cosmos with a built-in capacity for determining what fates people deserve and for ensuring they get what they deserve. The universe contains a heaven for those who have been virtuous, and a hell for those who have sinned. The idea of an afterlife has been infused with ethical significance. This is a fact of cultural history, but not a logical requirement of the concepts of afterlife and salvation. In other religions, a person may simply pass on to another realm or state of being in the afterlife, neither heaven nor hell; or sinners and the virtuous alike may be saved, or doomed (Obeyesekere 1968).

If a concept of justice—the idea that people should be punished or rewarded for their actions—shapes a person's fate after death, it also rules his fate in this life, according to many Newars. Newars frequently drop the idea of transmigration but retain the idea that sin will be punished without direct human intervention. Misery is sometimes defined as the just desserts for "sins" committed in this life; justice is immanent in the world (or perhaps mediated by the deities).

> (What happens if you commit sins?)
> If we commit sins, our affairs won't work out. Illness will come out from inside. I guess we can get leprosy too. If it is a great sin, we can get leprosy. . . . We can become poor. Whatever you do will not work out, and so you will be destroyed. If your wealth is destroyed, then you will be poor. If you are poor, you won't have enough to eat. . . . The gods have done this. [A low-caste Jugi]

Some Newars attribute people's current misfortunes to sins they committed earlier in their lives; these attributions resemble the depiction above of what will happen to a person who does not do dharma. They express both their disapproval of the acts such a person is alleged to have committed and teach others that misdeeds will be punished.

When acts that count as sin are thought not to have been done deliberately—as might be inferred, for example, when an individual has no history of acting so—they may be seen, rather, as simple errors, and may not be matters for punishment, for community sanctions, or for self-reproach, depending on the relevant circumstances, nature, and gravity of the offense. Even so, Newars speak of such sins as requiring some penance, ritual expiation, or plea for forgiveness.

Many "sins" or "misdeeds" can happen to anyone, no matter how guarded one may be. Sins may touch, contact, or befall a person; they are not necessarily something a person does, but something that happens to that person. The person may be defined as subject to sin rather than as the agent of sins. Sins may be removed, and a person may escape through various practices the consequences of sin. Reciting the names of god is one way; so is ritual bathing.[15]

In general sins are removed by doing dharma. A Newar untouchable describes ways of mitigating or removing the consequences of sin, and also makes the distinction between sins done knowingly and those done unknowingly.

> If, unconsciously, we do wrong, we must do dharma. To discharge sin, we must do dharma. . . . So what dharma must we do? Where must we go? We must go to God, we must approach the God who is everywhere. We must ask Bhagavan to save us.
>
> (Do you think a good person can commit sins?)
>
> He can. Mistakes happen. We can sin without knowing it, without meaning to do it. So we ask Bhagavan that our sin be discharged. What happened, happened unknowingly. We were not aware of it, we did not know — it happened. A sin befell us. Now I have done this wrong — so we think, "Father, what must I do? How can I make it right?" This thought (*kalpana*) occurs, and because this thought is with us, inside us, we go to Bhagavan's place and we ask — Today, I will go to that place and say, Discharge this sin. If I put this in my mind, my sin will be ended. We will not have sin.

Many Newars see "the mind" as vulnerable and self-created — the mind can be "spoiled" by "thinking bad thoughts." While a wrongful turn of mind is not an absolute prerequisite for sinful action (since anyone can be subject to sin, committing wrongful acts by mistake or out of ignorance), some people make themselves prone to sin. Thinking "bad thoughts," they generate within themselves mental states — desires, intentions, and attitudes — that lead to sinful action.

Dharma Raj, for example, contends that people can "sin" in word, in action, and in their minds. Of these, mental sins are the worst. When I ask what influence they have, he replies that if a person strikes you the action is done. What people have in their minds, however, goes on—and this persistence "is fright-ening."

> An action can be seen. [Making a hitting motion, Dharma Raj refers back to an earlier example of a sin.] Now he hit you, and that action is finished. But the mental sin is now too. And still it is, and later it is too. This is frightening. For if this happens, a person's mind [*man*] is spoiled. He could become crazy. Anything could happen. So for this to happen is very dangerous. If you do not do mental sin, then you will not sin in word or deed. The mind is the source. If [the mind] is made good, then the other sins will not occur.[16]

Since "wrong" desires may lead to sinful action, efforts may be made to eradicate the underlying desire as well as the disapproved behavior pattern.

> (If you have a bad thought, but do not do anything, is that also a pap?)
> We should not have bad thoughts to the extent we are able. We must think only about doing good actions. And then we can win. We can win over pap. We can make ourselves fight with pap. By dharma, we will win.

This low-caste Newar proposes that an "inner struggle" will be triggered by the presence of bad thoughts. Others (suggestively, often those who are not religious specialists, but members of castes conceived to have once had predominantly political roles in the caste system) discount the importance of thoughts without actions. Many Newars insisted that it is important to evaluate the motives behind and consequences of acts ordinarily deemed to be wrong. Whether an act was done knowingly or unknowingly, was forced by circumstances or not, are factors in evaluating the severity of a sin. Some Newars argue that people have the dharma they can afford; poverty forces some to commit transgressions. An untouchable Pore said:

> What to do if we don't have our own rice to eat? We will say to ourselves, "I don't know, now, whether to do dharma or to do sin. I don't know." It is all the same [for poor people]. I guess I have done dharma, I think, I think I have not done sin.

Newars recognize a person may be forced to act by circumstances. Asked if it would be wrong for a man to steal or accept bribes in order to pay for treatment of a sick wife, a Brahman replied that such acts would be sin "on the outside," but arose from a desire to do dharma. A puja asking forgiveness would make the matter right.[17]

> On the outside, . . . to take bribes, to steal, this is one kind of sin. To save his wife, to take good care of her, this is a kind of dharma. Otherwise it would be a pap. It is a pap. Even so, he was forced to do this. He steals, and that is a pap. When he sins, he does a puja for forgiveness. He does puja saying "I have sinned, forgive me."

Such *Chema puja*, which ask forgiveness for wrongdoing, are common. The informant's statement suggests how wrongs are relative to higher needs, and can properly be mitigated. One may be forced to commit acts that are bad; but the ultimate evaluation of those acts depends on the situation and not on the rigid application of the moral norms.

The Brahman told the following story to illustrate further the point that a person may be forgiven for sin to which he is driven by misfortune:

> A man knew great suffering. And because he suffered, he became a thief. When he went to Shiva's temple, there was an image of Shiva. Above the image, there were rich things. To get up to take these rich things, the thief stepped on the head of Shiva. For this offense, Shiva must feel angry; but Shiva was pleased. He thought, "This person is suffering, and so he came here to steal. To steal is a sin. For this thief to step on my head is an even greater sin. But although he has done two great wrongs, even though he has stepped on me, I will help him, because of his inner suffering." And so Shiva helped him. Although it was a sin, Shiva forgave him.

Note that theft is a sin, but stepping on the head of the god is the greater sin because it shows disrespect for a divinity, which threatens elementary sentiments of the moral system of this hierarchical society.

Major sins are wrong even if they were done by accident or unknowingly. Actions resulting in the death of a person are perhaps more prone to absolute judgments than theft motivated by real need:

> **(For example, if I unknowingly kill someone, but I did not know, I killed by accident — is that a sin (pap) or not?)**
> **It is a pap.**
> **(Although it was done without knowing?)**
> **It is still a pap. Once you kill, pap occurs. Even if you don't have understanding [buddhi], to kill is a sin.**

Mental incompetence does not remove the stigma of sin from killing, either. I do not think this is any different than one set of Western moral intuitions; the more serious the consequences of an act, the less it matters what the actor intended. When the consequences are grave, actors cannot escape responsibility by claiming they do not have a guilty mind and did not intend their acts to have the consequences they did. Nonetheless, motive or intent is part of the formula for evaluating all actions. In some circles in the West, I suspect that the notion of "sin" would not adhere so tightly to wrongs done by accident; only intentional or negligent acts of killing would count as "sins." In Newar eyes, certain acts are always pap. Where the West mitigates by assessing intention and competence, Hindu Newars declare a sin, but ritualize penance and forgiveness — judging intention is important, but intentional and nonintentional wrongdoing alike require ritual attention.

Though evil deeds deserve and receive punishment, in this life, in subsequent lives, or in hell, Newar culture does not rule out the possibility of escaping the (just) consequences of having transgressed. The possibility of salvation exists, for example, if one can call on Vishnu with one's dying breath, even if one is a sinner.

This leaves the question of why "a bad man is happy and a good man suffers" when status distinctions are not at issue. Here a Brahman expresses the belief that justice will be done after death, and reads merit into suffering.

> **It can seem that the deities do injustice, as when a bad man is happy and a good man suffers. Many followers of the dharma are not happy. If they were happy, they would sin. When they suffer, they are devoted to Bhagavan. Those who suffer are very**

devoted to Bhagavan, while those who are happy have little devotion for Bhagavan. Therefore when a person is suffering, when they appear to be in pain, although it seems he is suffering, on the inside he is happy. He is with God. So it is said. . . . After death, there is complete justice [*nyaya*]. . . . The King of Death, Yamaraj, approves of whoever has done dharma, and does not like those who have sinned. Yamaraj does justice.

Justice, here, is a transcendent fact, not a worldly one. The Brahman conceded, with a smile, that he personally preferred happiness, and did not wish to suffer. We can see his statement as an attempt to ethicize suffering, rather than as an invitation to suffer; he is attempting to give some meaning to suffering and to bring it within the scope of the moral system.[18] He proposes a transformation: suffering brings those who suffer closer to divinity. This represents a higher good. His view is consistent with his role as priest and an elder, although the theodicy—the justification of suffering or vindication of god in the face of the reality of suffering—that it expresses is not necessarily one the informant or any ordinary Newar would endorse except in special circumstances. As theodicy, it preserves justice: but instead of the sinner being punished by being made miserable (in hell, incarnated in misery, contracting a disease), justice is realized for the innocent who suffer in this life, since they acquire a sort of merit which will be rewarded after death.

Karmic Responsibility

A Brahman offered this reflective account of the karma doctrine, implicitly arguing against the proposition that people are self-makers, the products of their own actions, which is presupposed by the karma concept. He does not wish to give human agency free reign—unlike Dharma Raj, he would not deify the collective agency of a human community.

Now, no one writes their own karma on their foreheads, according to the Newar conception. In fact, "karma" means action or work (*kam*). Newars, whether they are Hindus or Buddhists, understand this word in terms of religious practices. For instance, if someone does not have offspring, the fault will customarily be given to karma. We blame karma for riches and poverty. [However, no one chooses their own karma] because we can only do what God desires. Without Bhagavan wishing it, we can do nothing. All castes have this conception. Whatever happens is God's desire. We are not the maker—we are only instruments. We are social beings—but as social beings we have different natures. We believe the differentiation of human nature is also God's creation.

Karma is not invisible, but we conceive of it as something that is invisible. Karma means only that you can judge someone's actions. Without action, you cannot judge. So it is said, as you do, so will you have the fruit. Without karma, the fruit [results] will not be forthcoming. We all trust that this is so. If you strive with little or no effect, then there is the conception that your failure is due to the sins of previous lives.

However, to connect every action with previous lives seems erroneous. That my situation is now this, mainly, can be explained due to the actions of previous lives. Low-caste people satisfy themselves by explaining their low-caste status in terms of their actions in previous lives. . . . So the natural creation of all things can be explained.

The linkage between acts—doing dharma or doing pap—and moral dessert is clear. Notice the proposition that would tend to reduce responsibility: "if you work with little or no effect, then there is the conception that it is due to the sins of previous lives." As the person transmigrates, his actions affect the conditions of his rebirth; acts have consequences across lifetimes.

Note, too, how this Brahman encompasses karma in divinity— does this convert responsibility into resignation? What place do agency and responsibility have? After all, the passage works out the relationships of action, nature, society, and divinity in terms that represent one influential strand of Hindu thought: what people do (which generates or embodies their karma) is a reflection of what they are—and here both nature (what they are) and action (what they do) are presented as the product of divine intent, built directly into the actor's nature and the structure of society. "No one writes their own karma on their foreheads"—God does. "We can only do what God desires." "Whatever happens is God's desire." "The differentiation of human nature" into castes, which people use the karma concept to explain "is also God's creation."

The unity of nature, action, and society is guaranteed by the divine. The way this presents the actors as the product of divinity would seem to limit human agency and reduce personal responsibility, introducing an element of conservative fatalism. Karma represents what people think and say, perhaps even represents how they experience their life situations—they satisfy themselves with it, he says—and may even be a proximate cause of their suffering, but the ultimate "cause" of every action and condition is God. I think this line of interpretation is present here because the informant is thinking about the structure of caste society (he refers to all Newars, and Newars of all castes). Looked at as a whole, this passage exemplifies the position that I suggest Dharma Raj more or less subverts in his testimony earlier in this chapter.

There is a gap, perhaps, between the cognitive claims of the karma doctrine and the way people experience themselves as intentional agents. The "sins" of this life, and their consequences, and the "sins" of previous lives are experienced in very different ways. To use Obeyesekere's key insight (1968), we can distinguish between psychologically *indeterminate* acts and psychologically *determinate* acts, between what doctrine suggests we have done in past lives, and what we know we have done in this life.

If I "sin" now, I can expect consequences either in this life or the next one. People may attribute my getting tuberculosis to some act I did in this life. But I may attribute my illness to some wrong act I did in a previous life. I may explain the suffering I experience now by postulating an act performed by a "self" that—while it is doctrinally ascribed to me—is not experienced by me as "self" in the way actions in my current live are. What karmic doctrine says does not necessarily mesh with my psychological sense of identity; and since I may not identify myself with the self I was in past lives, who sinned, I feel less responsibility. This splits up a very basic equation: intentions and acts (of previous lives) are divorced from consequences. The moral agent, the self who acted, exists only in the imagined past, not the real present, even though the normative doctrine of karma insists on the identity of past and present self. As one informant noted, "you do not know anything about what you did in past lives." Yet my suffering in this life is punishment for what the remote self of previous lives did. I suffer concretely in the present life, and yet my fate has nothing to do with my experienced moral self, the "I" that I am in the here and now. Self-blame is, paradoxically, diminished by making responsibility absolute, but indeterminate.

There does seem to be a residual sense of responsibility here, however—the concept of karma decreases, but does not do away with, felt responsibility. Attributing a misfortune to karma stigmatizes to a degree, although less so than attributing that same misfortune to a pap committed in this life. Hence Newars sometimes avoid ascribing certain conditions to karma. The concept of *dasa* can also be used to explain some suffering.

In a general sense, dasa means "condition" or "situation" of life, the "state" of a person, but is usually used to refer to states of ill fortune and mischance. Unqualified, dasa is bad dasa, a condition of misfortune, a state of bad luck or ill fate. Although dasa may have a number of sources—I was told dasa may result if you break a mirror or found gold and brought it home without putting a drop of your blood on it—dasa determined by the astrological influence of the planets (*graha dasa*) is perhaps the most important.

Dasa can be managed by going to an astrologer or worshiping certain deities; attributing suffering to a state of ill fortune or "bad luck" due to the negative influence of astrological factors does not carry a moral stigma the way attributing them to sin and karma would. Dasa is not generally judged in terms of intentions, motives, or purposes. Even a sin done by mistake, however, posits a responsible agent; but dasa explains people's suffering, not as the result of anything they did, not because of a moral agent's mistakes, but as the result of circumstances beyond their control. Invoking karma explains suffering precisely by relating it to the moral failings of a person in previous lives; and while karma can be mitigated in future lives by doing dharma in this life, it cannot be radically altered in this life (except possibly through appeals to the mercy of deities). Dasa and karma are, then, somewhat differently invoked as explanations, since they have different implications for responsibility. Individuals are not agents with respect to dasa (except in an indirect sense to be discussed below), but patients; they are afflicted with "ill" fortune or "ill" fate, victims of forces not under their control. As a result of these differing implications, the concepts seem to be used to explain different types of suffering. For example, what I term "incorrigible" suffering—blindness, the death of a spouse, stigmatizing deprivation—seems to attract karmic explanations. Accidents are more likely viewed as resulting from bad dasa. The different distribution may not be unrelated to questions of agency. Blindness may elicit irrational guilt, because it seems punitive (perhaps because seeing is implicitly equated with knowing), whereas slipping and taking a fall does not. Finally, dasa is psychologically determinate in a way karma is not; an astrologer can diagnose it, and suggest remedies.

Dasa itself *may* be ethicized, by encompassing dasa in the karma concept—your "bad luck" ultimately reflects bad karma. The reverse is not possible: karma and sin are not due to bad dasa. Dasa may, some Newars suggested, have a protective influence; if your dasa is good, it may save you from getting into situations where you might be faced with the possibility of doing wrong.

Newars did not spontaneously assert to me that dasa results from wrongs committed in previous lives, somehow encoded in planetary influences. Some saw the connection, but the notion that karmic explanation "includes" dasa, so that the planets merely "chart" a person's karma (as Obeyesekere [1984: 47] describes the views of Sri Lankhan ritual specialists) does not seem to be salient. I do not think this is what most Newars have in mind when they use the dasa concept to explain suffering or mischance. One Brahman priest, when prompted, articulated the connection with ease and fluency: "your dasa in this life reflects the sins of past lives," he said. I had the impression, however, that this was only a somewhat theoretical connection. So I asked another Brahman about it. He denied the connection, arguing that dasa and sin are distinct. He argued that a person who had done no wrong could have bad dasa. He said sins were violations of dharma and would be punished in hell. While many people suffered, he noted, few commit major sins. So most suffering, he argued, is due to graha dasa, not to sin. He summed up by saying: "Graha is graha, dharma is dharma."

For most Newars, I suspect, karma and dasa are alternative explanations of suffering, and not necessarily coupled as ultimate and proximate causes. Responsibility—and the absence of responsibility—in Newar culture is known and experienced in terms of multiple concepts that do not necessarily have a stable relationship with each other (as when sometimes dasa is viewed the product of karma, sometimes not). Rather, actors use different concepts for different purposes, according to the context they see as relevant, or want to make relevant (S. Daniel 1983). I would suggest one reason some Newars decouple sin and dasa is because not everyone is willing to accept the stigma and anxiety that comes with karmic explanations—especially not if it also calls into question the moral legitimacy of self and of one's place in society. After all, while the suffering of the low castes may be attributed to the sins of previous lives, suffering is not confined to the low castes. A karmic explanation of high-caste suffering is potentially subversive of the moral legitimacy asserted for the caste hierarchy in karmic terms. Moreover, when karma is used to interpret misfortune, a person's state of suffering may raise questions about his or her morality and place in the moral community. Thus, the unethicized concept of dasa can be used to explain suffering that people would prefer not to explain in karmic terms; invoking dasa also maintains the ideological potency of karmic responsibility.

The introduction of a God who determines human nature and action complicates the question of responsibility even further, seemingly introducing an unresolvable tension. Does the Brahman I quoted above mean that the will of God determines what our karma (actions) are? If so, does karma as action and consequence mean anything? Encompassing karma in divinity seems to dissolve personal agency altogether, absolving the person of responsibility—or defining it as a function of their god-given natures. One Hindu Newar concept of reality says that what people do reflects what they are, what their natures or essences are. Moreover, "as social beings we have different natures." If a divinity determines what we are (creates our natures) and this determines what we do, then the freedom of human agency is indeed an illusion. What we do cannot make us what we are; we cannot make our own natures. This Brahman's perspective thus seems radically opposed to Dharma Raj's thinking on action. In this Brahman's account, action is foregrounded with the concept of karma, with its implications of agency, personal responsibility, and self-making; but this action perspective is encompassed and transformed by invoking divine desire and will. A person's karma—and just place in society—is ultimately determined by divinity, not by self. This restores the conservative concept of society as a natural moral order (not a human construction), envisioning the human actors as products, not agents—as the Brahman phrases it, people are "instruments," not "makers."

Arguably, in this way the problem of the suffering inherent in society is doubly resolved—or doubly distanced—from self-responsibility. First, the karma doctrine justifies differences in caste and economic status (they deserve their fate); second, divine will justifies social differentiation (God desires this state of affairs, having created a nature for each social group that determines what they do, what place they have in society, and what their karmic fate is). Does this elaborate distancing reflect a sense of guilt at the suffering built into caste society—overcoming an empathy for suffering others that is experienced but not acted on? Does it also reflect several registers of fear—the fear it could happen to me, the fear of the resentment of those who suffer—that feed into a political and cultural hegemony? These are questions I will have to explore in other work.

The Nature and Culture of Moral Order

For most Newars, most of the time, morality is not wholly a human creation, but an integral part of the way the world is—at least until they shift perspectives and define morality as the product of human action (S. Daniel 1983). Newars, like people elsewhere, seek to see "what is" in terms of "what should be." Using culture, they recreate the "brute otherness" of reality, and see it as bearing the signature of a moral order. But there are complex cross-currents in their moral discourse, since different actors are prepared to map "what should be" onto "what is" in different ways. Dharma, we have seen, means different things to different actors. Even as some try to embed cultural practices in nature, making them objective realities, others will find ways to interpret culture in terms of human action.

Arguably, each human culture gives its own distinctive signature to the moral; moral knowing is in part transcultural, drawing on universal moral ideas. Yet, always, these universals enter into culture, are reshaped and redirected. Dharma is perhaps one of these culturally transfigured universals; it carries within it the idea of transcendent objective standards, of immutable "natural law." The paradox of dharma is, then, that it is known subjectively, by individual men and women, and given meaning that reflects their place in society. Social actors finds meaning in dharma in terms of their own experiences and perspectives—they bring their experience, their lives, to the concept. There is no way to disentangle the concept from these lives, and find some single, fixed meaning for it. Beyond signifying what people must do, dharma has an open texture. It can be embedded in a range of cultural scenarios, in a range of contexts. It marks a space in thought and life in which people construct moral meanings in terms of complex scenes, narratives, and images.

At the same time, dharma *is* society; life-in-society embodies dharma. To be a moral person, then, a Newar must both survive the scrutiny of "society," and nurture relationships. This, too, is dharma—there is an obligation to be responsive to particular others. In this context, conformity (or its appearance) is not itself a moral end, but a means of seeing that relationships—which define and nurture the self—are not ruptured, and that the moral order is not threatened. To break rules can be fatal. But the rules can be bent, and this is expressed in a pragmatic discourse in tension with the moral rhetoric of ideal practice.

Knowing what Newars believe ("marriage with people of lower caste standing is wrong") is not the same as knowing how they apply and live their beliefs. Knowledge of moral codes has to be translated into action, and this is not always a simple matter. Knowledge of norms and the actualities of life may face each other across a great gap ("my son married a woman of lower caste status"). For this and other reasons, Newars make judgments in context-sensitive ways, sometimes breaking rules and evading obligations they affirm as moral, natural, and necessary.

"Society" has priority over "self" in Newar moral thought, at least relative to the extreme individualism cherished by some in the Western world. The idea of "society" is used as an overarching frame for moral discourse. It is an active principle, known and experienced as an agency that embodies collective judgment on individual acts. All acts echo in society, which gives them meaning; the idea of "society" provides the essential grounds for interpreting actions. The "self" is not given equal weight—the idea that you can "do right, and do it alone," in opposition to the weight of social opinion does not receive, as far as I can tell, much cultural support, at least not compared with the elaboration found in some Western cultural traditions. Society is, for Newars, godlike and moral—an almost palpable and objective presence. The reality of "society" is felt; it bears on self—and this experience is constituted in terms of moral discourses. For Newars, society is not an aggregate of individuals, but a collective "Other" standing in judgment of self.

A person's relationship to this reified "society-as-Other" is in addition to particular relationships with concrete others. This complicates moral life. Tension may characterize the relationship of the more overarching and the more particular value: it may be wrong for anyone to violate dharma, but justified or excused in a particular case—as when your son marries a woman of another, lower, caste. The idea of abstract standards that can be applied to everyone, the concrete experience of particular others as worthy of concern and care, and the belief that society judges categorically, are modes of moral consciousness that coexist in Newar life. They may conflict, each in turn taking on evaluative life in the minds of individual actors, each tugging at the other with moral force and meaning: this is our duty, this is our dharma, this is love—what will society think?—this is my son, my daughter. Each mode requires compromises with, or a destructuring of, the other. Newars find ways to accommodate conflicting values, and to live with the tensions that arise between them. Sometimes Newars respond to the evaluative force of society; sometimes they affirm concrete moral relationships; sometimes they appeal to more universalistic principles. They have to juggle moral perspectives.

To Western eyes, the Newar respect for society, the way Newars let social groups guide their thinking and action, the way they acquiesce to social norms and fear society's disapproval, may look like unreflective conformity—and, of course, in some cases, this is exactly what it is. But not always.[19]

We need to recognize that, in cultural terms, Western minds and Newar minds are different historical and cultural phenomena. While both grow out of whatever innate powers of thought that human beings possess, minds absorbed in culture construe experience differently, drawing on different cultural presuppositions to bring forth different conclusions about moral life, different visions of moral order.

Consider the concepts of the person that shape Western and Newar thought. Shweder, Mahapatra, and Miller (1987) have grasped a key difference in these when they argue that Lawrence Kohlberg's theory of universal stages of moral development incorporates an ideology of individualism that would be alien to the moral code of many societies. In Kohlberg's account of the basic elements of a moral code, they argue, the individual has no personal qualities or social identity; this "abstract" individual is "conceived to exist as an autonomous entity prior to or outside of the social arrangements in which he or she is found" (1987: 21). Society is a product of individuals joining together in a social contract, a notion also central to the justice theories of John Rawls (1971). According to this perspective, individuals use reason to find and apply moral principles autonomously; the ability to do this develops psychologically. The person defines society and morality.

Whether this position corresponds in any meaningful way to the cultural premises of everyday life even in Western societies is open to debate. Perhaps Western individualism distorts Western actuality; I suspect the "Western" value of the individual self coexists with a kind of passion to conform and fit in, to seek definition from the mass media, the corporate workplace, experts, religion. Moreover, there are surely also many Americans who believe in a sacred natural law that defines what is good for persons and society. And even if the psychologist and the philosopher have elaborated tellingly on Western common sense, we can question whether this defines what the terms of moral thought must be everywhere.[20]

Other cultures—including Newar culture—conceive of the relationship of self and society in a very different way, not as the product of an agreement between individuals, but as an independent reality that exists prior to the individual. In this conception, the social order is a natural order, and a moral order. It is a sacred order. As such, it is person-defining.

Thus, for Newars, at least in much of their moral discourse, society encompasses the individual person. It does not reflect the self-constructed values of the individual mind, but mirrors the place of each individual in the natural and moral order of the world. Newars do not think one can stand outside of society, relying on one's reason or conscience, withdrawing into self, in order to make moral judgments about what is good, ethical, or just. More typically, they urge people to *generate* and *receive* what is good and ethical by immersing themselves in social action, sorting out moral perspectives on the basis of what works to bring vitality and harmony to the community, struggling from within society to make society good. For Newars like Dharma Raj, the experiences and reflections of the social actor, engaged with social life as a cultural being, provide a basis for determining what is good, true, and right—not individual reason alone. Newars respect the powers of the mind and intellect, but the individual mind, cut off from both the social and sacred order, is not for them the foundation of moral judgment.

Thus, in much Newar thought, moral consciousness is produced by society, which mediates between self and ultimate moral principles. The full development of moral character and consciousness can only be achieved in society. Society "connects" the self to ultimate sacred-moral reality.

Newars have other viewpoints as well, recognizing that their own society does not always reflect what they believe is moral; as Dharma Raj pointed out, when society is "bad," it can sever or distort the connection with moral reality, and so prevent the development of "true" or "real" moral conduct and consciousness. Society is not even the only connection a person has with moral truth—as we will see in chapter 4, Newars conceive of persons as sacred beings inherently attuned to the moral order. If social consensus and experience is not enough, if a mood of moral certainty, a conviction of virtue, does not grow out of participation in society, if they find that social conventions and institutions somehow still violate their moral intuitions, Newars have an alternative to social definitions of right and wrong, an alternative that is still not individualistic in a Western sense. Newars may shift from a social perspective to a sacred perspective; a person's connection with the sacred order permits reflections on the social order. If society does not provide a valid foundation for moral judgment, the sacred order can; and so moral consciousness is grounded in something outside of the individual and society. For them, moral consciousness is not solely a social product, but also formed within the sacred-moral self, preparing the self to be social.

In my view, Newars perceive society as the source of moral guidance, not because they confuse arbitrary social conventions with objective moral obligations, but because of the way they perceive and experience society as a moral order, as dharma. Dharma Raj, for example, both proposes that society is a natural, moral, and sacred order, and that people make society. He attempts to integrate and use conflicting perspectives at the heart of Newar (and perhaps any) culture.

It seems clear to me that Newars do not have a single understanding of their own moral order, although some understandings
may be more dominant, or have more "gravity," than others.
Rather, Newars "tell" several different kinds of "stories" about this
moral order. These multiple "tellings" are necessary for the construction of a moral order that is complex and nuanced enough to
hold and sustain social life. Thus, in the context of one "telling,"
Newars may define society as a moral order, possessing a godlike
authority to define what is right and wrong, as a natural and
divinely ordained order that is worthy of their respect and commitment, and so affirm conformity. In other contexts, they will,
like Dharma Raj, exhort people to do good, to make society good,
treating it as a human construction. They act as if they must
reshape society or themselves, and so affirm processes of society-
making and self-making. If they value conformity to social norms,
if they respect and fear the judgment of society, Newars also view
social life as a shared, constructive moral project. If they objectify
social norms, treating them as natural and necessary, they also
deify their own power to create society, treating society as the
product of people's efforts to make a moral community, to actual-
ize dharma within society. Newars make use of both perspectives
in their moral discourse; it may be that having such a dual perspective is a prerequisite of practical moral life in any culture.

If so, it would be one-sided to draw conclusions about a culture
based on how just one of these perspectives is formulated. If the
Newars need multiple "tellings" of the moral order in order to fit
their lives into it, then perhaps we need multiple accounts, too, in
order to understand what they think and feel, and how they
engage social life.

Part Two

Moral Knowing

CHAPTER THREE

The Web of Relatedness

Toward the end of his life, the French artist Paul Gauguin—living in Tahiti, working through the shock, perhaps, of his encounter with another culture, disappointed by the reception of his work, disconnected from his family (from whom he had separated himself in the course of pursuing his career), yet disturbed by news of the death of his daughter—painted one of his greatest works. The painting, a large, dark, somber canvas, shows twelve human figures ranging across the life span—children, youth, adults. An infant lying on its back in the right hand foreground, attended by others, part of a group, is balanced by an old woman on the left. Posed in an upright, but almost fetal posture, the figure of the old woman faces away from the others, and seems withdrawn—careworn or suffering. A young woman leans toward the old one, almost touching her with one hand, as if inviting interaction, or offering a connection with life and others. A statue—a religious image, possibly—stands on a platform behind them, perhaps suggesting another order of existence.

The painting is entitled *Where do we come from? What are we? Where are we going?* For Gauguin these were, perhaps, ultimate questions. In 1898, the year after he finished the painting, Gauguin attempted suicide by taking arsenic. He survived, the painting was sold for a thousand francs, and ended up in the Museum of Fine Arts in Boston, where I happened to see it, not long after finishing the first draft of this book. As I stood contemplating it, I was struck with the thought that much of the material I present in this book represents Newar answers to the questions Gauguin asks.[1] Newars would paint a different scene, but they recognize the same spectrum of life—in the lives they live—and they have formulated answers to the questions Gauguin asks, as part of their culture. Newars being a sophisticated people, I would expect them to give me sophisticated and diverse answers if I asked them these existential questions—when they got done laughing at me. But I believe these questions, for Newars, must be answered in part in terms of their concepts of person and relatedness.

Where do Newars come from? One answer is that they grow out of a "web of relatedness"—they are the products of life in the Newar extended family. Mothers and fathers, siblings and kin shaped them and nurtured them. What are Newars? Most of them are people bound to a family world, a world of kinship. Unlike Gauguin, who virtually abandoned his family to create himself as creative artist, and may serve here as sort of a wild caricature of the self-creating, autonomous person of "Western individualism," most Newars find value and meaning in family life, in connection. I believe their sense of self grows out of this. They are defined by their commitments to family and family line. Family love and empathy, family duty and necessity, family conflict and tension make them what they are.

Where are they going? The short answer is, they grow back into the family circle. They never leave it. It provides the structure and unity of their lives. Newars do not search for some authentic self that exists apart from their social relationships and place in social groups. They seem, rather, to draw their sense of self from their experience of relatedness and social constraint, from a sense of connection, from their identifications with particular others and social groups, especially their extended family. Where are they going? Most of them remain rooted in the family circle for all of their lives. Yet this is not stagnation. It is a process of becoming. They experience the unfolding of their lives within the developmental cycle of family life. Growing up and growing older, they experience transitions and assume new roles; the passage from role to role forms a spiral into the center of the family, a center which is also the apex of a social hierarchy. Ideally, the son marries, has children, and assumes a more central role, eventually becoming head of his own extended family. The daughter-in-law becomes a mother, and eventually a mother-in-law, achieving first a measure of security and then a measured power. With increasing centrality and power, comes responsibility—primarily the responsibility to nurture, protect, and care for children and younger family members, the responsibility to make a shared life possible.

The web of relatedness is as much a religious reality as a social one. The Newar family is a religious institution as well as a social one, and it nurtures the religious becoming of its members as well. If nurturing the process of becoming is central to family life, Newars conceive of this as centrally a religious duty. They undertake to reveal ultimate conditions—they "show" their children "karma," meaning the set of obligatory religious rites that define the human condition for Newars. The family organizes the rites of passage (to be explored in a later chapter) that define the stages of a life, give unity and meaning to that life, and prepare persons for death. In religious action, Newars reveal and make a person what a person is, revealing and transforming their nature, weaving them into the web of relatedness.

In all of this, the stress is on interdependence. In Newar life, the dependence of the individual on the domestic and kinship group is greater than in most Western communities—it is almost total in most cases. Looked at from a certain point of view, this seems to entail submerging the individual in the group. This point has been made by many, and even been identified as a key feature of the value systems of India and Nepal. Louis Dumont is, perhaps, the most important advocate of this point of view; he has argued that South Asian cultures do not acknowledge the individual self, do not grant it any value or meaning, much less cherish or celebrate it.[2] I can agree with this view up to a point—but only so far; after that I find that it distorts the reality of Newar lives. However, I do not want to reject Dumont's position altogether, for it captures an important aspect of things. Thus, the delicate task of this chapter is to at once confirm and qualify the perception of South Asian culture as characterized by holism.

In my view, the stress on interdependence in Newar culture does not obliterate the individual—the individual self has being and reality in Newar culture, but not in the same way as in Western cultures. Although Newars—as we saw in the last chapter—in their moral discourse often strongly stress the way persons are socially embedded, and often define persons in terms of the way they are positioned in social units, they do not absolutely and always deny meaning or value to individual life. Rather, within the web of relatedness, Newars have cultural ways of knowing themselves as individual selves, ways of expressing and developing personal autonomy, ways of forcing society to acknowledge their individual existence, ways of managing and subverting the cultural ideology that disowns the individual. While cultural beliefs restrict the scope of personal autonomy, people also find a measure of autonomy, and value what autonomy they achieve. Thus, I believe that any attempt to understand Newar culture in terms of a Western discourse that opposes Asian "holism" to Western "individualism" risks seriously distorting the cultural experience of Newars. In reality, Newar culture, like any culture, has several distinctive ways of imagining and organizing the relationship of individual and society, and Newar persons have their own culturally shaped ways of knowing and experiencing themselves—as social beings *and* as self-defining, self-making persons.

If this is so, we need to qualify and develop Dumont's insights into South Asian holism. To do so, I think we only need to recognize two simple— but fundamental and far-reaching—facts about culture, as a way of forcing ourselves to adopting a more flexible and multisided approach to depicting cultural reality. First, we need to recognize the "inner diversity" of culture. A culture can contain multiple values, a range of perspectives on self and society, activated in different contexts for different reasons. The Newar sense of self shifts across different modes, allowing Newars to know and experience themselves in different ways, both as autonomous individuals and as socially embedded persons. Second, we need to recognize the element of time. There are moments when social embeddedness is foregrounded in consciousness and action, when meaning and value is withheld from individual existence; and other moments when individual choice and action are stressed, the self nurtured and cherished.

My position here is likely to be misunderstood by some, so let me risk being redundant about my purpose. I am not denying that South Asians value social interdependency and relatedness. My goal is to restore some balance to our interpretation of South Asian cultures, by showing how what are often taken as mutually exclusive values often in fact interpenetrate and develop together in culturally distinctive ways. The individual self also has value in South Asian culture.

Of course, what it means to be an individual, the way individual existence is known and experienced, and the precise nature of the value of the individual self, vary from culture to culture. What it means to be an individual self, the value that attaches to individual existence, is not exactly the same in Newar and American culture. By arguing that individual existence has cultural meaning and value in South Asia, I am not saying Americans and Newars are the same. In fact, I find them radically different.

American popular culture, for example, often seems to treat self-identity and interdependency as antithetical; you can "lose your identity" in relationships; you "find yourself" by separating and distancing. However, even if this conception of the relationship of "self" and "relatedness" were characteristic of American culture (at least sometimes for some people), I am not convinced it holds at all for Newars. It seems more likely that Newars "find themselves" in relationships and "lose themselves" by separating.

Thus, cultural differences seem to make a psychological difference. In American culture, merging may be experienced as a loss of self, and interdependency may be experienced as threatening— the popular culture of self-help often treats it as a kind of dysfunction, as co-dependency. In Newar culture, self-identity and relationship seem less opposed. There seems to be a greater tolerance for merging; interdependency is highly valued. Newars do not seem to feel this necessarily obliterates self-identity. Interdependency is where you find yourself. In relationships, you discover what and who you are, where you are going, and what you need to do.

Newar concepts of person and kinship stress the way lives are joined together; they presuppose more basic concepts of "relatedness" that give meaning to social relationships and to acts that sustain, nurture or disrupt relationships. Newar concepts of relatedness join Newar lives together within a dynamic web of relatedness that shapes experience and action. This web connects selves. It does not, I think, necessarily devalue them, or deny them self-identity. Certainly, separating from, or cannibalizing, the web is not valued. Limits are placed on what individuals can do and be. Within these limits, individuality is possible and valued. Indeed, one possible psychological outcome of the organization and experience of this web of relatedness might be this: the richer and more responsive the connections, the more distinct and developed the sense of self. Despite the value they place on it, and the centrality it has in their lives, Newars recognize—often anticipate—the potential for conflict in the web of relatedness.

I intend the concept of the "web of relatedness" to stand as a meta-concept to concepts of holism and individualism. In the web of relatedness, Newar lives are joined together, lives lived in socially embedded ways *and* lived by self-defining, self-making persons. I derive the idea of a web of relatedness from a Newar figure of speech; they sometimes speak of the family as a "net"—a *janjal*— of relationships in which their lives and selves are entangled and shaped. In this chapter, I will explore this web of relatedness and interpret its relation to self.

As I do so, I will attempt to shed light on some aspects of the moral consciousness generated by the Newar cultural constructions of relatedness. The way Newars envision themselves is not monolithic, but multiple. Their vision of what they are and can be is not based exclusively on their cultural ideology of holism, as powerful as it is—it is not as if they simply internalized and enacted those values; nor is their concept of the person predicated simply on the mere existence of the powerfully constraining and person-defining social units given value and meaning by this ideology of holism. Rather, I wish to suggest, the Newar sense of self grows out of the cultural and psychological experience of merging with and emerging from the "web of relatedness." The experience of an interplay of merging and emerging produces and validates a coherent sense of personal identity—of the "self" as a unique, dynamic body of memories and experience, as a center of awareness and action, as an agent of a life, as an individual with a personal history, and as a nexus of relationships.[3] At the same time, the experience of merging, emerging, and remerging helps instill a deep consciousness of relatedness and interdependency, a consciousness that grounds cultural values of holism, giving them some of their sense of reality and naturalness. In Newar life, personal identity and social identity are continuously produced and shaped, stressed, displaced and muted, over time. The culturally mediated interplay of group existence and individual existence does not assume a single, fixed, final form. Personal identity and social identity are woven together into the web of relatedness.

The Sense of Connection

Some aspects of the moral meaning of kin relatedness are revealed in the following passage, taken from a longer narrative, an account of a ritual outing written out for me by a Brahman. It tells of how a man organized a trip to make offerings and worship at Daksin Kali, an important Goddess temple in the Kathmandu Valley. The man, his family, some of his friends, and his family priests, both a Brahman and a Tantric practitioner, leave Bhaktapur early one morning, taking with them food, the things they need to worship, and a goat to sacrifice. The narrative describes the pleasure of passing through fields, forests, and villages on the way to the temple. Arriving at the temple, they join the crowd of worshipers, and make ready to perform the puja. They overcome certain minor obstacles, sacrifice the goat, and eat at the shrine. Then, in a key passage, the narrative focuses on motives.

> We all ate at the shrine. And then the Tantric priest asked his client, "How long ago did you pledge to do this worship to the Goddess?"
>
> The client said, "When I was a child my father made this pledge."
>
> And the priest asked, "Then why did you not do it until today?"
>
> The man answered, "We have been poor for a very long time. We pledged that we would worship the Goddess when we became wealthy. My father, they say, made this pledge so that we would have good fortune."
>
> "So then you did not know why the pledge was made?"
>
> "I did not know about it. At that time I was only a child. But I'm unlucky. My father climbed to heaven, he died, without keeping his promise to the Goddess."
>
> "Then how did you learn that your father had made such a promise?"
>
> "When I grew up, my mother told me. My mother said, 'Ah, son, we have suffered so much. When you were very small, your father promised to sacrifice a goat to the goddess Kali. We must do this some day. My son, only when we have done this can we

receive the blessings of the Goddess.' And now my mother too has gone to heaven. I am a very sad person. I was not able to do as she asked. When she was alive, I could not do it. I could not keep my father's pledge to the Goddess. How pleased she would have been if I had been able to do this puja while she was alive. Now, what to do?"

The priests blessed the man, and everyone there rejoiced with him.

They said, "You have done a great, good work. Our Mother Kali takes delight in what you have done. From now on the Goddess will smile on you. Poor man, how you have suffered!"

And he replied, "Your words will be as the words of god. I have settled my debt. My mother and father are released from this pledge. Now I can stop worrying about nothing but when I can do this puja, for surely my mother and father have been saved. Your blessings will work for me."

His companions were pleased. They told him, "Through your act of dharma, we were able to come to the place of this great Goddess. You made it possible for us to come into her presence, and to feast on the food offered her."

Deceptively simple, this passage celebrates the qualities that constitute a moral person. Convivial, religious, and generous, the organizer of the rite brings his kin, his friends, and the priests together for an act of dharma. He acts in terms of an inner commitment to the forms of relatedness that join Newar lives together.

In the passage quoted, the narrative reveals the "moral self" of the ritual actor. Using the device of an inquiry into the actor's motives, it discloses a sense of duty brought into existence through the experience of relatedness. The actor's sense of obligation—of what must be done—is keyed to feelings and emotions about concrete persons. It is not based on some abstract, formal concept of duty, but on memory and attachment.

The narrative proposes that the experience of the ritual event involves empathy as well as duty. Duty is a central motive, because a father's obligation was kept by his son. The narrative invokes empathy in two different ways. First, the son recreates his mother's experience in his imagination; he reflects on how happy she would have been if she had lived to see him keep his father's promise to the Goddess. Second, the audience within the narrative acknowledges and validates his experience and emotions. They reconstruct and evaluate his experience and actions in terms of the moral code; they recognize the moral meaning he confers on his loss and suffering through his actions. They approve of his motives and affirm his act of dharma. They assure him the Goddess will smile on him.

At a third level, the audience that reads or hears the narrative may reconstruct and reexperience some aspects of the story. I have tried out the story on a few Newars, and the responses varied. But one reported a strong emotional response, saying it made him think of his own parents. The empathic possibilities of the narrative are quite complex. You can feel for the person in the story who feels for his father and mother—or the episode can resonate with what you feel for others in your own life.

The narrative suggests that a "moral self" is identified with, and known through, a structure of intentions and actions that were part of other lives. The commitment of the ritual actor to finishing what his parents set out to do, to fulfilling their desires, is what makes him a "moral person." He has identified self with the intentions and experience of others in culturally codified ways. He seeks to give closure to the moral "project" of their lives by keeping a promise his father made to the goddess Kali—a promise his mother conveyed to him. She made it clear that this was her desire, and that it would give meaning to their loss and suffering. Since she too is dead by the time the rite is performed, its meaning is redoubled.

The story suggests how the "web of relatedness" is composed of strands of obligations and empathy. Before he fulfills his father's pledge, the ritual actors felt burdened with an obligation, the kind of obligation Newars say you keep "worrying" about because of the way it connects you to significant others. Many Newars reported having this kind of feeling. Here, the ritual actor expresses a sense of release from the obligations in which he is entangled through his relatedness to his parents.

Before we discuss the way culture structures the fusion and separation of self and other, we need to know something of the general structure of Newar family life and of the meaning and emotional quality of relationships within households.

Relationships with Fathers

Although Newars sometimes say the relationship of a father and a son is ultimately grounded in "love," they do not believe that sons will necessarily have easy, warm relationships with their fathers.

They stress respect, rather than open affection, as defining the quality of the relationship. A son should honor and obey a father, and must be grateful for being taught and shaped. The father is a disciplinarian.[4] The father is responsible for the education and moral upbringing of the boy, and any violations of moral rules by the boy will reflect on him.

When young, daughters are treated warmly, but as they grow older their fathers may distance themselves, and treat daughters with a certain coolness. Asked how she would describe the relationship of fathers and daughters, a woman said, "Not much." She made a sort of shrug, grimaced, and went on: "When the daughter marries, her father will think—I have to buy this and buy that. They only think about the expense. Before marriage they will scold you, if you talk to a boy. (Is it always like that?) No, sometimes fathers respect their daughters." She went on to describe a father who liked his sons, but who also respected and liked his daughters. When I asked her how he demonstrated this attitude, she said that even though his daughters had already married out of the family, he gave them the key to the family treasure room, the repository of family valuables. This was a sign of trust.

Overall, the bond with the father is not obviously brittle, and is valued as fundamental, and often seems warm, if guarded, but estrangement does occur. Tensions were obvious in the way some Newars spoke of their fathers. Their fathers had punished them, and required them to do things they did not want to do, set out goals for them, chided and rebuked them, continually and harshly.

Newars whose fathers had died often expressed appreciation for what their father had done for them, and affirmed the value of his discipline or training. I had the impression that this was deeply felt. Some men had lost their fathers when they were young children; they stressed their father's love and concern for them. I was told that fathers (and mothers) sometimes appeared, hungry, naked, and forlorn, in dreams. This inspires a desire in the dreamer to help and nurture the dead parent by performing a puja for them.

To sum up, the Newar father is viewed as a nurturing authority (Kakar 1981: 119) for whom sons and daughters, reciprocally, are expected to feel deferential love. As Kakar (1981) says of India, tradition gives this ideal legitimacy. It has moral and emotional force. In actual families, this ideal synthesis of authority and nurturing, deference and love, may not be easy to achieve or maintain. There may be more coercive authority than nurturing affection, more outward deference than love. Authority may be subverted by affection, and efforts to maintain distance breached by love. Newars display a spectrum of emotions when they speak of their fathers, ranging from devotion to dislike. They remember fathers who took them places and played with them, helped them master social practices and "showed" them religion — or they recall fathers who neglected and beat them.

Krishna Bahadur, for example, was afraid of his father, who beat him while drunk. Krishna refuses to strike or physically punish his own children — a fairly unusual stand in Newar culture, where corporal punishment is generally accepted, but a stand consistent with Krishna's dreamy, gentle surfaces. He is not as authoritative and distant a father as some.

Less ambivalent relations are often maintained with the mother's brother (*paju*); this relationship is expected to be characterized by warmth, openness, and support. Krishna has warm memories of his maternal uncle. The intimacy and ease of this relationships contrasts with the distance and tensions of the relationship with a father.

In important ways, a father experiences a son as part of self. What Margaret Trawick (1990: 158) has said of the bond of son and father in South Indian Tamil culture works for Newars up to a point: "The father longs for continuity, but the son longs for independence." The son's life is a continuation of the father's life; the son's body is an extension of the father's body. Sons inherit the family estate — a powerful symbol of self. Culturally, a son will perform death rites necessary for the salvation of his father. He will assume his father's roles and duties. Given this longing for continuity, the son's strivings for a modest degree of independence may be disturbing, perhaps experienced as a loss or fragmentation of self. Any striving for separation may move a father to bring more pressure to bear on the son. This breeds resentment and an increased desire for autonomy.

While I think this is a basic tension in the relationships of Newar sons and fathers, it poses the question of how sons who want independence grow up to be fathers who desire continuity with their sons, and — in a crucial transformation — into adult sons who desire continuity with their fathers. Much cultural and psychological material points to this transformation, but how do we account for it? Part of the answer may lie in the fact that while a father's desire for continuity through his son is more overt, a son also identifies with his father. This identification is easily over-looked, by sons as well as observers, while the father is alive. As shown in the narrative above, a transformation occurs when a father dies. Sons then seek continuity, not independence. They begin to stress their continuity with their fathers by finding mean-ing in the ways their fathers restricted their autonomy. It is then that they speak of their love of their fathers, and of the value of their father's efforts to shape and educate them.[5] They place them-selves within a moral tradition by identifying themselves with their fathers. This act is crucial for the continuity of tradition; the way Newars identify with their parents mediates the way they identify with key cultural practices, and so shapes emotional commitment to cultural tradition.

Relationships with Mothers

Women's roles in Newar extended households are both like, and unlike, those of women in the extended patrilineal households of other cultures. In comparison to some other Hindu groups, Newar women have considerable freedom, power, and status within households (Allen 1982; Levy 1990). The relative freedom and enhanced status of Newar women are not derived from the basic principles of their kinship system. Households are organized in terms of patrilineal descent, virilocal residence, and the authority of males; daughters are given to other families in marriage, and wives are brought into the family. They are expected to show def-erence to the husband, his father, and his mother, to work hard, and to bear children—ideally sons—for the lineage. Newars share this type of patrilineal kinship system with groups where women's roles involve more social constraint and greater cultural disabili-ties than those Newar women experience. Newar culture mutes some of the implications of the patrilineal kinship system for women, lessening some of the disabilities imposed on women in other Indian and Nepalese groups with this kinship type (Bennett 1983; Levy 1990: 120–125).

Newars stress emotional and moral bonds with mothers. One Newar mother complained mildly of the dependence of her grown children, saying that whenever her sons entered the house, they asked "ma gwo, ma gwo ?" (Where's mother, where's mother?). Contemplating her own death, she wondered what they would do without her. As the female head (naki(n)) of the hearth group, she was the emotional *center* of the family, and wielded considerable power, not only within the extended family, but beyond, among client families and with her neighbors. My impression is that senior males are more likely to be emotionally isolated within the family, relegated to their hierarchical and disciplinarian roles, than are senior women. This may sometime work to enhance the power of women, and to diminish the influence of senior males, even though males are dominant in the "official" patrilineal ideology.

A mother's place in family life is not wholly defined by emotional nurturing, as significant as this is. In the case of the mother who found her children slightly too dependent, her extensive knowledge and good judgment were valuable family resources. She would sit with her sons as they ate, listen to their concerns, and be consulted on a range of subjects, from household and neighborhood affairs to aspects of city politics.

Daughters and sons are expected to love and to respect their mother, while mothers are expected to guide and nurture their children. We could use almost the same terms we used to sum up the father-child relationship—the nurturing authority of the parent is met with deferential love on the part of children—to describe the mother-child relationship. But this would not capture nuances of the relationships that make them different for Newars. One person suggested that father-child and mother-child bonds are the same in that they involve love and respect, but that mothers are gentler, fathers more distant. She also thought that daughters love their parents more than sons do, but that mothers and fathers love sons more than daughters. This asymmetry perhaps reflects the structural importance of sons in the patriline: the birth of sons enhances a woman's status within her husband's family, and helps her make a place for herself.[6] Daughters are aware of these structural preferences, and some are critical of the patrilineal system, stressing the unfairness of a daughter's marginality.

For these and other reasons, the mother-daughter bond is often ambivalent. Laksmi, a high-caste woman, was asked to describe the relationship of a daughter and her mother. She responded by saying that most daughters love and respect their mothers. "But sometimes," she said, "I don't even want to look in her face. I think she is cruel." Yet she went on to describe the kinds of things she liked to do for her mother, out of love, like bringing her flowers and fruit.

Trawick (1990) suggests that a basic tension in the mother-daughter bond in South Indian Tamil culture reflects a daughter's need for continuity in the face of a mother's lack of such a need. This seems to be true of Newars as well. Newar mothers may seek greater continuity and closeness with their sons, whose birth secured their place in their husband's family and who will help them make a life within that family. Mothers do not need daughters in the way they need sons, and must anticipate discontinuity in their relationship with daughters; for while sons continue the kul, the patriline, and will stay in the family home, daughters will marry and leave to live with their husband's family. For Newars, this mismatching of the emotional needs of the daughter for continuity and the mother's commitment to the patriline (and thus to discontinuity in her relationship with her daughter) is one element in a complex set of tensions that are experienced, expressed, and culturally formulated in various ways.

Laksmi, for example, clearly desires continuity with her mother, and with her natal family as a whole. She wants to be with them, and be there for them. But she also desires independence — up to a point. She recalls how bitterly she resented the way her mother disciplined her when she was young, and even now, as a grown-up, married woman, she sometimes resents the pressure her mother puts on her. She sees herself as being like her mother in some ways, but is ambivalent about this. She claims that the part of her that is like her mother makes her weak — and being weak, meaning being unable to stand up to others, is something she rejects in herself. Despite this ambivalence, Laksmi is determined not to let her own children be too independent; she says she will bind them to her, sons and daughters alike, so that they will take care of her when she grows old. At the same time, her mother's socially mediated detachment and separation from her daughter is contingent, notabsolute, despite the patrilineal values that define her sons as primary.

Most Newars would probably prefer to have their daughters marry into a family that lives close by; when this is feasible, a woman does not have to make as sharp a break with her family (or her family with her) as would be the case if she married into a distant community. Laksmi's husband is a government worker, however, and they often live for periods of time in distant government posts. This fact poses problems of separation for Laksmi and her mother. After her daughter has been away for a while, Laksmi's mother's desire for continuity and connection seems to match her daughter's in emotional intensity. She seeks to nurture and be nurtured by her daughter. She makes her daughter feel guilty by complaining that her sons' wives neglect her. She urges Laksmi to see her before she dies. When Laksmi returns, she brings her mother special foods, gives (and receives) emotional support, and pressures her brothers and brothers' wives to pay more attention to her mother. When Laksmi and her mother separate or rejoin, they cry together.

This suggests that the separation required by patrilineal kinship is mediated and overcome in emotional relatedness: daughter and mother come together to help meet each other's emotional and social needs. Paradoxically, their structural separation draws them closer. The fact that they are part of the life of different families means their relationship is not complicated by domestic concerns and politics. They can afford to be nurturing and supportive in ways that co-residents of the same household cannot always be. While other mother-daughter pairs may deal with the rupture that kinship structure produces in their relationship in other ways, Laksmi and her mother have responded by creating an emotional dynamic of mutual support and empathy enhancement. That is, they dramatize their domestic problems and triumphs to each other, and each is a responsive and sympathetic audience to the other.

Relatedness is desired, but experienced as a burden. Daughters and sons desire continuity, but also want independence. Reciprocally, parents want continuity *and* autonomy. Different elements come into play in different ways in different contexts. At some points in the developmental cycle, the daughter's desire for emotional continuity is salient, because of the structural discontinuities—she must go live among relative strangers, her husband's family. But she remains part of the emotional structure of her *tha:che*, her "own house," where she grew up.

Brothers and Sisters

Brothers and sisters often have warm, close relationships. A brother will, as paju, help perform necessary life-cycle rituals for his sister's children; a *nini* (father's sister) has similar roles. Sisters perform important rituals that are supposed to help ensure a long life for their brothers; the performance of these rituals stress the bond of brother and sister. Brothers help protect their sisters from "bad eyes," the sexual regard of men. The ethic of protection may be invoked to justify control, and women sometimes chafe under the criticism of brothers more concerned with the reputation of the family than with their sister's autonomy.

Brothers are an important source of political and emotional support for married women. Close relations with brothers are often a factor in a woman's status in her husband's family, especially in the period when the woman is establishing herself in the new household.

Brothers get along before they get married, I was told, while sisters get along after they get married. The implication is that the brothers' wives are at fault when there is friction between brothers. Asked why sisters would find it hard to get along with each other before marriage, one woman said that in her own case, she felt her family liked her sister better, and that her sister did not do her share of the household work. Sisters get along better after marriage, she suggested, because they have similar experiences and problems, and can give each other support. Since they no longer live together, they are not caught up in day to day discord.

Wives Come from Outside

The way that women join families is clearly a problem for Newars—a problem of integration and adaptation. Much moral discourse has to do with helping women fit into new families, or with justifying and making sense of failures, for marriages do not always work, and problems may arise in the relationships marriages create.

The Daughter's Position

The system of arranged marriages has moral premises, reflecting the nurturing hierarchy of family life. To arrange a marriage is a key parental duty, but daughters may resist. Personal choice is not part of the traditional cultural script; marriage is too important to be left to the dubious discretion of the young. The choice of partners, or the timing of a marriage, may pose problems. Ambivalence about separation (from the natal household) and commitment (to a spouse who is a stranger) may be a issues for daughters. The prospect of a marriage is sometimes distressing enough that a woman will resort to desperation tactics: being forced to marry is given as one of the major reasons for suicides, suicide attempts, and suicide threats by women.

The prospect of marriages does not always produce such severe distress or resistance; women often look forward to marriage with anticipation, even delight—if also with some anxiety. In other cases women put up considerable covert and overt resistance to arranged marriage in the face of great pressure; people will say (or she may tell herself) that she should respect the wisdom of her elders' decisions, that marriage is a duty and fate, and that being compliant is the proper stance for a daughter. The reluctance of many Newar parents to force a particular marriage suggests that the daughter's protests have some moral and emotional force.

Daughters-in-Law

Like a round wheel, it turns and turns [goes round and round] sometimes the mother-in-law's turn, sometimes the daughter-in-law's turn.

-A saying

Married women may have close, affectionate relationships with their husband's mothers. Newars see this as a potentially brittle relationship, however, and are not surprised when conflict breaks out. The precipitating surface cause may be disagreements over household work, or a mother-in-law's feeling that her authority is not accepted. But underlying this may be deeper concerns.

Conflict may be expressed in terms of issues of authority and subordination. Certainly, the mother-in-law's authority may be challenged in overt or subtle ways by her daughter-in-law. In many cases, however, there may be little basis for the conflict in anything the daughter-in-law does.

Conflict may grow out of the emotional meaning of relationships. In such cases, a state of perpetual tension may reflect not what the daughter-in-law does but "who she is" in relational terms—a son's wife. Even when specific behaviors are represented as the problem, they may serve more as a way of expressing a concern with relationship, as ad hoc mediating structures, than as a primary cause of conflict. A mother's desire for continuity in the bond with her son may contribute to tensions with her son's wife. A mothers may feel that her daughter-in-law has alienated her son's affection. Given the importance of a son to a woman's efforts to make a place for herself in the patrilineal family, a structural reality that amplifies the emotional significance of the mother-son bond, this may be experienced as extremely threatening. Such speculations are invited by the fact these tensions are perennial, and appear despite the fact the mother-in-law was once a daughter-in-law herself, and might be expected to temper her behavior and words because she remembers what it was like to be a *bhau maca*. The failure of empathy signals the working of other processes.

It is possible that the way women identify with their own mothers-in-law may undermine empathy for daughters-in-law.[7] The identification with their own mothers-in-law may be a kind of "internalization of the aggressor." As one Newar woman noted, a mother-in-law may justify her relatively harsh treatment of her daughter-in-law by relating it to her own experience. To illustrate her point, she assumed the complaining character of a mother-in-law: "If I had slept until the sun-god rose, like these bhau maca do, when I was a young bride, then my mother-in-law would have raised hell all the way to heaven." What all this suggests is not only identification, but a need to master the experience by assuming the power of the person who once punished and controlled them. In reaction, younger women may return to their natal households because they feel their mothers-in-law are too severe with them.

The presence of psychological motives does not mean that issues of dominance and subordination are insignificant. They are, as is suggested by the fact that "power" struggles emerge among the wives of brothers as well as with the mother-in-law. The psychological politics of attachment and jealousy do not cause domestic power struggles, struggles over the control of resources, even over power itself, but they do complicate them.

In other families, the bonds among women may be warm and nurturing for the most part, and the mother-in-law may be a key ally to a woman who marries into a house. In some households, the mother-in-law may help the daughter-in-law in managing and shaping her husband's behavior, especially in cases involving gambling or suspected or actual adultery. The shifting qualities of these relationships, at once emotional and political, are not easily caught in stereotypes—not even in the stereotypes Newars have of themselves.

The Failure of Marriages

In the traditional system, a woman who wished to go outside the house (except for tasks such as bringing water) would have to explain where she planned to go, and ask permission of her husband or mother-in-law. Even today, for a woman to venture outside the house on her own may be a serious breach. (One husband described his reaction when his wife stayed at her natal household without notifying him as intense rage.) In the traditional system, among high-caste groups, a woman who stayed away overnight, even at her parents' house, could not return to her husband's house until he sent someone (generally a servant or a client of the farming caste) to escort her back. If her husband did not want her back, he simply never sent for her. A wife desiring a separation walks out of her husband's house, and does not return.

Newars say women will leave their husbands if they are beaten, if they are unable to get along with their mothers-in-law, or if they are subject to economic exploitation—for example, when a husband's family takes a woman's dowry, self-acquired property, or personal earnings against her will. In other cases, women feel unloved or unable to cope. They may feel their husbands are unwilling or unable to work hard, to earn money, and to gain prestige for the family. Some women may leave, permanently or temporarily, because they, or their children, are not getting enough to eat. Even if they are not going hungry, women may leave because they believe they are not getting enough of the right kind of food, which they need to sustain themselves and their children. Claims that the husband's family did not feed a woman are hard to interpret; the idea of being hungry and deprived may serve as a powerful symbol of the malice or selfishness of the husband's family. In other cases, women flee real hunger.

A woman's natal household members may, depending on how they evaluate the situation, resist the return of a married daughter, reluctantly accept her, or welcome her. In some cases, they may actively encourage a woman to return to escape violence or deprivation.

Husbands also have varied reasons for separating from their wives. Feeling exploited is not as prominent a theme in their accounts, while feelings of estrangement seem more salient. They may express an aversion to their wives: as one man, who was often called on to help resolve marital problems, put it, "a bad smell comes on the breath of a woman you don't like," and "if you don't like your wife, there is no medicine."

The Cultural Construction of Relatedness

In their cultural emphasis on relatedness, Newars are similar to other South Asians. Some of their concepts of relatedness have a family resemblance to concepts found in other South Asian groups without being identical to these concepts.

Fruzzetti, Östör, and Barnett (1983: 17) see "blood" as a basic concept that Bengalis use to understand kinship: "*Rakta* (blood) is a Bengali construct referring to a substance, enduring and persistent, a permanent attribute that is recognized and transmitted in the male line through women." They argue that blood (rakta) is a fundamental value, a symbolic construct that defines the identity and continuity of the family line. Men produce their family line (*bangsa*) by means of procreation with wives who transmit their husband's male "blood" to children (1983: 17–18). "Blood" is thus a symbol of male essence, and, as such, constitutes relatedness in a patrilineal idiom.

Inden and Nicholas (1977) emphasize "body" rather than "blood" as the concept in Bengali kinship which represents a patriline's identity and relatedness. They cite Hindu texts:

The shared body relationship [*sapindata*] comes about by virtue of connection [*anvaya*] with portions [*avayava*] of the same body [*eka-sarira*]. Thus, by virtue of connection with portions of the father's body, the son comes to have a shared body relationship with the father and through the father with the set of those beginning with the father's father as well, because of the connections with portions of his body. Similarly, by virtue of connection with portions of the mother's body he comes to have a shared body relationship with the mother and through the mother with the set of those beginning with the mother's father. . . . So, too, the wife comes to have a shared body relationship with the husband by virtue of their reproduction of the same body [*ekasarirarambhakataya*]. Similarly, the wives of brothers also come to have a shared body relationship, the one with the other [*paraspara*], because they have the relationship of reproducing the same body with those men reproduced from the same body. (Vijnanesvara's Mitaksara, a commentary on the code book of Yajnavalkya, circa A.D. 1100, quoted in Inden and Nicholas 1977: 13; diacritics omitted)

In this commentary, the metaphor of a "shared body" has been consciously worked out and systematized. The Bengali family, Inden and Nicholas (1977) argue, is intelligible in terms of this metaphorical system; the "metaphor" stands as "reality" for social actors. Notice that the metaphor has both egalitarian and hierarchical implications. It expresses — or shapes — what Inden and Nicholas call the "generic unity and equality" of male kin and of female kin (p. 23) and the "egalitarian love" of spouses and siblings. These egalitarian modes of kinship contrast with the "hierarchical love" that reflects generational differences or birth order. The distinction works for Newars, as we will see below.

Whether "blood" or "body" is the most central and pervasive metaphor in Bengali culture for the perception of Bengali kinship is a matter for ethnographic review. They are not necessarily mutually exclusive. More than one symbol may be used to constitute a domain of life as vitally important as kinship. Different ensembles of symbols may be invoked in different contexts, may be more or less shared, may have different implications that serve different purposes — ranging from efforts to ward off psychological threats to self to strategic communication and moral rhetoric. Symbols may have microhistorical careers as well as canonical expressions in a culture. The search for overarching cultural con-

cepts may not be productive at all; the mental templates for relatedness and identity may be so abstract, pliable, overdetermined,
that they can be embodied in a variety of forms, symbols, and gestures. Different metaphors may point to the same thing in different ways. For Newars, I believe, the essential idea is that people in
families are joined together in a "web of relatedness." Various
metaphors argue for the way they are connected, but do not argue
against the essential unity of the family, its "shared identity." They
only phrase it in importantly different idioms; the phrasings fold in
other values. I therefore offer the following account of "seed" and
"blood" as a metaphor, not the metaphor, of relatedness—as one
"myth" of the origin and nature of the grounds of relationship in
the Newar family. The metaphor is a common one, and, like the
one body metaphor, is patrifocal, stressing male bonds and contributions. The male "seed" organizes female "blood" to make a person.

Govinda Raj gives this account:

(How does a child begin in the womb?)
The usual way is that a woman and a man have sex. During
sex, there is blood inside the woman. . . . And then the man's seed
goes—this is semen. When the blood and seed are well mixed
together in the woman's womb, in the child-house of the womb,
then a small person slowly develops. As small as a bug. Gradu-
ally it grows bigger, and develops a head, arms, and legs.

(So the mother gives blood, the father gives seed?)
You don't have to say the mother gives blood—she has blood,
she doesn't have to give blood. The only one who gives anything
is the father. The mother has blood, the man gives seed to the
blood. The blood and seed are mixed. Let me make an analogy:
think of a field. The field is the mother's womb. The man's
semen is planted in the field. After the seed has been planted in
the field, the mother gives birth. A tree comes, rice comes, grass
comes. Just as these plants grow, so the child in the womb comes
into being, grows and develops.[8] That is the way a child is conceived in the womb, develops, matures. This is the usual view of
the process.

(How does the blood, and the seed, influence the child?)
The child has only flesh, the flesh grows. As it grows bigger,
a head develops, a body. Everything. Blood is only soil. The
man's semen—this seed is the real person. Only the seed is the

real person; the blood is only the soil. To grow—inside the soil is nourishment. Blood makes [the fetus] happy and well-fed. The potential person is the man's seed. Not blood. If blood is the body, then seed is life [pran].
(Will you say that again?)
Blood is only like a body. Seed is the inner life [jib]. The inner life is pran. The same as living spirit [jivatma, spirit, soul].
(But how does the blood, the seed influence the child's nature [swabhav]?)
Their influence on the child's nature?—for one thing the concerns of past lives comes. There is a relationship with the past. [He is alluding to the karma doctrine here.]
(With the blood or with the seed?)
With the blood, and with the seed, too, there is a relationship.
(So the influences of the past also are mixed up?)
That happens. . . . [He goes on to speak of influences on the child not mediated by concepts of "blood" or "seed," e.g., the child may acquire the moral character of the parents.]
(Compared to blood, the seed is more important?)
Seed is more important than blood.
(Why?)
The seed is small, a tiny thing—but the land is vast. The most important part of the eye is the little pupil. Although it is small, it is very important, the pupil of the eye. The seed is like this. It is small but it has to do much. The mind is a product of the seed. Intelligence, understanding and knowledge develop from the seed. From the man's seed knowledge and intellect develop. From the woman's blood, only flesh develops.

There is a tacit rhetoric here, an implicit ideology that validates patriarchal patterns in the Newar family. The essential qualities of personhood—thought, knowledge, judgment—are constituted by the active male principle of "seed." Life and spirit reside in the seed.[9]

Govinda sees this as the ordinary concept of development. He contrasts it with a somewhat more esoteric doctrine calling on the man not to "spill his seed" because losing seed entails loss of life-force. He also notes the Newar belief that older men have weaker seed, and that this is likely to produce inferior offspring. He does not attribute all aspects of being a person to seed. "Desire," he noted, "comes later."

A Newar woman, asked to comment on all this, reframed and reformulated the question of what makes a person. She acknowledged that the male seed was a generative principle — before birth. After a child is born, she insisted, a mother trains, disciplines, and takes care of it. Once the child is born, she argued, the male's contribution is passive, while a woman's nurturing is active and shapes the child in fundamental ways. The father as a parent may not take responsibility for shaping young children or even for their care. To support her argument, she pointed out the likelihood that if a father dies, the mother will take care of the child, but that if a mother dies, the father's new wife may not; she drew the implication that a father may not be involved actively in the process through which a child becomes a finished person, while a natural mother is committed and engaged. While the "blood" of the mother may be a passive biological principle, the mother as caregiver actively shapes the young child into a full moral person.[10]

She also observed that not only parents are involved in the process of making a person. Society (samaj), especially kin groups, play an active role as the child grows up. She gave the example of life-cycle rituals (which I will discuss in chapter 5); these are a form of moral socialization organized in terms of kinship relations. "They must do these rituals for their sons and daughters. (Why?) To make them part of society, to make them complete persons."

Blood may not constitute persons, but it does connect them. One man recalled how his mother used to respond to her children's misbehavior by saying, "If the seed is good, then the plant will be good." His mother meant, he said, to imply the child's misbehavior was rooted in the "seed" that made them what they were. A second implication (which he made explicit) is that the father was also bad; the phrase picked up meanings in the context of a history of marital discord. When she was feeling more well disposed to her children, this mother would refer to them as *tha la hi*, her "own flesh and blood." This is a different metaphor in a different context; but the import is still one of connection. Blood in this idiom may not constitute a person's identity with his patriline, but it does assert an emotional bond.

Govinda defines "blood" as a passive, neutral material. It does not carry the meaning of patrilineal identity, solidarity, and continuity; it is less salient and less constitute a category than "blood" in

Bengali culture. Yet the fundamental understanding of "related-ness" is there; an idea of relatedness as fundamental is found across the very different cultural conceptions of the nature of biological and moral relationship. This basic understanding seems quite sim-ilar in both Bengali and Newar cultures. The two cultures share the metaphor that relates blood to soil and semen to seed, women to the field and men to the cultivator of the field.[11]

Underlying the important matrifocal or patrifocal emphases of "blood," "shared body," and "seed" is a vision of relatedness; these concepts assert the nature of kinship. The vision of relatedness these concepts help establish at once acknowledge and insist on emotional ties that are, at the same time, moral bonds. The con-cepts define the way that self is joined to other lives.

But this conception of relatedness does not diminish the impor-tance of personal identity. When relatedness is constituted in these ways, the individuality of a self is not abolished; in some ways, embeddedness may enhance individuality, not diminish it. The act-ing and experiencing self must have the capacity to be concerned about others, able to "feel for" them. The politics of relationships must be negotiated. A person must have a capacity for responsible action in a moral sense.

All this requires a "self" that is, more or less, a "dynamic center of awareness, emotion, judgment, and action" (Geertz 1984: 126). This "dynamic center" of experience and agency provides a basis for self-identity, for individuality. Geertz, of course, characterizes the "Western" concept of the person in these words only to ques-tion the universality of such a concept of the person. Newars have more than one concept of the person; the phrase "dynamic center of awareness, emotion, judgment," usefully characterize one mode of their experience. The reality of lived, individual existence may not be fully represented in cultural meaning systems, but is con-fronted by concrete men and women even in the web of related-ness (Roland 1986) .

Purity and Pollution

Newars also know and experience the web of relatedness in terms of concepts of purity and impurity. Of course, the English words *purity* and *pollution* are not precise translations of the meanings of local concepts and may not shed much light on what they label.

They may even mislead. In English, "pollution" is something to avoid, to keep away from self. In Newar culture, persons general-ly seek to avoid contact with "pollution," but at certain times they actively share "pollution," giving or receiving it. Some are required to absorb it from others, to make it a part of self. Household and lineage members may share "pollution" transmitted in the medium of food.[12]

In translating local terms, we run the risk of merely displacing the mystery of indigenous concepts by glossing them with equally mysterious English language concepts—at best, this adds little to understanding. If I suggest, as I will, that household and lineage members sometimes eat food that has been "polluted" by having been tasted by other members of their group, and that this sym-bolizes solidarity, I can make the argument without much of a the-ory of what "pollution" is for Newars—but I would leave much opaque.[13] To simply say that something, a portion of food that has been tasted, and so brought into contact with saliva, is "polluted" does not explain what "pollution" means, what import it has, why it might seem real to people, why it might engage them in such a way that it has come to form the basis of key cultural practices— or why they might at times want to eat "polluted" food. One can, of course, describe the social behavior that goes along with con-cepts of pollution without understanding what indigenous psy-chology or sense of reality it expresses, but this would tell only part of the story.

What makes "polluted" food a potent symbol—good to think and act out? Perhaps it is the images or schemas of person and relationship that are embedded within everyday practices. Here I will draw a line of interpretation put forward by McKim Mar-riott, which suggests we view purity and pollution in terms of a theory of the person prevalent in South Asia. A caveat: this the-ory, it seems to me, addresses the conceptual foundations of prac-tice, but does not necessarily correspond directly to felt reality. Newars did not typically speak to me in terms that derive direct-ly from the model that Marriott proposes, although many cultur-al constructs and practices seem highly consistent with the model. Newars most often spoke, though, in terms of feelings of closeness, intimacy, solidarity, exclusion, when they talked about food as a medium of relatedness. Ultimately, we need to bring into view the social context and the cultural foundations of concerns with pollution together with data on actual persons to achieve any real understanding—which I can do here only in the briefest way, and only as it may relate to the theme of this chapter.

For Newars, impurity resides in things like saliva, feces, menstruating women, untouchables. Concerns with purity and impurity arise within the Newar family primarily in relation to the body, food, water, death, childbirth, and menstruation. In each case, the beliefs and practices of the purity complex suggest something about the nature of persons and their relationships or potential for relationship. I will only consider the language of personhood and relationship that seems implicit in Newar concepts of "polluted" food (*cipa*) here, and not consider other types of impurity.

Like many South Asians, Newars often speak and act as if persons have fluid, permeable boundaries. As McKim Marriott puts it:

> Persons—single actors—are not thought in South Asia to be "individual," that is, indivisible, bounded units, as they are in much of Western social and psychological theory as well as in common sense. Instead, it appears that persons are generally thought by South Asians to be "dividuals" or divisible. To exist, dividual persons absorb heterogeneous material influences. They must also give out from themselves particles of their own coded substances—essences, residues, or other active influences—that may then reproduce in others something of the nature of the persons in which they originated. (1976: 111)

If this interpretation of the South Asian concept of the person is more or less correct—and it seems plausible, at least in some contexts—then we should find behavior organized as if a person can emit pieces of himself, of his essential, defining nature. Transmitted in various media—such as food—these constituent, organizing elements of one person may be incorporated by another, altering the second person in the process. Reciprocally, self may acquire "something of the nature" of others. This may alter a person's social standing, or, more importantly for our discussion here, signify the transformation of her identity and her incorporation into new relationships.

In the Newar case, cultural practices regarding the sharing of food within the family seem consistent with the concept of a "dividual" person with permeable boundaries. For Newars, food that has been tasted—and so brought into contact with saliva—is cipa. It is contaminated—but by what? In many ways, the concepts and practices associated with cipa seem to embody the notion that persons have permeable boundaries. Viewed in this light, cipa might be interpreted as food bearing particles of self, making food a medium for the transmission of the qualities and essences that constitute persons not only as bodies, but as social actors, as moral agents, and—embracing both these—as members of a family line.

Giving and receiving—or refusal to give and receive—in the medium of food also defines who people are in relationship to each other, declaring who is higher, and who is lower. Those who are ranked higher will often not accept food made cipa by those who are lower in rank. Although eating food made in "the same rice pot" conveys a sense of family unity, the state of the food, as cipa or not cipa, marks the way members of a household are positioned in relationship to each other. Cooked food is subject to rules that govern who accepts food from whom, and under what conditions. Thus, what is shared also marks differences, and helps constitute the internal hierarchy of the family.

As the hierarchical implications of accepting or refusing to accept some else's cipa suggest, having "something of the nature" of others reproduced in self may be desirable or undesirable, depending on the relationship of the persons involved. Social expectations define who should eat food made cipa by another (and thus make "the nature" of others part of themselves, if indeed this is the implication of accepting the cipa by others) and who should not accept food made cipa (and thus refuse to incorporate particles of others in themselves). Among Newars, these expectations may be modified to some extent by personal feeling, but the expectations have some force as norms. Those rejecting the transfer may experience it as a violation of self, should it happen despite their best efforts to avoid it. Those who welcome it may perceive it as expressing or creating intimacy or equality, may perhaps, in some cases and contexts, experience it as an affirmation of bonds with others.

How do Newars respond to this? Most conform to the practice, but it is a more serious matter for some than others. For many

Newars, not accepting others' cipa is largely a matter of convention, not of emotional commitment. They will avoid eating it in public contexts, but eating others' cipa arouses little in the way of disgust or uneasiness. Others react more strongly, with more self-involvement, in some cases reacting with physical revulsion, especially when they inadvertently eat the cipa of someone of lower-caste standing. I have heard stories of people vomiting in such cases, but this was considered extreme by some other Newars. Within households, I have the general impression that refusing to eat the cipa of those who are—or one wished were—more junior than self in the household more often reflects the politics of family life than it does profound anxiety about the integrity of self-boundaries. In a more general sense, however, the definition and defense of the boundaries of the family unit against outsiders—and the incorporation of women who marry in—do seem to be issues. The concepts of the person that cipa may reflect seem to have more to do with the social integration of the household than with the personal integration of individuals.

Cipa is contagious—it can pass from one person or object to another. As one Newar Brahman put it, cipa flows "like electricity" through various media. It can run from one person to another through touch, food, certain utensils, even, he indicated, through a table top. Cipa transmitted in this way causes others to become cipa, and contagious in turn. Since cipa diffuses in this way, a person may become cipa inadvertently. Some discipline and care must be taken to avoid causing others to become cipa; usually this involves eating in a specific order—and it often boils down to women eating after men.

As this suggests, cipa has much to do with separating men and women. Within households (the implications work out in somewhat different ways in the caste system), cipa seems mainly to separate people in terms of gender and age. Men will not accept cipa from their wives or younger household women. They may accept cipa from their parents or senior relatives, including senior women. Women will generally accept cipa from all males; eating their husband's cipa is, in fact, something they should do. They may accept cipa from women who are older, but may not accept it from the wives of brothers, or, if they themselves are wives, from the wives of husbands' younger brothers.[14] Women eat after men, which prevents women from contaminating men's food.[15] Men may eat the cipa of their younger children "out of love" or not do so, if they are concerned about maintaining a state of ritual purity. Some Newars suggested that eating a child's cipa is a way of expressing a special sense of intimacy and love; this is a gesture made possible by the existence of the norms prohibiting it—by setting aside the norm, you assert that something else is more important.

Young children are not expected to observe these rules. Measures are taken to see that they do not contaminate the food of others, such as warning them or picking them up, but the rules are generally relaxed.

Accepting cipa is most stressed in the case of women who marry into the family. A wife will accept cipa from her husband, her husband's father and mother, and his brothers. Only her own children, and perhaps junior women who have married in and sometimes the younger siblings of her husband, eat her cipa. It seems likely that this serves a way of incorporating women into their husband's family. We can provisionally interpret cipa as "substance," or a sign of substance, which can be shared or not shared. By accepting cipa, a woman who marries into a family makes the substance of the family part of herself, and thus incorporates herself into the corporate "body" of the family. The practice thus has special significance for the woman married to the youngest male of the household.[16] As a new member of the household, a stranger and outsider, this woman accepts the cipa of the widest set of other family members, and so comes to share their being or essence.[17]

The senior male of the hearth group tends to be sheltered from the impurity of cipa, as well as from other sources of impurity. This is consistent with the hierarchical authority of the senior male, but seems keyed to the performance of specific roles, rather than forming a general condition of being a senior male, since, in some families, men may eat the cipa of their children. Men who have undergone Tantric initiation, have mantras, and perform rites for the lineage deity, or are otherwise in a state of intensified purity, are required to maintain their purity by avoiding pollution.

The flow of cipa in the hearth group expresses the idea that senior males form the "body" of the hearth group. That is, they embody, and are the source of what the family is, its substance and being. The practices maintain the homogeneity of the family by requiring the most alien member to eat food that carries the sub-

stance of the most prototypic members of the family. The husband's mother, who was also once an alien, unrelated in a deep
sense, must be viewed in this interpretation as already having been
incorporated in the body or shared substance of the family through
eating cipa, by having sexual relations with her husband, and by
bearing a child for the family. If this interpretation is plausible,
then the impurity of food not only segregates, but incorporates—
it marks differences but makes a sameness.[18]

In theory, as was noted in chapter 2, the moral code that applies
to individuals is not separate from what they are, from their material nature as persons; it is contained in the constituent elements of
their being, makes them what they are, makes them do what they
do, and makes them fit for certain roles in life. Incorporating "the
nature" of others into self thus can signify a radical restructuring
of self and world for South Asian persons. In family life, this
apparently reflects some of the discontinuities of women's social
roles and experience.

In sum, by refusing to accept another's cipa, people assert differences, and embody hierarchy in a concrete practice, reminding
all of the way they are each positioned relative to each other in
terms of household power and priority. Others may be required to
eat cipa, thereby affirming their incorporation into the household.
By eating cipa, people feast on each other's essences in a way that
symbolizes their unity as a group and their places in the household.

The family has other self-images, of course. The image of the
family as "one hearth" or "one rice pot" defines the boundaries of
the household unit. The location of the hearth on the top floor of
the house and the concern for its purity separates the family from
others, who cannot enter it. Unlike concerns with cipa, these self-
images of family solidarity do not impose an internal structure on
the household. The symbolism is not hierarchical; these images do
not distinguish family members, but rather submerge differences.
If the idea of one hearth, and the daily practice of eating together
or from the same source, work to create a sense of mutual identity,
which has important consequences for achieving and organizing
solidarity and interdependence, they also, I would suggest, have
implications for the experience of empathy and an ethic of caring
within the family. Empathy and mutual concern, as well as hierarchy and duty, are experienced values in the kind of union of lives
that the Newar family is. A sense of solidarity, of being "at one"

with others, is central, in some ways transcending hierarchical differences.

Interpreting Moral Constructs

If "blood," "seed," and "pollution" are, in their different Newar and Bengali uses, "symbols," we can ask what they "stand for." Part of the answer seems to be that they "stand for" relationships that kin have with each other. One could, I suppose, argue that these symbols or metaphors are not only representational but constitutive: they not only "stand for" but "bring about." I am sympathetic to this idea — culture brings some things about, constituting them as "reality." But not all things. And I think these particular symbols, while they do shape relationships, also express emotion that is not brought into being by the symbols, but exists prior to the cognitive activation of the symbols. This body of emotion reflects experience in the family; people find meaning in symbols by relating them to their lives. The expressive dimension of symbols or metaphors may empower them — make them emotionally significant, and so especially suitable for representing or constructing relationships.

This is a crucial point. Emotion *is* mediated by symbols, I believe, but it is *more than* the product of a process of symbolic construction. Emotional experience and knowing is generated in the concrete social reality of ongoing life, reflecting the lived, practical experience of actual relationships, dialectically linked to, but not simply constituted by, symbolic forms.

Whether constituted by symbols, or expressed by symbols (or both), the sense people develop of themselves-in-relationships shapes the activity that goes into having and negotiating relationship. This "practical" consciousness is fundamental to social life anywhere; social life always presupposes reflexive self-knowing in social contexts where a cultural repertoire of concepts of relatedness helps define the possibilities of relationship.[19]

Maya: Love as Illusion, Illusion as Love

Cultural concepts of "love" also shape the way Newars experience, understand, and enact relationships. The ways they know and experience love help generate the web of relatedness.[20] The Newari word for "love" is maya. A second meaning of this word is

"illusion," and it is possible this second meaning has subtle resonances in the way Newars speak of love as an emotional and moral
force in their lives.[21]

When speaking of love, Newars may combine the noun maya
with the verb "to go" (wanegu), presenting love as something that
moves in the space between self and other. Love goes "out," and
doing so transports the mind or heart with it, making people connect, empathize, with others. Newars often speak of love in terms
that suggest that the experience of empathy is central to their concept of love. For example, Durga, a high-caste woman, describes
love in terms of what others feel and experience:

(When do you say, "love goes"?)
When you see someone suffering. When you see a beggar,
when someone is sick. When someone in the family cries.
(Do you feel it more for your own flesh and blood?)
Yes. But also for the poor. But it is different.

For Newars, empathy seems at once to animate and be animated by love. In empathic responses, the experience of another resonates in self. "When my child cries," Durga explains, "I also want
to cry." Another woman said, "I love the children. Because I love
them, I want to feed them and give them things."

A Brahman man, Shiva Raj, reflects on gender differences in
parental love. He argues that the greater love of a mother makes
her more responsive to her children:

A mother loves her children. And so does a father. But a mother has a greater love for her children than a father. The mother
cares for her children, and so does the father, but the mother
watches over the children more than the father. She watches
over them with as much love as she has.

Thus, children trust their mother—and their father too. But
they have more love and trust for their mother. There is no
doubt about a mother's love. There is no duplicity in a mother's
love. A mother's love is selfless. A mother's love is very holy.

Even though she has not eaten, a mother loves her children.
Even in sickness she loves them. She worries constantly. She
wonders, "What kind of ∂ukha [pain, suffering, trouble] will
come to my child?" She wants to prevent any suffering from
coming to her child. A mother is always thinking of her child.

She thinks, my child must not suffer. All mothers have this pure
form of love—it is their nature. This kind of pure love is found
in a mother's heart. A mother's love is as measureless as the
water of an ocean.

A mother is like a goddess. And it is said, the greatest goddess
is also a mother. She is the mother of the world. And the mother of the worlds is the source of all love, who gives love to each
separate mother. This is our belief. This is our belief according
to dharma.

This is a vision of perfection, a radical idealization of the mother as
a source of limitless, unconditional love. Shiva Raj spoke with considerable emphasis and emotion. Notice the emphasis on concern
and responsiveness; this passage idealizes the expectation that
mothers (and fathers, but not as much) will anticipate and focus on
the experience of their children, and will experience distress at
their children's distress.[22]

Asked what maya is, Devi Maya first identifies it as *prem*, another term that could be translated "love." (Others sometimes distinguish maya and prem by suggesting that prem has erotic over-
tones.) For her, the love is inherent in the relatedness of a mother
with her own children. She says that "you cannot stop loving your
own son and daughter no matter where they are or what they
are—this is certainly the way it happens" [said with emphatic
structure].

Explaining how she feels love for her children, Devi makes a
gesture to show how it is: she puts her hand on her "heart," the seat
of emotion, and then reaches out with it, showing the open palm of
the hand at the end of the gesture, suggesting a sort of opening of
the heart, a giving to the other.

Devi Maya then distinguished between love for one's own children and love for others. She argued that, in addition to this fundamental and spontaneous love for your children, if you see people over time, if you talk to them, and become friends, then your
love also "goes" to them. "Even if you live with just a dog for a few
days, you start to love it."

Asked to explain the difference between maya and *karna* [=
karuna, "compassion"], she says first that they are the same. Then
she reverses herself, saying that you will feel karna wanigu for a
child or a beggar you do not know, if they have a cut or wound, if

they are sick or suffering. For them, she says, you feel karna—in your own "mind," [*man*, "mind" or "heart"], karna "goes." Both karna and maya involve empathy, since they depict a psychological experience in which the "mind" or "heart" reaches out and brings self into contact with experience of others; but Devi distinguishes karna as what you feel for people you do not know and maya as what you feel for people you know. Thus, you have to know people, in the sense of sharing a life with them, to love them, but not to feel compassion for them.

Govinda Raj distinguishes "natural love" (*swabhabik maya*) that is felt for those who are part of the lineage and family from "love by association" (*nhapan cwana juigu maya*). In his view, love mirrors a natural hierarchy of commitment: you love your own family first, then affines, and next friends. Only after these might one feel "love" for others. Love by association develops through being together—it develops over time.

Karna differs from maya because it is felt when someone is suffering (*dukha siiugu*, to suffer). Govinda sees karna as an emotional response to a person's life situation or to specific events in their lives; you feel karna for someone who must beg for food, or when someone fails at some important task. When you encounter such persons, Govinda says you might describe them as *bichara*, a "poor one." For example, he says, if it is cold, and you see someone working in the cold, you would feel karna, and would express it by saying, "Bichara, how hard they are working in the cold."

Govinda adds that *karna wanegu* is for "humanity" (*manavata*). "If you do not feel karna and maya for others, you are not human (*manav*). Even animals feel love for their children."

> But although brothers and sisters love each other, sometimes they fight over the family wealth. If you do not feel love (maya) and sympathy (*daya*), then you feel that this is yours, and that is theirs, and it develops that people say, these are my people, and these are other people.

Although the ideal is that a Newar should love everyone in the extended family "the same," Newars acknowledge that is often not the case—a father might love his own children more than the children of his brother, sons more than daughters, or one son more than another.

While "love" has great ethical depth for Newars, the moral part of love is not the whole of love. Although I have stressed the way maya is a moral emotion, I do not want to reduce the complex cultural experience of love to just one of its many aspects. We would not be doing justice to Newar life by taking the Newar cultural idealization of maya for their actual experience of love and relatedness.

Even as a moral concept, love is complex. "Love" has moral force within Newar life, but this cuts two ways. If visions of love sustain relatedness, they can also undermine it; although love may reinforce commitments, it can also subvert them. Knowing what love should be, Newars may not accept what life offers them.

This was made poignantly clear by the way some of the Newars I knew seem to find more "love" in memory and fantasy, even in dreams, than in actual life.

A dream I was told illustrates the way Newars may imagine or remember love and relatedness in contrast to what they experience. A Newar woman, the mother of several children, dreams of her father, her mother, her aunts and uncles, all of them dead for many years. When they appear in her dream, they ask her to come join them—to die. They tell her that she has suffered much, and should not have to suffer anymore. The woman, in her dream, wants to go to them, but says that she cannot leave her young son and daughter. She tells her dead that her children would suffer as she has, if she left now. She assures the figures in her dream that she will come later, when her children are grown.

This dream expresses the central significance of relatedness in Newar lives; the dreaming mind holds on to, or recreates, a sense of relatedness, of being loved and cared for. In the dream, the dreamer renounces what she wants to do, out of her concern for her children. She would like to escape her life, and join her dead, but not if it meant her children would suffer.

This woman is deeply ambivalent about her actual family relationships. She feels her marriage is loveless, her husband weak, greedy, and self-centered. She characterized her husband by telling of his behavior just after they married. Newly married Newar husbands often bring their new wives small gifts and food. Such small acts of giving and sharing are done secretly because the joint family is wary of the new bride, and might disapprove of any show of commitment to her rather than to the extended family.

This makes such acts of giving and sharing all the more significant to the newly married woman. They make her feel that a personal bond might be possible with the stranger she has married.
But this woman's husband did not bring her anything. Worse, he
would buy and eat sweets himself, but make no effort to share
them with her. She was bitter about this, and held it as a griev-
ance over the years. It came to sum up her husband's character
for her, acting as a symbol of her life-situation, a telling image of
disconnection.

Her expectations about love and relatedness, based on cultural
conceptions and on her experience of kinship within her natal family, contrasted sharply with what she experienced after marriage,
when she experienced conflict with her husband and his family
over money and household work. In the early years of her married
life, she was deeply troubled because she felt her children were not
getting enough good food. She felt that her husband and his father
were unwilling to spend the money to feed them properly. She tells
her grown children of their miserliness, and how she fought with
them to get more food.[23]

Romantic and Sexual Love

Kin love is not the only kind of love Newars know. Even though
constraint characterizes the relations between men and women,
and most marriages are arranged, Newars do view sexual love as
having the power to form an emotional bond. Romantic love may
be a Western invention, but Newars recognize something akin to
it. They commemorate erotic and passionate love in songs and
poetry, acknowledge it in gossip, and speak of it as part of their
own experience. Such love is not the only or primary basis for the
marital bond; it is not exalted as the only natural basis for a relationship. For Newars, marriage is too important to be built primarily on an emotion that is unpredictable, volatile. The bonds of
marriage should not be based on physical attraction, but on the
developed good judgment of family elders, acting for the good of
the entire family. The marriage bond is a moral relationship before
it is an emotional one; it should be based on dharma, the moral law,
not passion. Thus, while Newars acknowledge, even celebrate, erotic and passionate love, they know that it can subvert key values.

Passionate love is dangerous, yet enticing and powerfully compeling.

In one folk song, a man is charmed by the sound made by the anklet bells of a young woman as she walks: "Taking away my heart, you walked away/ Please wait, you've caught my heart in a net of love [*maya jal*]." Her laughter is compared to a magic charm. The experience of love described in these songs has the quality of arising spontaneously, as a result of the presence of the other. It is unplanned, not deliberate and self-willed—it happens to persons, making them experience themselves as vitally connected to another.

Maya jal has a double meaning. It means "net of love," but also "net of illusion." This double meaning sets up resonances with another way of knowing the world, the way of the Hindu ascetic who seeks to escape "illusion" and "desire."

Although my informants stressed the first meaning, I suspect the ambiguity may add something to the force of the lyric. Other songs play on the contrast of the world of love and the world of love renounced.

For example, in another well-known song, a man pleads with his father to arrange his marriage to a woman named Rajamati, "the daughter child of a man from Sa(n)ku." The son warns that "If you don't give me Rajamati, it'll be time to go to Kashi [Varanasi]"—meaning that he will become a world-renouncer, an ascetic. The son promises, "if you give me Rajamati, I won't go to Kashi, father. Give me Rajamati." The song then describes how a go-between arranges the marriage for Rajamati with someone else; the song says Rajamati did not want to go, but it was her karma to have a hateful life in a house where her husband's family did not treat her well. In the song, desires and intentions are socially mediated: a man asks his father to arrange his marriage; Rajamati is given in marriage against her wishes. Others, not self, determine what happens.

Contact between unrelated young men and women is rather strictly controlled in Newar society. They will be reprimanded by their parents and kin if they are seen talking or walking together. Gossip acts as a control, too. Newars know that stigmatizing gossip about themselves might disrupt their vital social network, leading to social isolation. This makes them careful about having unsupervised contact with others, however innocent these encounters might be. Young couples might be able to pair off during certain festivals, taking advantage of the break with the ordinary these events represent. A few couples might arrange to meet secretly in the woods encircling a temple outside the city. Others, wealthier and more modern, might arrange to meet discretely in a curtained booth in a restaurant in Kathmandu (but they still might be seen). Modern college campuses create opportunities to meet and socialize. Relationships that develop in this way sometimes lead to what Newars call "love marriages," even though these may face considerable family resistance.

Some young male Newars report experiencing intense anger and jealousy when a woman with whom they have fantasized a relationship speaks with another man; the woman may not even be aware of, much less return, this interest. Unspoken expectations of this sort often complicate marriages. Some younger Newar women, like elite women in Bengal (Roy 1972), build up a romantic conception of love out of the emerging popular culture of movies and novels; they hope for emotional intimacy, and this may lead to disappointment in marriage, since the men they marry will often have different concepts of marriage, which emphasize traditional obligations more than emotional rapport. Some modernizing men, on the other hand, find that traditional women do not share their interests, concerns, and conceptions of marriage. Some educated women resist marriage with men who lack an education on the same grounds; they do not want to vanish into the traditional role of a wife.

Passionate attachments can end in tragedy. Adulterous relationships may lead to suicide, especially, perhaps, if they cross caste boundaries. A double standard leaves women subject to harsher criticism and sanctions should they have a sexual relationship outside marriage. The vulnerability of women to seduction — seen variously as resulting from their more intense sexuality, their innocence and willingness to trust in what men say, or their poverty — puts them at risk of sexual exploitation.

In the West, some people may perceive some form of romantic love as the best basis for forming a relationship, and hold that the emotional experience of love, alone, can constitute an enduring moral bond. Newars do not value passionate love in quite this way; despite their capacity for experiencing it, such love is not viewed as the essential principle of relationship on which a marriage must be based. Newar marriage is ethicized, I think, most forcefully in terms of social concepts of duty, not the personal experience of love. The dominant moral rhetoric is that the relationships of husbands and wives should be based solidly on the dharma, the moral law, of their roles. While Newars experience passionate love, and emotional intimacy often develops within marriages, they do not act as if this is a necessary and sufficient condition for joining lives together; a concept of love as intimacy, laced with erotic playfulness, is not indispensable to the way Newars understand relatedness. Sexual love itself is not, for them, the primary prototype for human relatedness. Birth is more fundamental, because it is the act through which a person comes into being, a person who *embodies* relatedness, creating the continuity of the patriline, the kul (cf. Inden and Nicholas 1977: 55). A woman's incorporation into her husband's family is not based primarily on the sexual love she feels for him, but on giving birth, on being a mother. A man and woman are united not by erotic love alone, but also by their duty to have children in order to continue the kul.

Of Empathy and Culture

Empathy is based on the ability to identify with the inner lives or subjective existence of others. This process is mediated by culture. While empathy may begin as a "natural" mode of moral knowing, based on cognitive and emotional capacities that develop universally, I believe empathy is shaped, enhanced, and completed in culture.[24] The ability to know something of the inner life of someone else, so that the flow of my inner experience reflects their experience, would seem to require a complex symbolic organization linking self and other, mind and society.[25]

Cultural concepts of love and relatedness have the power to give social and symbolic form to empathy, making it develop in certain ways within social relationships. Culture appears to shape, modulate, limit, and distort the experience of empathy; it may also organize the distribution of empathy across social positions and contexts.

Newars are culturally prepared for empathy. As kin, they identify with each other; their concepts of shared substance, embedded in the practices concerning purity and pollution, amplify and shape this identification. Discourse within the family and kin groups is laden with concepts like "caring for" others, and "remembering" them. As I have shown, the Newar concept of maya has multiple meanings, but it is often used to relate people to each other in terms of empathy and concern.

At the same time, one can argue that Newar moral tradition is reproduced in terms of these identifications. I believe this interaction is vital to the continuity of Newar culture: as empathy is symbolically constituted, moral tradition is reproduced. Identifying with significant others, Newars identify themselves with traditions and practices that these others made themselves part of; this ensures the continuity of tradition by establishing engagement with, and creating commitment to, the symbols, forms, and values of tradition. While culture serves as a mediating structure for identifications, the desire for fusion structures the reproduction of culture. Seeking connection with others through culture, the Newar self makes culture part of self, and self part of culture.

To fuse with the other—a father, a mother, a son—is to fuse with culture, as it flows from the past and continues into the future. It is precisely this organization, this process of identifying with others, of relating self to them in the flow of life, that make the elements of culture which mediate identifications cohere into what we can call "tradition."

The possibilities of empathy, the significance it can have in various lives and relationships, must be diverse: empathy's place in human social life can be elaborated or expanded, diminished or limited, in terms of cultural and biographical experience. Being symbolically "at one" in Newar culture at least throws up no barriers to empathy. In Western culture, empathy may become problematic, at least where individuals have learned to emphasize their uniqueness, where they seek to create a self by having rich, unique, private experiences.

The capacity for empathy is not in any simple sense associated with gender; Newar men as well as women have it and value it, even though it seems to be more stressed for women. But it seems possible that empathy is culturally more accessible to Newars of either gender than it is to many American males. We need systematic comparative research on "empathy."[26]

A capacity for empathy may be central to the organization of other moral emotions. One woman said, recalling her childhood: "When I was young, I used to fight with my younger brother, and sometimes I hurt him and then I feel so bad that I feel like killing myself. I know that he's younger and weaker than me, like a small fresh vegetable, a young squash." The image is of vulnerability: the idea of hierarchical relatedness (the other is younger and weaker) unfolds into a sort of impassioned remorseful empathy. Empathy can structure and amplify remorse.

There is such a vision of the hurt feelings, or of the prospect of hurting another's feelings, in the memory of virtually every Newar I interviewed.

The Dynamics of Relatedness

Govinda Raj once told me that family members are the same because they are joined by "love" (maya). And yet the Newar family is organized into a hierarchy, where some have more purity and power than others, and are owed respect and deference. Two ways of knowing relatedness coexist for Newars. Even love is twofold: egalitarian and hierarchical. Understandings of relatedness have to be flexible enough to permit people to find meaning in each of these perspectives.

How do Newars do this? Recall how they define the bond with parents. Emotional and moral bonds come in matrifocal and patrifocal versions, and link siblings; they are based on a concept of reciprocity grounded in a sense of natural moral identity and solidarity that may be inflected to propose a natural moral hierarchy. As one Newar put it: "You drink your mother's milk. You owe her for what made you. Your father gave you seed." The hierarchical love (as Inden and Nicholas aptly phrase it) of parent and child is based on this reciprocity. The bond entails giving obedience, respect, and deference to those who gave you life, nurturance, protection, and instruction. Siblings, the informant continues, are united by the fact that they "drank the same mother's milk."

Just as hierarchy can be introduced into the unity of individuals who share seed or share a body by ranking them in terms of birth order or generational precedence, so hierarchy can be introduced into the equality defined by sharing a womb or drinking the same mother's milk. Birth order refers to who preceded whom out of the same womb. The equality and solidarity asserted by the claim that they drank the same mother's milk is countered by the image of a used breast—"you must respect older brothers because you drink milk they have made impure." The import is that younger siblings share their brothers' substance as well as their mother's substance, since the older brothers have made the mother's milk "impure" (cipa). Thus, younger siblings are subordinate to them, and dependent upon them. They, in turn, must care for or "look after" [ʌwegu] younger siblings, instruct, provide for and help them in the same way that parents must care for children. And so siblings are equal, but also ranked; "hierarchical love" is introduced into sibling relations. The love understood to exist in the parent-child bond is here extended to siblings in a way that preserves both solidarity and rank, caring and hierarchy.

Newar concepts that seem to shape empathy and moral responsiveness include at least these: 1) the family shares the same hearth; it eats together from the same rice pot (family members identify themselves in these terms); 2) they share the same "seed," "blood," and "bone marrow"; 3) the family shares joy and pain; they "love each other"; 4) siblings were born from one womb, drank milk at the same breast, had the same father, all of which equate them as whole persons, and makes intelligible claims to equality; 5) the giving and taking of polluted food, cipa, and restrictions on its exchange, express the unity of the family (if we accept that cipa offers a way of affirming closeness, of acknowledging a bond, of incorporating a person in a group, as well as a way of excluding and ranking persons). All these propositions and images assert the ways family members have something in common.

Concepts proposing "sameness" run against the current of ideas and practices that constitute and express hierarchy within the family, such as birth order, ritual seating, bowing, access to and responsibility for lineage deities, impurity in the family. Brothers are equal in cultural perspective because they shared the same father and mother—the same seed and the same womb. Fathers and sons are united along another cultural "tangent" as members of the same kul, but ranked by generation. This perception, backed up by culturally coherent metaphors and propositions, poses an organizational problem: how are duties and tasks to be allotted? Ritual hierarchy, generational precedence, and birth order provide solutions. Duties and privileges go preferentially to the older, not only as the more mature, but as the one ritually and symbolically more closely identified with senior family and lineage males. This is expressed in terms of address, in seating at feasts, where the senior males eat first, in the division of the head of the goat at the annual feast celebrating worship of a form of the lineage deity, the digu dya:, and in the prerogatives, responsibilities, and expectations of deference associated with seniority. Hierarchy in the family is highly marked. It is clearly a crucial value.

But why? This hierarchy is distinct from the hierarchy of castes. Authority in the family could no doubt be maintained without the complex and highly structured ritual hierarchy of the Newar family—it is in other cultures. Is the organizational problem, the need for a clear division of labor, enough to require the degree of symbolically and ritually marked hierarchy that we find in the Newar family? Many Newars argue that hierarchy is necessary to maintain the harmony within the family. This is a plausible reason. But there is probably more to it. One possibility is that hierarchy reflects an underlying psychological dynamic. Another reason for the development of the ritual hierarchy of family life is the way that households and kin groups are embedded in the hierarchical world of the wider society. Levy (personal communication) suggests that the family must preadapt children to the values of hierarchy, to make later experiences with hierarchy seem natural. Adults might want to do this; after all, they have experienced hierarchy in a variety of forms, and it would seen natural to orient their children to hierarchical reality. However, this "socialization perspective" could only be part of the answer. The ritual structure of family life may perform this function, but it does not exist in order to do so.

Perhaps the ritual practices of family life reflect the ideology and interests of the state. In this view, state power penetrates the family by promoting ideological formulations of the natural order of life. Such views are propagated in rhetoric and narratives that people hear. In the past, households were disciplined when they failed to maintain the purity of the family (as when they permitted an inter-caste marriage). The Hindu state in Nepal viewed inter-caste relations as a legal matter. The articulation of households with larger economic and systems may force them to have particular hierarchical structures of authority and control—to internalize, as it were, the state. The internal adjustments to external realities takes form in terms of the ritual hierarchy of the family.

The political economy perspective on family structure allows, even requires, a socialization perspective: hierarchy is organized and reproduced in the family in ways that reflect efforts to maintain and reproduce hierarchy in society. The systematic historical sociology needed to verify and ground this thesis is beyond the scope of this work, but I think relations with state power are central to household organization.

But even so, this does not rule out cultural and psychological perspectives. All historical and political formations have a psychocultural organization. They are experienced and may pose problems of meaning and self-identity.

Concepts of hierarchy and duty support role-definition; without this support, power and authority in the family might collapse, leading to conflict—as we shall see it often does when families divide, usually after a father's death. By creating and sustaining hierarchy in the family, role differentiation is possible within an empathic matrix, allowing for adaptive role behavior and authoritative planning and definition of situations within the family. Empathy and equality provide no structure, no basis for order or collective action. Hierarchy does. But, though the hierarchical authority of active family leaders and elders is seen as maintaining order, this is justified on moral grounds. Hierarchy is based on love and responsibility in the context of family relatedness; it is constructed in terms of an ethic of protection, nurturing, and caring. It is the duty of the older and more experienced to care for ("to feed" and "look after") those who need care, young or old.

I have argued that cultural ideas about shared substance may increase people's ability to experience empathy. They are, after all, in terms of these beliefs, the same. But people also know themselves in other ways. I think that self-identity has a psychological reality independent of cultural concepts of the person. Granted that individuals experience themselves as having self-boundaries, the cultural amplifications of the capacity for empathy may be threatening. Empathy involves the loss of self in the other. Such merging is at once desired and feared.

But if merging threatens self-identity, so may separation. Being detached and apart from others may also be experienced as a loss of self, as dissolution, because the boundaries and value of self are found in the self-confirming presence of others. Others give meaning to self; without them, self may be experienced as having no value, as being nothing.

This need for confirming presence is expressed in a number of surface behaviors. Newars dislike being alone; they dislike living alone. I have seen Newars experience what I judged to be anxiety and depression as a result of relative isolation from others. Even sleeping alone in a room is viewed by some as disagreeable. Solitude and privacy are not highly valued, while the presence of others is. Newars are gregarious and convivial; they like to do things in groups. I have seen Newars, who I thought disliked and had no use for each other, break down and weep when separated. The Newar sense of self requires the presence of others; self and other are often experienced as interdependent. Far from diminishing the significance of individuals, this ensures that individuals—specific, whole persons—are valued, for it is concrete individuals who have emotional significance for each other in the realms of relatedness.

I would speculate that the structure of Hindu beliefs allows people to avoid the painful extremes of individualism (isolation) and holism (loss of self) in culturally structured ways. The conceptions of shared substance permit people to find a range of ways of relating self and other. Separation and blending are both possible. "Substance" can be received from others; this expresses and organizes the psychological experience of merging through empathic identification. This is valued, in some contexts, but it may also be threatening, and individuals may seek to defend against receiving the substance of others. People can modulate merging and differentiation, finding a balance for themselves. The hierarchical self is differentiated; it invokes cultural defenses against the possibility of merging with another, of dissolving into otherness. It experiences empathy as hierarchical nurturing. The merging self is receptive to sentiments of solidarity and relatedness. It experiences empathy as mutuality, or egalitarian love. However, this tendency toward psychological equilibrium is complicated by social and political circumstances. An orthodox Brahman cannot very well experience the mutuality and emotions of merging with an untouchable; the social and political reality of the caste system encourages a strategy of differentiation. But he can seek to merge with a god. Or special institutions may permit inter-caste blending in special contexts.

FIGURE 21   An image of Shiva and Parvati. Shiva is the most important of the "ordinary" gods for Bhaktapur's Hindu Newars. Parvati, "daughter of the Himalayas," has special significance for Nepalese women as an idealized representation of female personhood.

FIGURE 22 Research assistant Rita Shakya with several Newar children. Notice how they relate themselves to each other through touch and proximity. Touch is an important medium of relatedness in same-sex groups.

Obligation and Relatedness

So far, this chapter has explored something of the ways in which Newars see their lives as joined together in families. This has much to do with empathy and relatedness, with the way that people understand the lives and emotional worlds of others, modifying their own psychological world in light of what they understand about relatedness. I have argued that culture mediates this, and also draws commitment from it.

So far, however, I have not stressed duty as a moral bond. It is a vital factor, however; the way Newars see themselves as part of families has much to do with a sense of duty. This involves a different kind of understanding, although it is linked to maya, and it joins lives together in a different way. Duties relate people in terms of obligations; they grant assurance that people can carry on their lives because others will do what is expected of them. Duties organize action into knowable configurations, so that one knows how lives intersect; this makes living life together coherent and viable. Obligations are felt; they shape desire. Just as a family member, experiencing maya, wants to comfort or help another — generating responsiveness—so Newars feel they "must" do certain things, and "want" to do these things, motivating them not just to be responsive, but to build and maintain the structure of life, for others as well as self. Let us turn to this configuration of experience—duty and desire interfused—now.

Duty Within the Web of Relatedness

Recall that Mahila, as an untouchable, lives in a very humble house by the river, outside the symbolic boundaries of the city. When I ask Mahila if there is something he wants to do, but cannot, he gives the following answer:

> The way it is, you see, I must build a house. I don't have any money, so I can't do it yet. It is a dilemma—I don't have money, but I must build a house. Other people, my friends, say the house I have now is old and falling down. So I have to build now—but with no money, it's hard. How easy it is, if you have money. I don't, and so I can't build a house . . . and yet I must do it! Otherwise my neighbors, the people of my ward will say to me, you should build a house, build a house. But what can I do without money? [He makes an exclamation of self-reproach.] I am in a hurry to build, to build. . . . Now even if it rains, even if the wind blows in, we must live in this old house.

Mahila feels limited by poverty and threatened by social pressure. He fears others will think badly of him, and he finds it hard to think well of himself. Later in the same interview, I ask him what his most important duty in life was, what it is that he "must do." Still thinking of the condition of his home, for his house is a crucial self-image, a metaphor for his life-situation, he replies:

> What I have been saying. Today, while I am still strong, I must leave things right for others. I must build a house, marry my son, and give my daughter-children away in marriage. If, in our house, my family and my children are all together, and fed, we will be happy together. Now, today, I cannot feed this family, these children—and you can't just feed yourself. We don't eat alone, no, all must be fed. And I have to build a house to leave for [them]. Then when I die, and you ask, Who built this house? Whose house is it?—they will say, Oh ho, it was his house, it is

Mahila's house, he built it. He left a really good thing behind. They will say he was a good man.

This is a moral fantasy, since it is beyond his means. It reveals Mahila's desire for recognition, fused with his sense of duty.

Shiva Bhakta, as a successful high-caste man, lives quite a different life. In many ways, Shiva Bhakta has found fulfillment. When I ask him what he "must do" in his life, he expresses satisfaction with what he has accomplished. He sees himself as having done what the Newar moral world requires, from making sure that his family has enough to eat, to performing the domestic and life-cycle rituals that reveal and affirm the sacred, moral character of their way of life. He also knows he has the resources, economic and psychological, to complete the moral project that a life is in Newar culture.

In reflecting on what he "must do" in his own life, Shiva Bhakta strongly emphasizes the continuity of the family line, and the rites of passage that mark it, the *samskara*, and the rites for the dead, the sraddha. In the following passage, he describes, not what the rites for the dead mean, but what they mean to him.[27]

> What must be done in my life? While I live I must do the death rites for my mother and father. While I am, I must follow tradition. I must do what has come down from long ago. If I did not perform the rites for the dead, I would not be satisfied in my mind. My father and I have performed these rites—because I saw my father doing the rites for my grandfather, I must do these rites, too. I perform the same rites for my father. Because my father did it, and I saw.

"This," he concludes, "is kuldharma." Kuldharma means the dharma of the family line, a code of conduct based in sacred reality. Shiva experiences kuldharma as a deep, personal obligation—"I must do now as they did, I must do as much in my life as they did"—an obligation which links him with his family line. He identifies with the kul, and this extends the horizons of "self" into the future and past; his sense of self rests on the continuity of the lineage.

And then, if I have done that much, if I die, I die. I mean that I will have that feeling in my mind, then—after my son's marriage, if my son has my grandson, then although I die, it is all right, I will have no regrets. But I don't want to die. What can I see? What can I see? I have this feeling [*mati*]. If I live, what won't I see?. . . Whatever happens, people don't want to die. What will I do, what will I do? How many pleasures will there be? So I don't want to die. The mouth says, "Although I die now, it is all right." But no one wants to die.

Here we see how Newars conceive of lives as joined together within a framework of duties, a code of conduct, associated with the family line as it crosses generations, from the dead to the living, from father to son, from those living to those yet to be born. Shiva Bhakta weaves himself into this symbolically constituted moral order, into the kul as transcendent family line, by invoking the image of his father as part of that line. "Because my father did it, and I saw."[28] Shiva identifies with his father, and this act of identification shapes his commitment to cultural tradition. He also sees his son and future grandson as part of this tradition, as part of himself.

If he has a grandson to continue the kul, Shiva says he can die with no regrets. He qualifies this declaration, however, and this reveals a tension. Shiva knows himself in terms of kuldharma. As a religious and moral concept that embraces the duties and moral ends of life, kuldharma defines a crucial moral context for self-knowing. As such, it shapes the development of the Newar moral self. But Shiva knows himself in other ways, too, just as Mahila does. If Mahila is not reducible to "untouchable," Shiva is more than a Hindu "householder." The life of a householder, with the duties, goals, and self-concept it confers, is central to his self-identity. It forms the core of what it is to be Shiva Bhakta. Shiva Bhakta reaches beyond this, however, reaches for new experiences. He senses that there are other horizons for self. While he foresees personal closure in terms of kuldharma, with a son and, he hopes, grandson to continue his line, making it possible for him to die with no regrets, he does not want to die, because he feels something else—that the possibilities of the world have not been exhausted for him. He can renew himself in new experiences. "If I live, what won't I see?"

The Structure of Intersubjectivity and Concepts of the Person

Duty and love, empathy and obligation are modes of thought, feeling, and action within Newar families that organize commitments and shape the way lives are joined together. They constitute two of the ways in which members of Newar families know each other and themselves, organizing two ways in which the morality of family life is conceived and lived—a dual structure for intersubjectivity.

This dual structure of intersubjectivity is reflected in two kinds of love in Newar families: hierarchical love and a merging, empathic relatedness.[29] Hierarchical love reflects a sense of duty, and involves a hierarchical relationship, such as between parent and child, justified by an ethic of protection, care, and reciprocity, while empathic relatedness limits or subverts hierarchical distance, and evokes a sense of identity with others, of oneness with them that suspends hierarchical differences. The distinction is often blurred.

Does the material on the Newar family tell us anything about the concept of the person in South Asia? If the question is what has priority, the self or society, then Bhaktapur is clearly a city of families, not of individuals who seek to create and isolate a self apart from social relationships. Their sense of self is founded in relatedness within the family, and this is what is valued.

Lives Split Apart

Given the way Newars value embeddedness, how do they experience the unraveling of the "web of relatedness"? In Bhaktapur as elsewhere, families fail, and people try to cope with tasks and crises inherent in the developmental cycle of families. The responses to failures reveals something of the system of moral values. Reflecting on such failure, Newars rehearse and reconstruct the circumstances and values of family life in terms of their own experience, goals, and place within families. They shift between different interpretive perspectives, invoking constructs concerning duty, love, hierarchy, solidarity, equality, equity, and self in order to define situations and evaluate actions. The failings of families are understood and experienced in light of these multiple points of view.

A Family Divided

The following account by a high-caste man, Bhimsen Lal, illuminates some of the tensions of family life. He narrates his version of the conflict that began sometime after the death of his father and ended with the division of the extended family he grew up in. We can read it as an account of events that happened, as interpreted by an actor involved in "what happened," a positioned actor who understandably advances a personal version of events. Since it is a deeply interpretive and evaluative account, we must also read it as a moral narrative, an attempt to view "what happened" in terms of "what should have been." The narrative is composed by drawing on implicitly moral language, and contains, at various levels, a moral point of view. The narrative holds an actor's voice, a moral voice—a more or less reflective voice, but one reflecting lived life, speaking of significant moments in his life experience, rather than recounting abstracted ideal norms. He tells of how his web of relatedness dissolved, describing how lives, once joined together, were split painfully apart. The voice is problematic, as all voices are, when speaking of their own lives, but conveys a sense of the personal reality of cultural experience.

A Newar family will labor, as this account suggests, under various strains until the only option is separation; the values of family solidarity, of connection, are not sufficient to keep a group of brothers together after their father dies. Somehow, the values fail; they dry up or fail to "connect" people. Far from being "at one," united in the family, family members have trouble placing themselves and others in the ongoing economic, emotional, and moral project of the family. Individuals have their own point of view, and what they make of the family scene involves placing themselves— with their own emotions and personal sense of what is a wrongful and a rightful turning of life in relationship to themselves—in tension or opposition to others in the family.

> I have three brothers. We have divided into three separate
> households. . . . After our father died, up until the time we sepa-
> rated, I was the one who did all the work for our joint household
> [by going outside the household to earn money and by organiz-
> ing the social and economic activity of the family and managing
> its affairs]. My brothers, they just sat in the house and ate.

The implication is that the brothers were lazy; solidarity entails a
commitment to sharing the burdens of life. The narrative takes us
back to a time when Bhimsen's family was composed of three
brothers; that family is defined by the loss of the father. The narrator, Bhimsen Lal, defines himself as the one who did all the
work—he sets up an "I," himself against his brothers. He justifies
himself in a preemptive claim: "I was the one who did all the
work," who went outside the house to make money to bring home
to support everyone. With this claim he is beginning to compose an
authoritative and independent voice for his audience. He is a practical agent and a locus of moral experience. He is telling his story,
not speaking of how a family is unified. He begins with a rational
social and economic assessment.

> I told them a long time ago, we have to work separately. If we go
> on working together [in the way we always have], we won't be
> able to eat. As three brothers, we won't always be together. One
> day we will separate. Must separate. They did not accept the fact
> that one day we would separate.

Here Bhimsen tells of confronting his brothers with a future of
naked need—"we won't be able to eat." He defines the division of
the family as inevitable, as something that the brothers should prepare for, a structural certainty. Meanwhile, life events intervene to
complicate things:

> I kept saying [this]—later my first wife died. My brother's wife
> also died. My younger brother married and I remarried. We got
> married at the same time. Even before that I did most of the
> work. Although my older brother, as the eldest, became the head
> of the household, he couldn't work. Inside the family, I was actu-
> ally the leader. Up to then, two uncles, our father's middle
> brother and our father's younger brother, were still alive. Now,
> our uncles did not know how to do anything, either, anymore

than any of the others. I respected them as parents. They had gotten old and were not able to work. I was the one who went everywhere. I had to do all the work. If it was necessary to go to a friend's place [to see to some obligation], I was the one who went. I was the one who had to earn money. I had to bring home what we needed to eat. For everything, I was the one. My brothers did only what I told them to do.

The ability to work empowers; it confers responsibilities that do not correspond to the ideal framework of responsibilities in the family.

I told my brothers, "You take on some work too. I have some money. What work will you do? Will you sell rice? Sell straw? Some other work, then?" Sometimes they said they wouldn't do it, sometimes they said they would. They did not take the work. Everybody must do some kind of work. But whatever my brothers tried, it did not work out.

After all three of us were married, all three of us had children. We got married with women from different places. My woman is from Kathmandu. My brothers' wives are from Bhaktapur. We brothers, we had all drunk my mother's milk—drunk the same breast's milk, our mother's milk. And then we fought. Like so [he makes a fist and swings his arm], we beat each other and said, "I'll kill you." So we fought. The next day it wouldn't matter. The next day, we would greet each other [as if nothing had happened].

The brothers are supposed to be "at one," a unity, cooperative — the idea of unity is here evoked in the concept of mother's milk. Despite the ideals of unity, the brothers fight; the situation is very divisive. They threaten each other with violence. Something of unity is reasserted, however—the next day they would continue as if nothing had happened. Note how Bhimsen introduces the contrast of ideal unity with actual divisiveness in the context of saying something about wives. Wives are outsiders, and the extended process of bringing them into the extended family can incite conflict. This theme is developed—with wives come more responsibilities, and more tensions:

The wives came from outside. They didn't get along. When there was only one, it didn't matter. Then we had children, I had two children, then four. My younger brother had two children, and so did my older brother.

Even before that my younger brother would whine that he should only have to feed himself. . . . Emotion [*bhabana*] you see, extremely bad emotion was brought [into the situation]. Even so, I endured. "Wait [I said], we should not separate. You will suffer if we do. Let's make a lot of money first. If we make at least 200,000 or 300,000 rupees, then you can do whatever you want, and it all will work out."

The tensions within the family—brothers fight, their wives fight, children have to be fed, the work of sustaining the family is hard and family members do not feel it is equitably shared—are stressed here. So are the moral faults of family members: his brothers are "lazy," and one of them "would whine that he should only have to feed himself." In the context of Newar culture, this is one of the most powerful moral reproaches possible: that you only want to feed yourself. Food is one of the most important mediums in which to express relatedness, and so to "feed only yourself" is to deny others and break the web of relatedness out of selfishness and greed. Providing food is at once an urgent economic problem, and a way of loving and nurturing others. Bhimsen Lal characterizes his brother as unable to sustain relatedness, as unable to master practical affairs, as unwilling to share family burdens, and as concerned only with themselves: "In this way, I endured, but I had to work and earn money."

Bhimsen returns to the way in which he was pitched out into the world of work: the insistence on "being the one who had to work" perhaps constitutes a subtext of autonomy. Work bears the signature of autonomy; it means being responsible and capable, ready and able to act. His wife bears burdens as well (marriage is the sharing of burdens):

My wife, she did all the work in the household. What my wife figured was, my husband is the one who earns money. That was my wife's opinion. My husband, he is the one who suffers [in this situation]. My wife said this, that's what she thought. She felt, my husband makes the money [that supports this family], and yet I have to do the housework, clean the utensils polluted by eating, wash the dishes, cook the meals, everything. I have to do it all. This is what she thought [*man tae-gu,* "placed in her mind"].

The moral question, and the emotional reaction, is a matter "placed in the mind" (man). Newars locate this in the chest. The use of this construction here proposes that the emotional and moral core of a person is involved. The wife's reactions parallel and confirm those of the husband. This itself reflects, or confers, solidarity: the wife and the husband share something—they share a sense of being burdened. The scene described might be labeled "unfair" in Western terms; no single moral word analogous to "unfair" is used here, but the description of the scene itself, in relation to "mind, heart" evokes the problem—an impasse or tension in the flow of everyday moral life. The enumeration of tasks as burdens is important: "I have to do the housework, clean the utensils polluted by eating, and wash the clothes, cook the meals, everything." It asks for an accounting. Why should this be one person's lot? Bhimsen then says she "put this" in her *man,* her mind; it becomes a problem in her relationship with the world, a question of how self enters into the everyday world, of the rightness or morality of that entry. This is Bhimsen's narrative, and the fact that he narrates it so, indicates he still thinks of her doing so; what enters her mind (which has to do with how she experiences and evaluates the world of everyday family life) is important enough for him to place his construction on it. An image emerges: wife and husband suffer, work hard, and think of each other. They are connected. This is an interesting construction of a domestic reality. It is not the only possible way of viewing the family scene:

What my sisters-in-law said was that it is not just hers, not just mine. "It is just yours?" they said. "Is it just hers?," they said to me. "Is it only hers? It is mine too, this. Is it only her fate? It is my fate as well."

There was a struggle over the moral definition of the situation. If Bhimsen's wife "held in mind" a set of concerns and identified herself with a concrete view of the situation as inequitable, then her sisters-in-law also staked out positions—an equality of fate and burdens. They said they did the same work, experienced the same

hardships; since they all had the same life-situation, and its burdens were shared by all alike, no one could claim to be more
oppressed by it. Bhimsen's wife had no call to complain, because
her situation was not any worse than theirs. Bhimsen is, of course
narrating this, but I think we can take him as a reliable narrator
here, as long as we appreciate that by having his wife respond in
just the way he describes he saves himself from isolation, from carrying a position alone. He rejects the claim that burdens were
shared equally.

> **In my view, they did not do even a straw's worth of work. They
> only showed off. They talked without doing anything. . . . For
> fifteen, sixteen years they cried—and ate. This didn't work out.
> Now we live separately.**

This is bitter talk. He accuses them of being fundamentally false,
of pretense where reality most matters, in a situation where he and
his wife felt overwhelmed, were struggling and suffering. Bhimsen's grievances are many: his brothers did not work; they showed
off, they falsely presented a good image of themselves; they resented their life-situation and complained of their circumstances, yet
reproached others for doing the same; they ate (consumed what
others provided, benefited from what others did), but they did not
contribute to the sustenance of the family. As Bhimsen says, it did
not work out. (The verb I have translated here as "work out" is
complex and has many implications and resonances having to do
with successful matching, fitness, harmony, and integration.)

The cultural structures of empathy and solidarity failed to keep
lives in this family joined together. Bhimsen tells of how he resisted the idea of splitting the family apart, yet was under great pressure to do so. His wife threatened to leave.

> **I really didn't like [the idea of dividing the joint family]. "I will
> live on warm water" [rather than stay in the joint family], she
> said, "I won't stay with you."**
>
> **My older brother's wife and my younger brother's wife didn't
> like it either. "We won't live with them, we don't like living with
> them. We will live separately," they said.**

In the next passage, the subtext of justified autonomy breaks out as what it probably was all along, a sense of being in possession of personal authority:

> However many times I said something, they did not follow me. Then how to do it, because I could not go on enduring so much, it was very wrong. My younger brother and my older brother's wife said false things and used bad words. "Come, if you people are so much against it, then I don't want to stay together either." And then we separated.

From Bhimsen's point of view, the family was not "connecting." They did not listen to him or follow his lead. He sees himself as bringing himself (and them, consistent with his implicit sense of himself as an authoritative man) to the crux. The experience of emotional and moral tension is stressed. The decisive moment — "then how to do it" — is entered by saying he was no longer able to suffer so much, by succumbing ("I could not go on enduring so much") and by declaring the fundamental wrongfulness of the situation — "It was very wrong." He uses emphatic language to express this; it signifies the crisis. He blames his brother and one of the women of the household for creating this morbid atmosphere, accusing them of lying and using invective. A release of tension — in life as in the narrative, one suspects — follows. The division is proposed, and it happens.

Bhimsen relived some of the emotion of that part of his life during the interview, and if this is any evidence of authenticity, then I would say he deeply felt the contradictions of the situation: he affirmed family loyalty, and had a real sense of the extended family as ideally "at one," a natural union of being, formed on the basis of absolute and unalterable bonds, in which lives are joined together for the sharing of life's burdens and joys. While the division of the joint family is a predictable natural process, the emotional violence he experienced violated his sense of the moral bonds that connect brothers.

His empathy for his wife was, I believe, powerfully motivating, and her suffering confirmed, focused, and helped valorize his sense of burden and autonomy. Wives, when they arrive in families, are marginal figures, often viewed with suspicion; as a consequence, they are sometimes used as scapegoats. There is some of this in

Bhimsen's account of the breakup of this extended family, but clearly he is not exempting the brothers. He felt the pain of the process more keenly, and he could make a better narrative of it, because of the contrast with the way life should be. Lives are often not joined together in an authentic and powerful moral union, as Newar concepts of kinship and relatedness declare they should be; lives are rather divided by human failings, by painful tensions. People may lack responsibility, may not love each other as they should, may be cruel, envious, and selfish.

Newar families may divide with less bitterness than this, but Newars feel that the process of division often involves conflict and emotional tensions. Marriage complicates interests, and wives are often blamed for tensions or contradictions that marriage perhaps intensifies, but does not create. Although Newars often stress the way they are socially embedded, the needs and interests of individuals are present, and these form fracture lines, places where relationships are vulnerable and can be wounded. These vulnerabilities emerge strongly for Newar men when their father dies, which requires a restructuring of the internal hierarchy of the family, and when they marry and have children, which shifts their view of self from dependence and subordination toward generativity and nurturing. The hierarchy of birth order among brothers does not have the same significance, either cognitive or emotional, as the generational hierarchy of authoritarian father and dutiful sons. With the death of a father, each son becomes, at least potentially, the head of a family. In this context, Newars have stereotypes about sibling rivalry. Given the assumption that brothers are "the same," for one brother to achieve more wealth and prestige, to do better in life as Newars understand it, by having a better house or undertaking religious work, is potentially threatening to the other brothers, especially since their wives may make invidious comparisons.

Holism and Self

The Newars are famous as wood-carvers, and Bhaktapur is still full of homes with beautifully carved wooden windows. There was a very old and unusual one on a side street not very far from the royal palace square where I lived. The window was round, composed of an intricate filigree circle set in a carved frame with

FIGURE 23 Newars say
this window was cut in
half when a family divided.

carved figures (the old windows had such lattice work and no
glass). It was a bit dilapidated, and not as grand as some, but I
liked it because of its wholeness and proportions, and because I
could not quite make out what some of the figures were—Vishnu
on a lotus? a goddess with a musical instrument? The carvings
were too worn to make out clearly, but I liked to try to see what
they were, early in my stay. I experienced the window as a kind of
"natural" symbol; the perfect circle affirmed wholeness and unity.

Then one day as I walked by, I saw that the window had been
cut in two—only half survived. A brick wall had been mortared
into place where the other half of the window had been. The old
half stood out oddly next to the new brick wall. When I described
this to a Newar friend, he suggested that a family of brothers had
divided their house. He went on to describe the fights and bitterness that sometimes break out when Newar families divide. The
half window, a delicate lattice-work circle sawed in half, became
for me a symbol of the struggles that go on within families. Newar
moral consciousness flows from the experience of union and dis-
union within the web of relatedness, as Newars position and reposition themselves within the developing contexts of domestic life.

Thus, while relatedness is a central cultural value and psychological reality for Newars, I want to stress that it involves the joining together of individual lives. Dumont (1980, 1983, 1986) argues that holism is a paramount value in South Asia — he argues that the "social whole" has value, but not the individual. Holism, the opposite of individualism, "neglects or subordinates the human individual." He once claimed that while particular persons exist within the South Asian tradition of caste and interdependency, they have "no reality in thought, no Being" (1960: 272). Shweder and Bourne (1984) also suggest that "sociocentrism" informs Indian thought: the group has more value than the individual.

I think the material I have here presented and interpreted at once richly confirms this recognition of South Asian holism, of the primacy given to social groups, to society over the individual, and yet strongly underscores the need to explore and conceptualize more deeply the place of the individual self in these cultures.[30] As we have seen in the last two chapters, Newars often stress society over self, often exclude the concept of the individual self from discourse, and at times seem to assign little or no value to the individual person. "It sometimes happens," P. F. Strawson (1965: 113) has written, "with groups of human beings, that, as *we* say, their members think, feel, and act 'as one.'" Newar culture prepares Newar women and men to think, feel, and act "as one" with their families and castes; and yet, as Strawson reminds us, such being "as one" is a state the self achieves "only sometimes."

I have shown here that Newars know and experience themselves in terms of a "web of relatedness." The cultural experience of life in the family, the hearth group, has a crucial role in shaping the way Newars view themselves. Such culturally constituted domestic experience provides the grounds for the development of conflicting self-images — merging relatedness coexists with emerging self-identity. Newar self-images stress a "connected self," viewing the person as caught up in family relationships that are at once *felt*, since the relationships help shape, satisfy, and frustrate psychological needs, and *known*, through symbols, ideas, and metaphors that express and organize emotion, empathy, and the quality of relationships. Newars know themselves as part of families, as lives joined together in a network of relationships, and not solely as self-made, self-possessing individuals. While their self-images reflect the way Newars are embedded in social relationships, Newars do not lack individuality, autonomy, and self-identity. Individual existence has reality, meaning, and value for Newars. If Newars sometimes seek to weave themselves into the web of relatedness, at other times, like Bhimsen, they disentangle themselves from it, achieving an autonomy that they may or may not desire.

Thus, although relatedness is a central value in Newar culture, this does not mean the individual self has no value.[31] The individual self can be, and often is, valued within a system of relationships, and constructed in self-narratives that are also social stories, tales of family life.

Consequently, I do not accept the view that the South Asian tradition obliterates "the individual." Rather, I believe the sharp contrast of individualism and holism is a Western discourse that obscures and distorts Newar cultural experience. Newars know and value themselves as autonomous individuals and as social beings. They find meaning both in their own individual actions and in relationships. They value social embeddedness and individual existence.

What I see in Newar experience is a cultural dialectic—a process in which men and women merge, blend, and unite in "relatedness," emerge as "selves," then merge again, and re-emerge, producing the subtle, powerful, cross-currents of moral consciousness. If Newars see themselves in terms of a union of being with significant others, embed themselves in social groups, and identify with moral traditions, they also value who they are, what they have done, and what they want to do. They know themselves in terms of their own identity and purposes, value their own existence and actions, and are often acutely, painfully, playfully, ironically, and self-reflectively conscious of the way "self" is entangled in a living "net" of relationships. Newar life cannot be reduced to either holism or individualism.[32]

CHAPTER FOUR

The Sacred Mind

For Newars, mind, self, and emotion are sacred and moral; the "inner" world is absorbed in a religious ethos. This sacralization of mental life in Newar culture is consistent with the way religious forms—sacred beings and symbols and a moral order based on a religious world view—provide the fundamental grounds for the Newar construction of reality. Newar life has not been secularized; the world and the mind have not been disenchanted.

The concepts of person Newars bring to the experience of an inner life, of mental existence, help Newars create themselves as moral beings. As Newars evaluate and experience themselves in terms of cultural theories of mental life, they produce states of moral consciousness, ways of knowing themselves as moral agents. Their concepts of an inner life, formed within a religious and ethical world view, mediate the development of a moral self. Their cultural vision of psychological life sensitizes them to moral emotions, inspires self-reflection, shapes insight into self, and structures efforts to alter self, helping generate what I term "moral knowing."

My discussion of these processes—the sacralization and ethicization of an "inner" world and the production of moral consciousness—will underscore the need for more flexible and less reductive accounts of mind, self, and emotion. Some theorists, reacting to a tradition in academic psychology that reduces emotion to a material entity or psychophysiological process, have played down the importance of affective experience, of feeling as a core aspect of emotion, emphasizing instead the way emotions are cognitive and social judgments (Solomon 1984; Myers 1986). While I also view emotions as judgments about the relationship of self to world, and reject theories of emotions that reduce them to nothing but physiological processes, I think we miss something vital if we treat emotions as nothing but discourse. Emotions are social judgments, but judgments embodied in affective experience (Rosaldo 1984; Levy 1984). That emotions are affective rather than discursive judgments makes a difference: I may use emotion concepts without feeling them, but when I feel an emotion I am more completely and powerfully engaged with my world. Emotions prepare people to be agents. The experience of emotion mediates engagement with life, priming social actors to find meaning in events and experiences, preparing them to know themselves in certain ways, and readying them to act.

Other theorists ignore the role of culture, stressing instead psychological processes. They view cultural models of psychological experience as unrelated to the processes that generate that experience. For example, the psychologist George Mandler (1975: 5–10) has argued that the examination of "phenomenal selves" and "ordinary language" offers no real basis for the study of mind; his view is that mind can only be understood apart from culture in a technical language that transcends ordinary language and cultural consciousness. He argues that "folk theories" of ordinary language and thought fundamentally misrepresent psychological processes. And, indeed, experimental psychologists should probably not look to ordinary language or to cultural models for "distinctions and concepts" that can stand as "ultimate descriptions" of emotion, mind, and self from the point of view of academic psychology (Mandler 1975: 8). In contrast, it is people's beliefs about psychological life that pose fundamental questions for anthropologists. Ethnographic research makes it clear that emotional experience is culturally embedded; it is more than a set of psychophysiological processes.[1] Since emotion has cultural meaning, we are compelled to ask: What place do "folk concepts" of mind, emotion, and self have in people's lives and experience? Although these cultural concepts may not be "true," from the perspective of experimental psychology, neuroscience, or analytical philosophy, they may reflect significant aspects of social, cultural, and personal reality.

The ethnographic data to be presented here point out the need to bridge the gap between two opposed approaches to emotion. These opposing approaches force the analyst either to decontextualize emotion or to disembody it. Both strategies are reductive, one severing the connection of emotion with sensation and feeling, with the actual self-experience of human bodies, while the other eliminates the need to explore cultural and social context. As useful as these strategies may be for very limited purposes, I believe the Newar material presented here makes it clear how emotional life is both intricately embedded in culture and dynamically embodied in affective experience. Since people make their lives within the world created by the interaction and interpenetration of culture and experience, it is there that the analysis of emotional *life* should begin.

The Knowing Heart

In Newar culture, the "heart" (*nuga:*) embodies a person's feelings and sense of self in ways that integrate self and moral order. Newars place much that Western culture conceives of as "mind" in this "heart-self,"[2] and also much that Western culture conceives of as belonging to the separate domain of religion. Newar concepts of the person do not recognize this separation of religion and psychology.

Newars take it for granted that people experience mental states something like those indicated by the English words *desire, feeling, thought, intention,* and *memory;*[3] many Newars locate these in the chest. Thus, if these states or processes constitue "mind," then Newars locate "mind" in the "heart." This psychologically active heart is not necessarily identified in a literal way with the anatomical heart, although it may be, at least implicity. The nuga:, itself, actively feels some things, but it is also viewed as a site that passively houses other mental processes, such as perception, memory, and emotions.

So far, perhaps, nuga: may sound like "mind" in Western parlance, moved from the head/brain to the chest cavity, but otherwise not very different. Nuga: is not mind, however; while there is some overlap—since mental processes like perception and memory can be conceived in terms of nuga: and mind alike—nuga: and mind belong to different cultural worlds and represent radically different conceptions of the inner life of self. Nuga: has features never contemplated in the models of mind prevalent in Western cultures (D'Andrade 1987).

Europeans, Americans, and Newars might agree that people think and feel, experience emotion and have desires, want and believe, remember and imagine—for all of them, these are obvious facts about persons, even if the meaning, the cultural significance, they attach to these mental processes vary to some extent. For Newars, however, it is also an obvious fact that a god is present in every person, that this divinity dwells in the nuga:, and that this god is responsible for much mental activity, animating key aspects of what we call "mind." Since the divinity that exists within the self is a moral god, the efforts of individual Newars to monitor their inner lives often draws on a sense of the presence of this god, as a kind of moral witness and support. In fact, this god within is at once the ultimate moral judge of the person, and, in some formulations, the ultimate self of the person.

Thus, this ethnopsychological belief in the inner god constitutes a sacred self and a sacred other within the person. Western concepts of the mind do not invoke the divine within the person as part of self.

This inner deity, the "heart -god," "god dwelling inside," or "god who dwells in the heart," is thought of as Narayana, a form of Vishnu, by Hindu Newars. This heart-god makes possible, or empowers, perception and cognition. The high-caste Newar Shiva Bhakta puts it this way, stressing the identity of the inner god with the ultimate form of god:

> The god who dwells in the heart . . . is the same as [the god] Bhagavan. How do we serve Bhagavan? We chant god's names, Bhagavan, Narayana [in prayer]. We pray to the very same god on the outside. We Newars feel [bhabana yai] that this same god is in our hearts. . . . The god who dwells in the heart, and who, it is said, sees with our eyes, is Bhagavan. Bhagavan is every place. He is here in the heart too.

Here Shiva alludes to the idea that the god in the heart makes perception and attention possible. A person sees because the god sees through his or her eyes. Another Newar clarified this by giving the example of a person who is not paying attention to what someone is saying. The speaker may scold the inattentive listener by saying "where is the heart god?" or by remarking that your "heart god is not still, and so you don't understand." These statements declare them "not there," metaphorically "away," by drawing on the belief that mental states have a source beyond the empirical individual in which mental life is embodied. Shiva Bhakta elaborates:

> This is your own idea—we think of Bhagavan. Like this [he shuts his eyes.] While our eyes are closed shut—let's say we think of the god Pashupatinath [Lord of Creatures, the deity enshrined in a nearby temple]. He has four faces, right? Just like that, if we have our eyes closed, here an image comes. Of that god. . . . With our eyes closed like this—suddenly he comes before us. It does not come before us—it appears in the heart. While our eyes are shut, it appears. Even with your eyes closed, you can still see it. In the same way, I can see your face, your eyes, your nose—inside, with my eyes shut, I can see your features. This is what we call the god who dwells in the heart.

Other Newars interpreted this to mean that the power of recall, the ability to see a face in memory or thought, derived directly from this deity. The idea of "god dwelling within" or the "Narayana dwelling within" helps explain the experience of psychological phenomena.[4]

Clearly, nuga: is a seat of cognition, memory, and perception. Nuga: is also the locus of emotional experience. The heart may be "easy" or "uneasy." Pain, sadness, fear, and grief are spoken of in terms of a heart in distress: a heart may sink, tremble, throb, flutter, or burn like fire. A heart can feel as if it has been pierced through, or as if it has been torn to pieces. The Newar heart can open and blossom like a flower in joy. It may fly away in fear or confusion, or burst in envy. It can feel pricks of pain or uneasiness for another person's plight. It can be bound and controlled, kept in balance, or stamped with lasting impressions. The heart can weep, and be wounded. "My mother's heart went weeping," said one Newar, speaking of a family tragedy, "her mind (*citta*) could not be happy." The language of the heart is thus the language of emotional experience, making it possible for Newars to speak of their heartfelt engagement with the social world.

The qualities of nuga: also express the moral qualities of a person. To say that someone has a "smooth mouth" or a "smooth face" but a "blue heart" is to warn against impression management that masks malice or manipulation. A cruel person has a hard heart, an evil person is black-hearted. There are persons with small, deceitful, stingy hearts. A person may be made of proper flesh and bone, like everyone else, Newars say, but lack the "heart blood" that animates moral commitments; Newars assert that such individuals do not possess the conviction or energizing feelings needed to do what is right or necessary. Moreover, if persons, viewed as moral selves, are sometimes passively incomplete, they may also be actively wrong in their inclinations, since sin (pap) can inhabit the heart. "Who," asked one Newar, "will trust a person who speaks with sin in his heart?" But a heart can also be generous and pure, clear and open.

Speaking in terms of the nuga: signals engagement in specialized kinds of discourse. In my view, the nuga: is a multiplex, metonymic sign—a sign of the self. The part stands for the whole; but the whole has many facets. It encloses a range of ways of being and knowing. Thus, talk of the heart helps Newars know themselves, by providing ways to formulate and evaluate experience and relationships.

When Newars speak of the states of the nuga:, they express their emotional worlds. The heart may be present or absent, intact or incomplete, whole or compromised—the discourse of the heart discloses the self. The feelings, rhythms, movements, conditions, and colors of the heart are cultural ways of speaking of critical aspects of individual experience and agency, of social embeddedness and constraint (McHugh 1989). The concept of nuga: allows individuals to represent their personal experience—feelings, emotions, intentions—to themselves and others in cultural terms. Thus, the discourse of the heart helps mediate self-awareness and self-identity.[5]

The concept of the nuga: also helps Newars place themselves within a religiously conceived moral order. The idea of a god who dwells in the heart does more than explain behavior; it represents and invokes the moral order within the self.

If you ask, "This Narayana who dwells in the heart, what does it do to you? What does it cause you to do?" [the answer is] "he is

in every thought. He has caused you to act." We think that he caus-
es us to do things. We think that. People think to themselves, "Our
Father, Bhagavan, has caused me to do this. What I am doing now,
I was brought to this by Bhagavan." [Shiva Bhakta]

But the deity may react to wrong actions and reproach the actor.

You think of the god who dwells in the heart and act. Don't do
wrong acts. If you do something wrong this Narayana who dwells
in the heart will curse you. The Narayana who dwells in the heart
will curse you. Curse, meaning rebuke. [Shiva Bhakta]

The imagery here is of a kind of moral monitor, of an agency paradoxically identified with, and yet separate from, the self. This dual
state of identity and separation makes it possible for this agency to
cause persons to act, and to judge them for those acts.

Newars often speak of an external deity as a moral witness or
judge, rather than of the "god who dwells in the heart." They may
assert that Bhagavan "sees" wrongdoing. When conceived of as
Narayana, the "god who dwells in the heart" is also a form of (perhaps the right phrase is a station of) a transcendent and omniscient
deity. God is both immanent and transcendent, at once part of self,
and yet separate, a larger whole in which the self is embedded. This
does not necessarily mean the two forms are have precisely the same
significance for people (that they feel and think the same things
when they invoke either form of the god). It seems likely, for example, that the immanent, in-dwelling form relates to concerns with
experience; it symbolizes and supports self-monitoring as a moral
activity. The idea of a transcendent judge of a life shifts the scale and
focus of moral reflections toward ultimate concerns, — the prospects
of death and salvation given the objective existence of a moral order.
Perhaps this idea of a moral watch kept in heaven also helps give
shape to the intuition that a life is a totality, a moral career that is the
object of moral judgment. We can speculate that there is a kind of
division of labor that reflects two orders of biographical time: a life
is both witnessed in its passing moments (by the heart-god) and
judged in its totality (by the god in heaven).

Self-Monitoring

In an interview with Krishna, focusing on the Hindu concept of
the soul (*atma*), he invoked the concepts of sin and dharma. He

argued that it is a sin not to believe in the existence of the gods. Since one can refuse to believe in the gods in the privacy of one's own thoughts, I asked him, "What if no one knew—would that be a sin or not?" He replied,

> It is a sin to lie. . . . That the gods do not exist, if we put this in our hearts, the god will know. In the sky, in the domain of Indra, King of Heaven, in the place of Yamaraj [the god of death], an account book is kept. The keeper of this book . . . counts our dharma and our sin. He continually considers and weighs [our acts]. He weighs our dharma, and our sin, in a balance and then records all in this account.
> (If I understand this, if no one in society knows, god will know?)
> Yes. With us in our heart, soul, is Narayana.

The point here is that Newars do speak of behavior and mental acts as being monitored and judged by supernatural agencies, and one of these is immanent in the heart, sometimes playing the part of an "ego," sometimes of a "superego."

In part, I interpret the god who dwells in the heart as a cultural representation of the way people experience mental processes of self-monitoring. In Western parlance, we might say that the heart is a place where part of the "self" observes and evaluates what an individual thinks and feels, experiences and does. The conscious self does not experience this self-monitoring part of the self as directly under its control. Rather, it may experience this part of the self as virtually an independent agency, and itself as the object of the actions of this other part of the mind. Thus the image of a divinity immanent in the self at once captures a sense of the experience of finding yourself the object of another part of your mind, and ethicizes it.

Cultural models take account of the fact that people do not always view their inner experiences as part of themselves. The mind can be viewed as divided into parts; only some of these parts may be viewed as self. You may reproach yourself for some act, at the same time that some other agency in the inner world reproaches you, and you passively experience this rebuke. Your self-reproach may only be a kind of echo, set off by an unexpected surge of remorse, which you may attribute to a culturally defined

entity—the heart-god, or the voice of conscience. People sometimes evaluate and interpret themselves spontaneously, despite
their expectations, even against their will, as well as volitionally;
you do not have to will yourself consciously to feel bad when you
believe you have done something wrong, though you may consciously resolve to never again do what makes you feel bad. The
image of the god who inhabits the heart reflects the way in which
some mental processes are not directly controlled by the conscious,
core part of the self. Perceptions, feelings, emotions, desires, are
not willed or directly controlled by self (D'Andrade 1987: 119);
the idea of the god who dwells in the heart as the source of psychological states explains how processes that happen inside a person, "happen to" a person.

The idea of the heart-god is not "psychological" in a narrow
Western sense, since it does not *only* relate self to entities and
processes within self; it *also* relates self to entities and processes in
the world, and this world is conceived religiously and ethically.
The Newar heart-self is permeable, not rigidly bounded, and is not
entirely dependent on the senses for knowledge—it has direct,
"inner" access to the religious source of moral being. From one
point of view, the religious construct, the god, is viewed as projected into the self, where it is held to produce thoughts and feelings. From another point of view, "self," the "I," is identified with
this being, and so transcends the bounds of mind, body, and personal identity as understood in Western terms. But these concepts,
although implicit in Newar thought, may not be active in a given
person's thinking about self. Much of the time, an individual
Newar may be content to live as a "bounded, unique, more or less
integrated motivational and cognitive universe, a dynamic center
of awareness, emotion, judgment and action organized into a distinctive whole," as Clifford Geertz (1984: 126) has described the
Western concept of the person. Newars have not just one, but multiple ways of viewing self.

In less Western terms, rather than thinking in terms of "parts"
acting within a self-contained, bounded whole, we might think of
the nuga: as *a place where* various forces, processes, agencies,
essences, and beings meet and interact. The nuga: provides a location for interactive psychological processes—it is where warring
forces of emotion and desire, of thought and understanding, confront each other and are transmuted and redeployed, but it is also

a place where self meets with god, where a dialogue with god and self is held. The nuga: is a receptive and permeable field, not a self-contained entity. Furthermore, the Newar heart-self is poised for merging with a higher-order reality—the self through the heart-god is identified with godhead—even while it enables persons to view and experience themselves as dynamic centers of awareness, and as morally responsible agents.

The "god who dwells in the heart" is not always taken by all Newars in a literal sense, as an actually existing divine being. Nevertheless, even some of those who do not believe that the "god who dwells in the heart" actually exists say that it represents a psychological truth. In the following quote, for example, a high-caste Newar denies the heart-god actually exists, but maintains that the "heart" knows what is going on within the self.

> **Although there is no god in the heart, the truth is always spoken in the heart (nuga:). Never is a lie spoken from the heart. If I tell you a lie, I will feel with my heart that I am telling a lie. Though the mouth tells a lie, the heart tells the truth. Although there is no god dwelling in the heart, your own ideas and truth are spoken in the heart. When you feel sad, if you cry, that too is in the heart. Since it occurs mentally in this way, there is the idea that, it is said that, there is a god in your heart.**

This statement suggests that the "god who dwells in the heart" is a cultural representation of the way "part" of the psyche monitors self and is the source of thoughts and feelings. This Newar prefers not to speak of a god within, but of a more abstract entity that observes and knows what self is thinking and feeling, *bibek*. This term designates a faculty for understanding. "The heart-god is bibek. With bibek you think."

Bibek literally means something like discrimination or the power of discrimination, or the power of reason. Here this person is, I think, positing the existence of a part or region of the self that monitors the larger self in action. The term acquires a kind of evocative force because of the way people experience their minds working. Moral judgment of self is possible because some part of the mind or self knows what is going on within a person, and so can separate lies from truth. The fact that "the mouth" told a lie while "the heart" knows the truth indicates that intentional acts are observed and evaluated.

Newar informants often treat bibek as a moral faculty. Not only have they posited a mental agency that engages in self-monitoring and self-evaluation, they have ethicized it. Bibek, too, prompts moral behavior. One Brahman told me that his bibek made him feel "soft" toward others, so that when he saw them suffering or in need, he would try to help them. Another noted that bibek makes you think, "only good things."

By seeing people as endowed with bibek, a cognitive power, and as having a moral god immanent in the heart, Newars see people as capable of moral knowing in a broad sense. Some individuals may be entirely indifferent to such conceptions, but these ideas can be used to raise the level of consciousness about moral life, to encourage sensitivity to moral norms, and to evoke commitment to values. These concepts of mental life do not function directly as moral controls, but provide the foundation for moral controls. For they define persons as moral beings, capable of moral knowing, creating the expectation that they should act in moral ways.

Cultural concepts such as these introduce a theme, a nuance, into the way people view themselves and others. The concepts mediate between a postulated moral order (what is known) and individual consciousness (the knower); they provide the minds capable of moral knowing required for persons to live moral lives.

This does not mean that people will behave in a moral way. Newars see mental life as subject to many different, often conflicting, influences, and the crosscurrents do not necessarily result in moral behavior. Newars know this from what they observe of others, and from their own experience. Newar culture takes account of this, and provides ways of thinking about the fact that people can want and do things that are wrong. As Newars see it, wrongful acts, or sin, begin in the heart, and must be resisted in the self.

So, while Newars ethicize some mental processes, they see others as morally problematic. Some mental dispositions or desires, for example, should be eliminated, or if that is not possible, then "tied up" and held in check—that is, Newars posit the need and ability to control mental states.[6] Moral controls and the resistance to mental tendencies to sin or to have "bad thoughts" are understood to involve psychological states and processes. Cultural conceptions of moral controls and of self-control are based in part on understandings regarding the *relations* of different mental capacities, states and processes.

Moral Emotions 1: Lajya

Emotion, as cultural experience, can help create moral orientations. For Newars, a key moral emotion is *lajya*. Although other emotions play important roles in the everyday morality of the Newars, lajya is a key emotion, embracing the range of emotional experience usually designated by the English words "shyness," "embarrassment," and "shame."[7]

Of course, while we need translations for orientation, they can be misleading. Lajya is not transparently the same as the "feelings" designated by the English words "shame" or "shyness." While lajya bears a family resemblance to these emotions, it is culturally different.

Lajya combines feeling and evaluation; it is an emotion and a moral state. The noun lajya is used with the verb *cay-gu*, "to feel." Newars do report body-feelings and sensations linked to lajya; they associate lajya with blushing, sweating, altered pulse, and similar psychophysiological phenomena, which are general signs of psychophysiological arousal or anxiety. Lajya is not, however, reducible to these physical states: while Newars report these bodily sensations, lajya also has meaning for them even in the absence of such signs of bodily arousal. Nor do they think of, or experience, the emotion outside of cultural contexts. Lajya plays a key role in Newar life because it defines a moral state of being, not because it identifies physiological states. In fact, lajya has no identity, no cultural or personal reality, and no moral significance, solely as a result of its association with somatic states. It has crucial evaluative and social regulative uses, which shape and evoke experience and action.

The totality of the experience of lajya, the way the experience is shaped by cultural and personal meaning, and the place of such experience in social life and individual existence, can only be fully understood in the context of cultural life. Emotions are felt cultural experiences, not just felt physiological states. Viewed from one angle, emotion is culture embodied in feelings. Looked at from another, this requires a human body biologically prepared to embody culture in emotional states.

By showing the contexts in which Newars speak of lajya, I will show that this emotion, like emotion in general and moral emotion in particular, cannot be simply identified with bodily feelings, reducing the emotion to a state of physiological arousal. However, to say symptoms of general arousal or anxiety do not define lajya as a total field of experience does not mean that we can or should ignore what Newars actually do feel and experience. Newars do point to affect, to what their bodies "feel," as part of their personal experience, after all. I contend simply that we should treat their feelings and sensations, their embodied inner experience (which seems to be more than physical states), as elements in a far more complex field of experience, not as the single defining essence of the emotion.

Using an enlarged concept of experience, I would argue that the ways Newars experience lajya as feeling is central to the organization of the larger, evaluative sense of the concept of lajya, and to its role as a moral state of being and consciousness. To disembody lajya by defining the emotion exclusively in terms of its cognitive content and structure, treating it as a semiotic system, a set of meanings, while ignoring the feelings and experience that energize and ground it, would also deeply distort what lajya is for Newars. What lajya embodies in felt emotional states are moral judgments based on cultural meanings. In emotion, meanings are infused with feelings, feelings infused with meanings.

Lajya relates centrally to issues of self-control. Newars sometimes assert: If you are a person, through shame (lajya) you must bind yourself (*manu kha:ṣa tha:yata lajya(n) ci-ma*). This maxim says something important about the morality of everyday life in Newar society, and about the sort of person required by that everyday morality: being a moral person means regulating the self through *sensitivity* to the emotion lajya. Self-control requires the capacity to experience lajya.

In the Newar case, the connection of lajya with "energizing" feeling seems critical. Although an actual state of feeling—an emotional experience—may not be present in a context where lajya is a key concept, the ways Newars associate lajya with an enlivening sense of self-worth and the distress of loss of self-worth is crucial to the understanding of the concept in general.

For Newars, as others, what people feel or experience may be understood to supply a motive; emotion animates the actor, leading to action. Since feeling and experience are central to lajya, and link it to action, lajya can be used to assert a number of things about moral behavior and moral personhood. The person with lajya (the self, that is, who possesses the capacity to experience shame, who is sensitive to the possibilities of shame) is seen as motivated by lajya (as feeling) to act in a manner consistent with moral norms. A person who lacks the capacity to experience lajya is, as Newars often put it, "like an animal." The idea is that animals have no moral standards, and do not live in conformity to a moral order. They will "do anything."

Thus, one of the central features of the Newar cultural concept of the moral person is the idea that all people are (or should be) subject to lajya as a feeling or emotion. Lajya is a moral state of being and consciousness; the capacity for lajya helps define what a moral person is.

But the capacity to experience lajya, the disposition to know shame, is conceived to be more developed in some people than others. A greater degree of lajya is held to be inherent in the personalities or natures of women, children, and youths.

Newars often define lajya as a special virtue of woman: "lajya," they say, "is a woman's jewel." A series of constructions of gender seem to converge to define lajya as a special virtue of women; the idea that women naturally have more lajya than adult males makes possible the feeling that they should have more. This generates an expectation about behavior, and expectations can be enforced in a variety of ways. This turning of lajya into a defining feature of womanhood is further developed by making lajya a standard of beauty, i.e., possessing lajya is said to make women beautiful. This links the capacity for lajya with the cultural control of female sexuality. The beautiful and virtuous woman is one who does not express her sexuality in overt, aggressive ways, but shyly, indirectly.[8]

This set of gender constructions exemplifies a larger process — the integration of social structure and affective experience. In Newar culture, the hierarchy of social life determines the social distribution of lajya.[9]

Women, children, and youth are particularly prone to lajya because they are subordinates — their lives are ruled by others. They owe respect to those who are their hierarchical superiors in the family and caste system. They know and experience this in the idiom of lajya, which shapes what they do in the presence of those deserving respect. When a hierarchical superior enters the field of action, the lesser person, the younger person, the woman, defers; a woman or youth makes room for persons higher in the social hierarchy, lets them take over, take charge. Lajya sensitizes people to hierarchy; it prompts a surrender of social space, of control over the course of interaction. A person who is properly sensitive to lajya withdraws to the social margins when a superior is present. In social terms, they yield control. In a psychological sense, they relinquish their desire to assert themselves autonomously, which means they must be able to retract their self-will and self-pride into the recesses of self. In essence, they silence themselves. As one Newar put it, when people experience lajya, they often "go quiet." They do not set things into motion, do not assert themselves as independent doers, do not give voice to their own desires and opinions. They do not struggle to make room for their point of view in social space.

Thus, lajya helps shape the way people respond to hierarchy. This involves a degree of self-suppression. As a Newar Brahman said, "Society makes you suppress some kinds of desires and thoughts." Lajya helps a person do so; it creates a mode of self-silencing, as the following testimony suggests.

> **When your mother and father talk about you getting married, you feel lajya. Of course, you are eager and excited. But you also feel lajya. You don't want to say anything. You hide your happiness. [A high-caste woman]**

Note that this statement implicitly accepts the nurturing, hierarchical authority of parents, acceding to them the right to make vital decisions for self. Notice, too, how lajya governs the formulation of a response to this. Put yourself in the place of the woman to be married: others are making decisions about your fate, about your future. Do you speak up? Do you voice your desires? Do you speak of your eagerness, your excitement, your happiness? No, not necessarily; you feel lajya, so you "don't want to say anything." You hide your feelings, rather than express them. You accept what others decide, deferring to the wisdom and authority of your elders, not intruding even happiness onto the social scene. While she was constructing a hypothetical example of when and how a person might feel lajya, she was also, I think, drawing on her own experience, and I think the example shows how lajya involves self-restraint that withholds personal desire from public interaction.

Of course, as we saw in chapter 3, women will sometimes resist unwanted arranged marriages. Lajya creates a mode of self-silencing, a habit of self-restraint, but Newars do not always let lajya govern them, and they may be critical of some of the implications of lajya.

As one high-caste Newar woman pointed out, since lajya is expressed by being quiet and unassertive, a woman with lajya will not challenge those who have power over her, such as her husband, her mother-in-law, her father-in-law. While, as another woman said, "You feel lajya in front of everyone," including the neighbors, a woman who has married into a family feels the greatest lajya with these members of her family: "it is a kind of respect" (*mane yaegu*), concluded the first woman. This woman, asked to explain the meaning of the saying "lajya is a woman's jewel," said it meant that a woman has more lajya than a man. Elaborating, she explained that lajya gives a woman beauty, makes her demure and quiet in ways consistent with women's subordination:

> If you have lajya, you look beautiful and attractive. When you have lajya, you blush and look down. This makes you beautiful. The other thing, is that you won't talk like a man, direct and outspoken. That [talking like a man] is kind of rough. For a woman, having lajya means that you should not laugh and talk in front of people.

Encouraging women to have lajya, she concluded, was a way of controlling them: having lajya means being quiet, not voicing one's opinions or taking independent action. While this woman chafes under these restrictions, she nonetheless views lajya as essential — without it, there would be chaos, and people might "do anything."[10]

Several Newars pointed out that men are not—and, in their view, should not be—as sensitive to lajya as women are, especially in the role of head of household. Men must be able to act forcefully for their households; they need to be able to assert themselves in an uninhibited, relatively aggressive way, to get their families what they need. Thus, Newars view too much sensitivity to lajya in young *men* as a problem, not a virtue.

As an evaluative concept that expresses disapproval, lajya is used to point out violations of norms, and to affirm standards of behavior by contrast with the violation. When a person does something wrong, disapproval may be expressed by saying that the violator is without lajya (*lajya marumha manu*). This assumes that lajya (as sensitivity to shame) would cause a person to behave in conformity to norms: if the person had lajya, they would behave in a proper way. There are degrees of sensitivity to lajya. One person might be moved by feelings of shame to stop behaving in a way that violates a community standard. But another would never have begun to behave in a way that would inevitably elicit disapproval, because he or she would anxiously anticipate that such acts would be greeted with shame-inducing criticism.

The kinds of behavior subject to evaluation in terms of lajya are diverse. One can be ashamed, for example, because one is poor.

> (You sometimes have lajya?)
> Sometimes.
> (Why?)
> You are a have [lit., you have-person become.] I am a have-not. As you have, so do you eat. I have nothing, there is nothing to eat. I cannot come up to your level. Since there is not enough to eat, there is lajya. If you cannot go in society, it is lajya, isn't it? ["to eat" has extended meaning of "to have," "to experience"]
> [Ganesh Lal, a farmer]

The "shame" of being a have-not has to do, I think, with perceived failure to be the kind of person who is socially valued. It is not just that he is poor, but that being poor points out, for others to see, that he is inadequate, a failure as a person or, as I heard other Newars put it, that he has not yet "become a person," and that he knows others see this. Note the reference to hierarchy: "I cannot come up to your level." Lajya expresses hierarchical respect and avoidance, an attitude of nonassertiveness "in front of" those who are defined as higher in the social hierarchy. A lower status person cannot fit in with those of higher status, cannot "go in society with them," or act to "become a person" in front of them. The lower status person is vulnerable to shame in his contacts with hierarchical superiors, and so may elect to navigate such encounters in terms of the etiquette of distancing, self-muting, and respect in order to avoid being exposed as less than an equal person.

The following were cited as producing lajya as well:

To be caught in a lie or deception.
To be forced to beg for a living.
To be seen eating at the door of a house (which suggests one is
  not sharing the food with the household).
For certain parts of the body to be exposed or mentioned.
For an unmarried woman to be seen in the company of men.
To make a mistake or misspeak in the presence of others.
To be seen urinating or defecating.
To use obscene, rude, or improper language.
To fail to show proper respect in speech or action.
To be rebuked in front of others.

One basic criterion for inclusion in this list is being seen, being in view, publicity: in each instance, something becomes known to others. Each act is publicly in violation of a norm. The feeling of lajya is triggered (or at least is most acute) when others know of a breach, and may be felt in its most powerful form when others confront a person with a failure or transgression. The norms or standards themselves are not of equal importance and have different sorts of meaning; social mistakes and inadvertent mishaps as well as moral offenses are grounds for lajya.

Lajya has to do with intersubjective integration into public life: lajya is felt when a person knows that others know that a breach has been committed. When asked if lajya would be felt if no one would see, a high-caste man replied: "if no one sees, why would they feel lajya?" Other high-caste Newars agreed.

(If you were at a place where no one else was, and you made a mistake, or did something wrong, but no one would know, would you feel lajya or not?)
I would not feel lajya.
(What if at that time you thought of others?)
I would not feel lajya. I'd be afraid—what if others knew?

Fear is an important moral emotion when it is linked to a set of moral standards. Newars report they worry about the disapproval of others—and the idea of lajya creates a fear of exposure. This anxiety is one of the main components of sensitivity to shame: one fears that others will know, and this fear acts as a check on behavior. The idea that others "might see" is an important control in Newar culture. As Obeyesekere (1984: 503) notes, people may fear exposure even when alone, to fantasized others who are psychologically present.

As a high-caste Newar pointed out, sometimes it does not matter what others see or think; what matters is what a person thinks they see or think, or what a person thinks of self. He concluded his argument that lajya is internalized by giving this example of a student who cannot come up with the right answer to a teacher's question:

> When you cannot give your guru an answer, you may feel lajya. When someone cannot say something in front of other students, he will only feel lajya himself. The others will not tease him. . . . It is not lajya, except in his own judgment. [He says to himself] "I could not do even that much." It is not lajya, only for himself is it lajya.

Lajya here is more like embarrassment over a flawed performance than it is like shame felt because others accuse self of a moral transgression. Others are not holding self to any standard in this example; they do not care. The idea expressed is that individuals may hold themselves to certain standards, and feel lajya as a result of their failure to meet these standards.

Lajya applies not only to social mistakes and lapses or inadequacies in the presentation of self, but also to serious cases of wrongdoing.

Lajya as Response to Wrongdoing

How do Newars experience lajya? Let me take the case, not of minor social mistakes or lapses in the presentation of self, but of serious transgressions. By violating important moral norms, Newars risk their social identities; and they may seriously complicate their views of themselves. A high-caste Newar makes this point by describing a hypothetical scenario, a situation to which lajya applies both as evaluation and as an emotion:

Let's say that I told you that you owe me money. But you don't owe me money. But what I say is, you owe me money. Will you pay or not? An argument starts. You do not owe me any money. Without justification, I say, Give the money to me. While we argue, having no proof, our friends will ask, what money? [That is, they demand an explanation.] Since I lied, I now have to make something else up: isn't it lajya? This is a very low thing. If I could, I would have taken your money. If I could, I would have taken it by fighting. I would try to get it by taking your watch. If I'm stronger than you, I'd take it. But my friends and neighbors will ask, what money? If I can make up some proof, whether it is true or not, I can take the money. So I would be a liar. One without lajya. If someone then says, he is a liar, then I will have lajya. I am as good as dead [literally, I am equal to dead]. A person who lives by lying may as well die, no?

This account shows how lajya is central to moral discourse. Shame is not *only* a feeling here; *it also* organizes and animates moral judgment, helping to define the wrongfulness of coercion, force, and intimidation. It is thus a moral/psychological concept— the evaluative and the psychological senses of the term support each other. The violation given as an example here is serious; the stakes are high. Lajya is conceived of as a basic standard of conduct, closely associated with right and wrong (a person with lajya does what is right, while the person without lajya does wrong); it is viewed as a motive for moral behavior (a person who lies has no lajya, while by implication a person with lajya will not lie, steal, or do "low things"); and it is conceived of as an experienced feeling (a person caught in a lie feels lajya).

The thread I want to pursue here is the expression "as good as dead," or "the same as dead." By using this expression, Newars say something about the organization and meaning of the experience of lajya.

Another high-caste Newar, commenting on this expression, suggested that persons who lied would feel "as good as dead" because of the shock and pain of the experience of great lajya. "When people say you have no lajya, you feel lajya." The notion of a kind of social death seems appropriate. Newars who ignore standards of conduct risk loss of social standing and prestige (ijjat). They may face ostracism, which can have devastating social and economic consequences. The threat of social death, like the threat of physical death, is a shock; it can cause a state of depersonalization, a loss of confidence in self, a loss of meaning for self, experienced as emptiness, withdrawal, and confusion.

Yet another high-caste Newar elaborated on the idea that a person shamed is "as good as dead" or "already dead" by speaking of the way he experienced lajya. He said that lajya felt "cold—like you did not exist." This indicates that lajya may, in certain situations, have a cold, withdrawn dimension, drawing on, or providing an experiential base for, the death metaphor.

This contrasts with hot, flushed, red-faced feelings of embarrassment that are also part of the experience of lajya. When the presentation of self as a proper social person slips, not coldness, but blurred perception, a red face, and blushing are attributed to the experience.

The loss of meaning associated with an intense experience of lajya may be profound. One high-caste Newar said:

> As long as you are alive you must do your rituals. The only people who don't do rituals are the dead—no one says anything to them. So if you are alive and don't do the rituals, you are . . . [drifts off] . . . (You are what?) You are the same as dead. You feel that—because you know society will say that you are bad. And society won't count you as a person. And that is like being dead. Having no significance [*chu(n) he mahatwa maru*].

The combined loss of self-control and social meaning experienced when intense shame is felt result in intense disorientation, since a relationship with the social world and the capacity for intentional action have been called into question by the emotion. The sense of self is threatened; a moral emotion can be a dangerous way to bind the heart.

Discussion: The Structure of Shamelike Affect

Lajya seems to involve not one, but several ways of evaluating and experiencing the relationship of self with the social world—the "embarrassment" of social failure or flawed interaction, "shyness" before strangers, "respect" for hierarchical superiors, the "shame," "humiliation" or "social death" of being caught doing wrong or harming others. In an earlier discussion of the issues posed by lajya, I suggested that "depersonalization" or "loss of self" where self is evaluated and experienced as diminished, as having reduced value or reality, might distinguish true "shame" from embarrassment and shyness, although all three are labeled in Newari by the same word. Much of what Newars say about lajya suggests a loss of self, or a devaluing of self, which occurs when a person is confronted with an inadequacy or transgression. I still think that the "shame" of transgressions involves the most intense "loss of self" in Newar culture, but some devaluing of self is involved when Newars err in social interactions; these errors undermine their sense of who they are, of being competent social actors. Being confronted with a transgression is thus not necessarily a different kind of experience, but perhaps only a more intense experience—being exposed as a bad person, or a total fool, threatens the core of a self-identity, calling into question what one is as a person. Such exposure also threatens the relationships in which one has found value and meaning for self.

This does not mean we can conflate the different kinds of experiences Newars describe as lajya; the "shame" of wrongdoing can be distinguished contextually from social embarrassment and shyness. The meaning of acts, and the engagement of self, vary; lajya is more intense and shamelike in the context of moral transgression and humiliation because the involvement and loss of self is greater.

A vulnerability to some manner of depersonalization or loss of self seems integral to emotions usually glossed as "shame" in a range of cultures; the exact form this takes seems specific to the emotional meaning system shaping shamelike affect within a particular culture. Geertz (1973: 401–402) says that the Balinese emotion lek, often translated as "shame" is better glossed as "stage fright," since it has "nothing to do with transgressions," but with performance in social interaction that is culturally constituted as depersonalizing ceremony.

> What is feared . . . is that the public performance that is etiquette will be botched, that the social distance etiquette maintains will consequently collapse, and that the personality of the individual will then break through to dissolve his standardized public identity. When this occurs . . . ceremony evaporates, the immediacy of the moment is felt with an excruciating intensity, and men become

unwilling consociates locked in mutual embarrassment, as though
they had inadvertently intruded upon one another's privacy (1973:
402)

This points to a destructuring of the meanings through which
people integrate themselves into a public world, introducing an
element of incoherency into life and causing a disruption of the
sense of public self. To take another example, Keeler (1983) has
argued that the Javanese define themselves through interaction.
Status is fluid and, in important ways, self-constructed, rather
than fixed by social roles or formal attributes. Hierarchical status
and a sense of self are mutually constituting, dependent on the
display, interpretation, and experience of emotion in social interaction. The operative emotion in this context, *iśin*, is similar in
some respect to the Balinese lek and the Newar lajya. In Javanese
culture, Keeler says, if a person has status, "Others should feel *iśin*
to eat or speak too familiarly in his presence. If they do not, he
feels *iśin* because they have shown him incapable of arousing fear
and respect in them. If his power does not impress itself upon
those around him, his status has been impugned, and he feels *iśin*"
(1983: 160).

Such acts of disrespect threaten a loss of self. They subvert self-
identity within a culturally constituted social order. In Javanese
culture, Keeler (1983: 162) argues, the "awkwardness" that flows
from "inappropriate" social behavior does not, as Geertz maintains
for Bali, threaten to dissolve a public identity and expose a private
self. Instead, Keeler says, "it threatens the dissolution of several
people's identities in the collapse of all social order."

The Newar data suggests that a culturally constituted self is vulnerable to derealization in terms of some range of circumstances
involving the integration of self into the public world. As we have
seen, the meaning of lajya, and the contexts in which it is imputed
or experienced, range from something like "stage fright" (where
the emphasis is on performance in social interaction) to "shame"
(associated with transgressions that threaten the moral order).
The disturbance of the sense of self varies in intensity: the self may
be rendered mildly problematic in "embarrassment"; it may be
threatened with dissolution and incoherence in more intense states
of "shame." If intense enough, one may become nothing — "as good
as dead" — as some Newars put it.

I suspect that some of the confusion and controversy regarding shamelike affect has resulted from a failure to recognize the complex structure of the emotion. Thus Geertz says of lek that:

[it] is neither the sense that one has transgressed nor the sense of humiliation that follows upon some uncovered transgression, both rather lightly felt and quickly effaced in Bali. . . . It is, on the contrary, a diffuse, usually mild, though in certain situations virtually paralyzing, nervousness before the prospect (and the fact) of social interaction. . . .

Whatever its deeper causes, stage fright consists in a fear that, for want of skill or self-control, or perhaps by mere accident, an aesthetic illusion will not be maintained, that the actor will show through his part and the part thus dissolve into the actor. (1973:402)

This exegesis — apart from the underlying dramaturgical metaphor — is not inconsistent with aspects of the shyness or embarrassment dimensions of lajya. But Geertz (1973: 401) denies that lek has anything to do with feelings of "shame" resulting from transgressions, whereas lajya encompasses experiences of "shame" associated with transgressions and humiliation. Unni Wikan (1987: 360–361) challenges Geertz's interpretation of lek on the basis of fieldwork in another part of Bali. She reports that she found that the Northern Balinese concept of *malu*, which her informants identified as synonymous with the Southern Balinese lek, "does indeed have to do with transgressions and humiliations, not at all lightly felt or quickly effaced in Bali." I suspect that the Balinese terms lek and malu tap an "emotional space" with complex dimensions, as does the Newar term lajya. "Stage fright" may be an apt description of one dimension of lek, but the context-sensitive emotional meaning system that generates stage fright may also generate shame/humiliation. People — Newars, Balinese, and Australian Aborigines — seem to recognize some kind of family resemblance among shame, shyness, fear/fright, and embarrassment, and make use of a single context-sensitive term to refer to a range of related experience. Perhaps the unity of emotions like lajya and lek has to do with the vulnerability of the self in a world of others, who observe and evaluate self. Within the framework of the public world, self-esteem and self-image are modulated and vulnerable in a number of ways, given the vicissitudes of the flow of social life. The complex structure of vulnerability is reflected in the range of meanings attached to these emotion terms.

The English emotion term "shame" seems peculiar in cross-cultural perspective, because it does not seem to be semantically and socially organized in terms of conceptual links with "timidity," "fear/fright," and "respect" in the way that the emotion terms often translated by the English word "shame" often are. To put it another way, English speakers apparently discriminate lexically what other cultures seem to discriminate contextually—if at all.

Wierzbicka (1986), for example, discusses some of the ways the meaning of the English word "shame" contrasts with Australian Aboriginal emotion concepts, such as *kunta*, often translated as "shame" (Myers 1986: 120–124). Wierzbicka (1986: 592) asks, "are the feelings corresponding to concepts such as 'shame,' 'fear,' and 'embarrassment' discrete?" She suggests (1986: 593) that if a language does not discriminate between emotions, such as shame and fear, then the speakers of that language may not be able to perceive them as two different feelings.

This may be true to some extent; linguistic categories can influence cognitive and perceptual processes (D'Andrade 1990: 73). Even if bodily sensations do not provide the grounds for perceiving emotions as distinct, however, there may be bases for discrimination other than language. People may know more than they can put into words (Nisbett and Wilson 1970); they may experience and act on mental states for which they have no words. Psychological experience is not always mediated by language.

Obeyesekere (1981: 76–83), for example, argues that guilt may be experienced and symbolized, even when there is no word for guilt in a language. Interpreting spirit attacks on Sinhala women who will become ecstatic priestesses as a symbolic representation of guilt—in these attacks "the dead reproach the living for betrayal and filial impiety"—he notes the absence of linguistic resources for speaking of and conceptualizing guilt: "Though the data indicate guilt, there is no word for guilt and no associated vocabulary in the Sinhala language," except neologisms coined by missionaries (1981: 79). Guilt, Obeyesekere argues, is a universal emotion, but it may not be "externalized" in language. Instead, people may experience more than they can say, expressing feelings of guilt in the form of culture specific symptoms, symbols, and visions (1981: 78).

Emotional understandings may also be encoded in visual images, or keyed to smell or touch, potentially bypassing the constructions of emotions in language. There are nonverbal or partly nonverbal modalities for socialization, communication, and expressiveness that rely more on showing than telling (Briggs 1986: 62–65; Forge 1970). Emotional meanings may be keyed to concrete practices in which words have only a limited role. Secular and religious rituals, for example, may "say" something about emotion and self without declaring all of their meaning in words. In art, feelings and felt self-images may be painted, carved, or danced (as Hindu myth is in Bhaktapur). Gregory Bateson (1972) quotes the dancer Isadora Duncan: "If I could tell you what it meant, there would be no point in dancing it."

Even if words exist in a culture's vocabulary to label particular emotional states, people may not make use of them very often, or may not have them in mind when they actually experience an emotion. Persons who do not discriminate between emotions by using different words may still be able to discriminate emotional states on the basis of judgments about the contexts of their experience. I may be afraid of ghosts when I am alone at night, and acknowledge this; I may fear intimacy (or loss of relatedness), but not acknowledge it. In either case, I experience fear, but I do not think the most important component of the experience is my ability to name it; I may flee ghosts or intimacy without stopping to describe my emotional experience to myself in words. My assessment of the world in relationship to myself, embodied in an emotion, can take place without my appealing to, or producing, words or discursive judgments (Levy 1973, 1984).

As Levy (1973, 1984) has argued for the Tahitians, the way people speak of what they feel, of their inner experience, may misrepresent what they actually experience. Levy says Tahitians often report feeling "fatigue" or "illness" when the Western observer has information about the person that would suggest a loss that might produce "sadness" or "grief" (or possibly anger or rage if the loss is blamed on the other rather than the self). While this poses difficult methodological problems—how do you assess a person's emotional states if they are not what that person tells you they are?— I do not think we can assume that the words people use to speak of their feelings transparently identify actual emotional states, natural *or* cultural. The words people use to identify their feelings to others and to themselves may disguise their actual, culturally generated, emotional experience, misrepresenting emotions that are based on the way they are involved with others in ongoing relationships. Such emotional states may be fully integral to cultural life, but not recognized in cultural theories of emotion.[11]

Moreover, people may also be able to discriminate cognitively, even when they do not discriminate lexically, if they can tap alternative cognitive schemas or cultural scenarios for a single emotion word, as they do with lajya. Transgression scenarios, social inadequacy scenarios, and understandings about hierarchy may be linked to a single word, providing a basis for experiencing shame, embarrassment, and respect/deference as distinct, felt relationships of self to world.

Emotion concepts, as elements of cultural theories about emotion and self that reflect key aspects of *experienced* social life, do, I believe, powerfully shape potential emotional responses, sensitizing people to possibilities inherent in their relationship to the world, others, and themselves. This does not mean that these more-or-less explicit concepts and theories exhaust all the possibilities of emotional life. I have discussed emotions which Newars label with single words here, but although these linguistically "marked" emotions are central to Newar moral knowing, I want to stress that there may be unspoken theories and "unmarked" feelings, for which people may not have words, but which nonetheless color moral knowing. Even culturally marked emotions are constantly reforged in terms of life experiences.

Emotion words are typically invoked in commentary on experience, not necessarily in the act of experiencing; but emotion should also be understood as a kind of action — *not* just as motivation for action, or as explanation of action, as important as these perspectives on emotion are. Emotion as a form of action is as central to social life as emotion talk: action infused with emotion can occur without much explicit commentary if people have been primed for it (perhaps in ritual or unspoken family experience, as well as in emotion talk). Clearly, cultural conversation about self, and discourse about emotion, orient self to action; but as crucial as talk about emotion is as a mode of socialization into emotional life, we should not ignore the ways emotion is embedded in action and practice in ways that go beyond what cultural theories of emotion say.

People do things with emotions; by experiencing or displaying emotion, they transform themselves and restructure the immediate context of action in significant ways. Maya and lajya, for example, are more than theories; they are felt, but also acted out, acted on. This quality of being intrinsic to action within relationship is arguably central to what they are for Newars. As F. G. Bailey (1983) suggests, emotions have tactical implications—a display of passion, whether felt or not, can make a difference, perhaps shifting the course of an interaction. Simulated or actually felt, emotion can bring about a restructuring of the meaning of a situation and a redirection of behavior. Ashamed, a person withdraws; feeling maya, they comfort or nurture. A Newar may be moved to responsiveness with maya, or be moved to flee the scene of social or moral failure because of lajya; this interpretation treats emotion as motive. With their feelings, however, they may also declare a context for interaction (keying it to compassion with maya or karuna, or to hierarchy with lajya in the respect/deference mode), define a relationship, or define self. They relate themselves to the social world in definite ways; these are acts, not motives for acts. Emotion sometimes fuses action and motivation, acting reflexively on self, and affecting others when displayed.

A Sense of Moral Virtue and the Pain of Moral Failure

It is worth stressing that lajya as an organizing element of cultural life can generate a sense of virtue or yield a painful sense of failure. It is desirable to have the capacity to feel lajya; to lack this capacity is a defect in moral character. The experience of the "raw" sensation of lajya, in its psychological immediacy, its "pain," is highly undesirable, but essential to moral life. Newar moral and emotional discourse presupposes that moral behavior is grounded in moral pain, and in the fear of moral pain. What Newars know, as moral beings, is mediated by this pain and fear. I think that it is fair to say that part of the reason moral emotions work as behavioral controls is because they are painful to experience, and that this experience of distress influences how agents place and present themselves in the social world. In my view, hot, flushed, red-faced feelings of embarrassment, and cold, metaphorically deathlike, empty feelings of shame, *embody* moral evaluations: to *feel* moral judgments of self in this way alters the way people know moral values and know themselves.

In the absence of emotional experience, people in any culture may cognitively know and use the knowledge structures that constitute the moral code. They can answer hypothetical questions about the moral code. But a cognitive or discursive rehearsal of their moral knowledge may have little impact on how they live their lives and organize their behavior. In contrast, painful emotional experience commands a greater degree of attention, and may initiate processes of psychological work, through which a person attempts to reorient the relationship of self to social world, and of self to self. Emotions engage the self more completely and more reflexively, bringing to life what was known about, in a passive way, but not known in terms of self-experience.

Thus, moral emotions are moral judgments, but they are not just cognitive judgments. They are, or have the potential for being, *felt* moral judgments. Such judgments have motivational significance. Simply knowing about a moral norm—being cognitively acquainted but not emotionally engaged with it (Spiro 1984)—is not as likely to motivate social action and psychological work as powerfully felt, emotionally embodied, judgments are.

For many Newars, the perception of self as perceived by others as being without lajya produces the kind of pain, the feelings of distress, they speak of as lajya. On the one hand, lajya is identified with feelings felt when social norms are violated; on the other, lajya is the disposition to uphold such norms, a commitment to a code of conduct integral to lajya itself. The notion that you "feel lajya" when you do not "have lajya" may seem paradoxical, but apparently makes sense to Newars, perhaps because of the way it links emotional distress to failure to uphold social norms: you feel distraught when you do not do what you should do. If, as a social actor, you lack lajya, as the virtuous self-control that enables you to live according to a code of conduct, and you do wrong, then feelings of lajya, surges of painful affect, will fill the gap between what you have done and what you should have done.

Note that the distress of lajya is not a single kind of distress. There are hot, flushed, feelings of embarrassment, perceptions of self as worthless or no good, as having no value or significance, even cold, deathlike depersonalization. Thus, I do not think that lajya can be identified with a single state of feeling. Multiple feelings embody lajya.

If so — if, in fact, no single affect is definitive of lajya — then we should not attempt to treat it as if it were. We should avoid classifying a protean, context-sensitive, culturally experienced emotion as a single kind of feeling or psychophysiological state, as an invariant, universal, basic emotion.

While lajya is associated with multiple feelings and meanings, not all of them are painful. While Newars often stress the pain or awkwardness they feel when they fail to live up to the standards associated with lajya, and even identify this distress as lajya, they also associate lajya with more pleasant mental states. They "feel good" when they have acted in an appropriate fashion, living up to the implicit moral code of lajya. By behaving appropriately, by having lajya, they can not only avoid the different kinds of distress associated with lajya, they can also "feel good" about themselves. The glow of positive feelings, however, is not the result of what self thinks of self, in isolation, but the result of what others think of self, just as is the case with the distress associated with lajya.

> Mostly, when you have lajya you feel good because people expect you to have lajya. There are two ways of feeling good. One, when you do what you want to do, not caring about others or lajya. The other, when you are able to do what you are expected to do, and are praised for that. [I know] people will say good things about me, so I feel good about that.

I believe the seemingly paradoxical statement that a person "feels lajya" when they do not "have lajya" actually conveys a deep and accurate understanding of the nature and scope of the emotion. In terms of lajya, the person may be integrated into social life as a moral actor with an enhanced sense of self, or be threatened with dissolution and abandonment. Having lajya, a person finds confirmation for self in the esteem of others, real or imagined; without lajya, a person faces a loss of self and a loss of relatedness and risks being left with no meaning or value. This dialectical dance of moral virtue and moral failure seems central to the concept of lajya and to the place of lajya in Newar life.

Moral Emotions 2: Pastae

Lajya is not the only emotion that a moral person feels. A person with the capacity to feel lajya, Newars say, will also be subject to *pastae*. Pastae, then, like lajya, is a moral emotion. It is painful to experience, and evaluative in nature. Pastae designates an emotion resembling "remorse," "regret," or "contrition." Like lajya, pastae results when a person violates a norm, or fails to live up to expectations about his or her conduct. As Ganesh Lal, a farmer, put it, "Pastae means, if we do something that is not appropriate, we have pastae." But the concept of pastae is apparently narrower than lajya. Pastae, unlike lajya, is not experienced for mere solecisms or minor improprieties. Acts resulting in feelings of pastae often involve some actual harm or infliction of pain (dukha) on others. Newars give examples like lying to someone, or hitting or beating someone, as acts that might produce pastae.

Unlike lajya, pastae seems to be what people expect to feel after they have done something wrong; it is not felt in anticipation of wrongdoing. Nor does pastae establish conventional standards in the way lajya does. There are separate terms for legalistic guilt, such as the word *dosh*. It refers to the condition of having violated some norm or law, of bearing the blame or fault for some act, without having the emotive sense of remorse that pastae possesses.

Pastae is not used in reproaching others in the way lajya is. This may reflect the definition of pastae as something felt after an act; it lacks the anticipatory value of sensitivity to shame. Newars say you may feel pastae and lajya at the same time about the same action. Krishna Bahadur has a keen sense of the pain of remorse, and views pastae as an emotional response to harming others.

> **Pastae means that we for no reason — unnecessarily — do something that gives pain (dukha) to others. We hit them, and then this is a sin. Because you struck them. Pastae means reviling [yourself]. For no reason you did that — do you have pastae? If you did not do that, you would not need to have pastae. You do something wrong, and then have pastae.**

Pastae, in his view, flows from acts that hurt others, when those acts are not justifiable ("for no reason"). Krishna grounds pastae in sin (pap). Pastae is felt when some act causes pain or injury to another; the act itself is a sin.

The notion of harm to others is not central to the concept of lajya. Exposure to the sight and verdict of others, not harm to others, unifies such diverse acts as being seen eating, public nakedness, and other improprieties.

The notion of harm may be picked up in other Newar moral concepts: "If I do dharma, I don't hurt anyone. Only if I sin do I hurt someone" (a Jugi). Pastae conveys, as part of its central meaning, the feeling associated with harming others.

Pastae often results from actions that were undertaken in the belief that they were warranted, but later were determined to lack justification. "Pastae means I made a mistake. Later I know my mistake, this is pastae." One example cited by several people was punishing a child in the belief that the child had done something wrong. Should they find out later that the child did not do anything wrong, they agreed that pastae would be experienced. Some reported that they had been in that situation, and had experienced pastae; others simply maintained it would be the appropriate emotion. Informants pointed out that a person feeling pastae in these circumstances might feel lajya as well, if others knew of their actions, since others might call you a bad person for striking a child without sufficient reason.

Pastae does not always designate a feeling that follows from a perception of harm done to another. It may be used in the sense of "regret" where there is no implication of moral fault, no sense of having done wrong. In such cases, it sometimes seems to play off a sense of empathy and connection, marking not perceived harm to another, but a sense of loss, of diminished relatedness, perhaps filtered through feelings that self did not do enough to sustain and nurture the relationship with other.

The Problem of Self-Control

If you can't control your own heart, who can?
— a Newar saying

Despite the power of these emotions, even the fear of shame and the pain of remorse sometimes fails to inhibit people. At times, there are deeper problems of self-control; some Newars, sometimes, engage in behavior that causes them deep shame and remorse, but find they cannot help themselves. Cultural responses to this state of affairs are revealing of further assumptions made about mental life.

Newars have ideas about what causes, and how to respond to, what might in Western folk models be termed "weakness of will," an inability to do what one wants, to live up to one's own or others' expectations. For example, sometimes Newars who drink heavily want to stop, but find that they cannot. For this, Newars propose various cultural remedies. One response, a kind of ritual therapy, involves mobilizing religious ideas to support resolve or to counter desire.

The therapy proceeds along lines consistent with the Newar view of the nature of mental life. The Newar cultural model of the person proposes that desires (*iccha*) are important mental states. Desires are states of wanting, needing, wishing, or liking (D'Andrade 1987). These may be seen as arising from within the self, from feelings, emotions, and thoughts, or as arising from outside the self, through perceptions of and experiences with things in the world. In either case, they are not fully under the control of the individual who experiences them, though an individual may be expected to make an effort to control them. In certain cases, desires may be viewed as entirely outside the control of the individual, and as caused by external forces. If not checked or regulated, desires tend to cause behavior. If you want to drink, and you let yourself, you will. To control yourself you have to regulate your desires. Dharma Raj, a Brahman, describes the process as follows:

> You can choose desires [iccha]. Slowly. So here we practice austerities [*vrata*].[12] [People] are taken to a god place to have these bad desires removed. They enlist the aid of the god or goddess. They swear, "From now on I truly will not drink alcohol." At the god place, they say, "Oh Bhagavan, Oh Goddess, I swear not to drink spirits. If I drink spirits, it will be as if drinking your blood." . . . And in that same way, to their friends they say, "Friend, if I drink spirits, it will count as drinking your urine." To the god, it will count as drinking the god's blood. Drinking blood is a great crime [*aparaдh*]. Drinking a god's blood is an even greater crime. Should I drink alcohol, it will be as if I committed that crime. They make this vow.

Viewed as a mental state, the vow expresses a resolution; D'Andrade (1987: 117) remarks that resolutions are "second-order intentions—intentions to keep certain other intentions despite difficult and opposing desires."

The vow can also be viewed as a social act, since it is publicly declared to other persons—to friends, family members, or deities (who count as special, divine persons). Notice the performative utterance—the vow taken is the speech act of promising. Speech acts may have a close relation to beliefs about mental states. D'Andrade (1987: 146) theorizes that "speech acts are one of the major classes of public events used as identifying marks of internal states and processes." What goes on in speech, in acts such as promising, commanding, requesting, may map out ideas about what go on in the mind.

In the resolutions in the above passage, there is more involved than swearing off drink; the speech act, or vow, is followed up by saying that any lapse will be the equivalent of some socially abhorred act. To drink alcohol is equated with drinking the goddess's blood, a fearful moral crime, or drinking urine, a disgusting or degrading act. (There are cultural performances in which ritual actors drink the blood of animals, so the notion of drinking blood is a familiar one, but one does not drink the blood of deities.) Drinking alcohol may also be equated with drinking mother's blood. Or people may ask that they be made to die vomiting blood if they drink again. In this way, the "bad" desire is countered by utterances that express "good" intentions or resolve, and we can speculate that the added notion of drinking blood is meant to arouse emotions that will lend strength to the resolution. This corresponds to a proposition in their model of person that says that desires reflect emotions or feelings, and intentions follow from desires. So to combat a morally wrong desire, a person must resolve not to do wrong, and this must be supported by desires, which develop from emotions. The imagery in the Newar resolutions supplies emotion; the desire is a desire not to do wrong, which is lent strength, in a sense, by the desire to avoid committing such an elemental crime as drinking blood. Arguably, feelings of anxiety and guilt are intensified by equating a wrongful act (drinking alcohol) with a far greater wrong (drinking blood) and by asking to be punished for the former as if it were the latter.

Vows or pledges made to deities thus express positive intentions or resolutions. The god is the guarantor of the consequences of breaking the pledge; the person who wishes to stop drinking organizes his intentions in the act of pledging. The equation of drinking spirits with drinking blood heightens the sense of consequence; it constitutes an effort to frighten self out of the habit of desire.

There is also, perhaps, an attempt in all this to leverage intentions, to make them stronger by making them public and linked to consequences so horrible as to render doing what would engender such grotesque consequences unthinkable. To increase the severity of consequences of an action is to arm a person with counterintentions, with resolve against desire. The more wrong the consequences of an act, the more wrong the desire to act in that manner — making self-control more important.

So the resolutions of the vow can be viewed, in reflexive terms, as efforts to manipulate or manage the mental processes that lead to unwanted behaviors. The ritualized resolutions presuppose that the mind is organized as an interactive system of different states and processes, and that people can willfully or deliberately influence the mind by formulating different goals. It is from this perspective that they can be seen as therapeutic discourse.

It is probably unnecessary to say that such procedures do not seem to be entirely effective.[13] But they do point out what people believe about states of self: the Newar cultural model proposes that there are links between mental states and processes that result in behavior; these beliefs about the links between mental states, processes, and behavior are the basis for therapeutic interventions. Self-control means being able to take an intentional stand regarding mental states (desires) that organize behavior.

Newars and Americans think that you can think about what you think and feel, and they believe this capacity to reflect on "inner" experience makes a difference. They believe you can act, mentally, to alter the self; in their view, self-control involves active deliberations about mental states and processes. D'Andrade (1987) points out the way the links between elements in the American cultural model of the mind make possible a concept of self-control:

> The folk model treatment of desire and intention as states that take propositionally framed objects or states of affairs means that what can be wanted, aimed for, and planned depends on what is known,

or believed, or understood . . . since what is wanted, aimed for, and planned are things thought of, one may "deliberate" about these wants, aims, and plans. These deliberations may, in turn, lead to other feelings, such as guilt or doubt, or other wishes, which may counter the original wish, or may involve various second-order intentional states, such as resolution or indecision. Were this feedback loop, in which one can think about what one feels, desires, and intends, not present in the folk model, there would be no mechanism of self-control in the system, and hence we would have no basis for concepts of responsibility, morality, or conscience. (D'Andrade 1987: 126)

This is a cultural process—the way these deliberations are couched and framed draws on cultural resources. When I asked Krishna, "If you have a bad thought or a bad desire, what do you do to stop that bad thought or desire?" he responded by describing how you should deliberate about these bad thoughts or desires, and resolve to give them up:

To unmake a bad thought you have to think, to concentrate in your mind, with your spirit, "I must not do this, it is a sin. If I do that, a great sin will happen to me, a mistake will happen." And if, in this way, we think thoughts of god, then god will be in our minds. . . . If we keep having this kind of mind [wish, desire], this kind of sin in our mind, then we should give it up. Cause ourselves to forget it. And then we decide by our hearts, by our soul, I should not do this, it is not done. Thinking so, we won't commit sins.

The language of self-control here is religious. As we saw in earlier passages from interviews with him, this man believes that inner moral struggles for self-control have a kind of transparency—they are known to god. This transparency, where you know that you are known, perhaps lends something to reflections on what one wants and desires; inner deliberations are undertaken with a sense of the moral presence of god. For Krishna, the ultimate goals of self-monitoring are religious—to think thoughts that bring god to consciousness, to avoid thoughts that lead to sin.

Newars judge themselves in moral terms. The process of self-judgment is a subjective experience. Inner deliberations may be motivated by moral feelings. I have described how Newars experience what they term pastae, a concept that designates something like remorse or regret. When I ask Krishna what pastae is, he speaks of it in terms that weave together psychological, moral, and religious ideas.

> (What is pastae?)
> There is worry.
> (How?)
> By his heart, he knows, Now he has done wrong, made a mistake, and he says to himself, "Oh, my god, damn." [That is, he reproaches self.] So he has worry in his heart. However great their understanding of dharma [the moral law], people sin too.
> (What happens inside you when you have pastae?)
> In the heart there is our Bhagavan, this heart beating. And then we do wrong; pastae means a mistake happened. I did wrong, why did I do that . . . so pain comes.

Cultural ideas shape how people view themselves and how they reflect on their moral intuitions, and so shape the way they experience themselves, even as what they experience shapes the way they understand culture. That people experience moral pain because they have done something they view as wrong lends meaning to the idea of a knowing heart. But the connection can be traced in the other direction as well: moral knowing grows out of the way culture and experience re-create and animate each other. The idea of a knowing heart, and the concept of a god within, are cultural representations that give meaning to moral experience; they give people's feelings and intuitions explicit ethical significance. Not only are they a way of speaking of what people feel, they articulate personal experience with the idea of a moral person and of a moral order. The Newars, like many people in many cultures, tend to see morality as an objective part of the world, rather than as a human construction — morality reflects natural or sacred law (Shweder, Mahapatra, and Miller 1987: 4; Mackie 1977: 30–35). Newars also see society as ideally embodying this law. We have seen that they also connect morality with personal, subjective experience. By understanding that the nuga: knows what is moral, that a witnessing god dwells within this heart-self, Newars are able to know that they are moral persons, at least in potential, capable of moral feeling and self-judgment. Their morality reaches into the heart, seizes the self.

Transcultural vs. Culture Specific Features of Emotion

Newars understand and experience mental life in ways shaped by their distinctive cultural tradition; their ethnopsychology is a local form, based on "local knowledge" of self that in part constitutes their psychological world for them. And yet some of what Newars say and assume about mental life seems familiar: many of the categories and concepts used by Newars correspond roughly to what is designated by such English psychological terms as desire, memory, thought, emotion, shame, intention, and resolution. The social and cultural meaning of the states and processes that correspond to these terms are not precisely the same as in English (Wierzbicka 1986). But there is at least a family resemblance.

Agency vs. Passive Experiencing

Not just discrete concepts, but also some of what is posited about the organization of psychological experience seems in some ways similar in the American and the Newar models. One interesting cross-cultural parallel is the way that some mental states can be represented either as involving parts of the self, or as engaging the core of self (D'Andrade 1987: 118–119; Levy 1984: 221). This shapes the ways a self can relate to itself within the bounds of intrapsychic life: people can be seen either as passive experiencers (as the objects of other part of their minds) or as agents of psychological states (having intentional control over aspects of mental life).

Both Newars and Americans seem to assume that people may experience themselves as being the agent of some states of mind, but as the passive experiencer (or object) of other states (D'Andrade 1987: 118–119). Newars do not will themselves to feel ashamed; the emotion originates within them, but is experienced by them. It happens to them. But when Newars resolve to stop drinking alcohol or thinking "bad" thoughts, they are attempting to do something to themselves, rather than passively experiencing something happening to them. They relate to themselves as agents in mental acts of intending, deliberating, and choosing.

In Newari, as in English, there are verbal forms and expressions that reflect the distinction of "a passive experiencer," and "intentional agent." D'Andrade (1987: 118) gives the examples of "the thought struck me" versus "I thought," and "I am afraid" versus "I fear." The Newar model seems similar to the American model in that it too "treats the self as an area of focus that can expand and contract, but the limit of its contraction lies outside the core act of intending" (D'Andrade 1987: 119). The core of the self can be experienced as inside or outside an emotion, so that self may be identified with an emotion, or viewed as passively experiencing it. For example, Newars seem to sometimes view anger as involving the intentional core of the self, the intending "I," while at other moments they may conceptualize it as a process happening to a person, in which the intentional core of the self is not (yet) fully engaged—but might become so.

Newars have two ways of speaking of anger. To say "anger came out to me" (*ta(n) piha wala*) is to indicate that a process of anger is happening to self; to say "I felt angry" (*ji ta(n) caya*), according to some informants, seems to involve more of a commitment of self, and seems to shift the semantic focus from process to action. One Newar explained that when a person throws things, or yells, or fights, "he [or she] feels angry" (*wa ta(n) cala*) is the appropriate verbal form; the anger is shown in the actions. This suggests that this expression refers to intentional states. One informant characterized "anger came out to me" as happening before such angry acts; a person might warn another not to speak or do something because "anger comes out to me." This suggests that anger is viewed here as a process happening to the self that might lead to actions; anger is treated as something that is "building up," but has not yet involved the intentional core of the self. When it does, the emotion will be acted on; a shift occurs, so that anger is no longer something happening to the self, but something self is doing. It becomes intentional.

The conception of anger as something that happens to the self, rather than something the self does is perhaps more salient for Newars, because frequent or excessive anger is subject to disapproval. Only justified anger is likely to be seen or portrayed as involving the "I," the intentional self. Typically, this involvement must be explained. One informant noted that it felt unnatural to say "I felt angry," without giving an account of why you were feeling angry. You would, he thought, ordinarily say why you felt angry, and then conclude by saying "and then I felt angry" (*ale ji ta(n) caya)*. When anger is justified, the experience of anger can be reconceptualized: anger happens to the self, but, under some conditions, the intending core of self is identified with the anger. A commitment to being angry arises, and anger becomes an intentional process. The person becomes involved as a whole—as an agent, not just as passive experiencer.

This may hold cross-culturally. For example, Lakoff and Kövecses (1987) examine the metaphorical structure of ways of speaking of anger in American English; the cognitive model of anger they identify resembles the "hydraulic" model of academic psychology in that anger builds up, creates pressure, and seeks release in an outburst or explosion. I think the metaphorical structure of these models may culturally represent and map out the process-action sequence, that is, the movement from passive experiencing to engagement as an intentional agent. The notion of self-engagement seems equally relevant to alternatives to the hydraulic model. Sabini and Silver (1982), for example, discuss the possibility of a "moral account" of anger, where anger (and the shift from process to action) has to do with transgression and retribution, rather than with frustration and aggression. Even more than the hydraulic account, a moral analysis of anger would seem to presuppose some concept of agency.[14]

Thus, I would speculate that the engagement of the "whole person" or "intentional core of the self," is a precondition of moral action, in Newar society and elsewhere. Take the example of shame, or lajya, as a response to wrongdoing; this feeling seems to happen to a person, but also engages the core of the self. Shame is something that happens to the self as a passive experiencer. One does not will shame to happen, and a self does not have direct control over it. And yet shame is not a moral emotion only because it serves as a kind of external force acting on self. People do fear being shamed and feeling shamed; shame does act on the self, producing anxiety and distress. But there is (at least sometimes) a deeper engagement of the self. Although one does not will shame to happen, and has no control over it, once felt, the person may respond not only by avoiding actions that induce shame (making shame a kind of aversive conditioning) but by intending not to do wrong (making it a matter of self-control). The person can respond with deliberations, reflections, intentions, resolutions—that is, as an intentional agent. The feeling may be unwilled, but the core of

the self can be involved in taking a stand on the breach of the relationship of self and world that gave rise to the feeling. The distress
associated with moral feelings—the pain they cause—pushes the
core of the self to respond, to commit itself to some course of action
that may resolve difficulties that have arisen in the relation of self
to social world.

What Americans call "shame" and what Newars call "lajya" may
thus have a similar, even identical organization, at this level. Cultural *differences* in the way emotions are known and experienced,
however, are at least as important as cross-cultural commonalities,
as Richard Shweder (1992a, 1992b) has pointed out in his investigation of South Asian emotions. If the "deep" semantic or psychological structure of these emotions (the way people conceptualize
shame and lajya in relation to themselves) are similar in some
important respects, in ways that may help shape the way the emotion may be experienced and acted on, the cultural contexts within which Americans actually experience and evaluate shame, and
Newars, lajya, seem radically different.

One key difference is the relationship of these emotions to the
culturally constituted moral order of their respective societies.
Newars typically view lajya as a moral state; but shame, for many
Americans, is not a moral state; the capacity to feel shame is not
treated by American culture as an essential attribute of the moral
person, and no cultural consensus exists that shame is necessary
for integrating the experiencing self into the moral community. As
often as not, for Americans, shame is a problem—it makes the self
less than it can be. Some Americans apparently possess a model of
shame that defines shame as a form of "low self-esteem," or as the
cause of low self-esteem; as such, shame saps a person's will and
drive, and thus it can stand in the way of the individual achieving
his or her goals, of reaching his or her "full potential."

Perceived in this way, shame is not a moral emotion. It is not a
moral state, but a psychological state that stands in the way of realizing key moral values, of becoming the kind of person valued in
American culture. To an American who experiences shame it may
make sense to try to eliminate the capacity to experience such
painful feelings; the emotion may trigger an effort to alter the relationship of self and world by altering the experiencing self, making
it shame-free. To most Newars, and the people of many other cultures, the desire to be without shame would not make sense, since

the capacity for and sensitivity to shame is part of what makes one a person, a moral person, more than an uninhibited animal who will "do anything."

Diversity

It is worth stressing that any culture may contain a range of ways of knowing self. This is certainly true of Newar culture. Often, postulates about self that seem to be based on universals can be reframed in more culturally specialized terms; people can shift between different perspectives on personhood, relevant in different contexts. For example, Newars see desires as a given of personal existence; having desires is necessary and natural. They can shift perspectives, however, and drawing on their cultural tradition view desire in other ways. "If a man has no desires," I ask a Brahman, "what would he feel?"

If there were no desires—if a man had no desires—it would be like being sick. There would be hopelessness [*niraj*]. There are two kinds of hopelessness. There is suffering [dukha] and [so] hopelessness develops. There is knowledge and hopelessness develops. A renouncer [*jannyaji*] is one who experiences hopelessness through knowledge. He has knowledge but he has no hope for the world. . . .[This] is hopelessness, but even so for the *paramatma* [soul, oversoul of which the individual soul is part], there is hope. While a renouncer must hope with [in terms of] the paramatma, he has no worldly hope. . . . But a sick person, a man who suffers greatly, he despairs because he has no money, no medicine, because he is ill, and has no rest. This too is a kind of hopelessness. In these there are no desires. [The informant qualifies his remarks.] There can be desires in sick people.
(What is the relationship [of hopelessness] with desire?)
Desires are for oneself.

In Newar culture, the desire to be without desire makes sense. It is a religious value, even though few Newars desire to be ascetics—or lack the desire to enjoy the world. Even as nonascetics, they see renunciation as radically reframing the way mental life is conceived, and as giving it a special ethical and soteriological twist. Ordinary models do not apply to special cases. Informants insisted that ordinary people, nonascetics like themselves, would have desires. Some found it hard to answer the question of what would it be like to be without desires. One person remarked that even very sick "hopeless" people have desires—they want to die.

Culture and Self

D'Andrade (1987: 146) suggests that even if parts of cultural models of mind are based on universal psychological experience, other parts may be related to the ecological and social structure of a community, and still other parts may be "legacies from the past"—historical formations unrelated either to current conditions of life or to universals of psychological experience. The Newar case leads to similar conclusions. Some elements of Newar conceptions of person, mind, and self seem to be due to social and political factors, while others can be seen as reflecting the cultural history of the Newars, especially the way they have made cultural and religious developments in South Asia part of their own worldview and cultural selves. Other aspects of Newar concepts of an inner life seem to reflect universals, near universals, or probable forms of mental experience.

The Newar material suggests that fully understanding how people understand psychological life (and use their psychological theories to understand themselves and others) will involve a range of approaches. It will certainly require examining the local organization of mental life and the way psychological experience is grounded in specific historical conditions and cultural frames. In the Newar case, this includes attention to religious and moral ideas. I believe it will also require that this body of data and theory be related to more universalist perspectives on mind, which take account of the way mental life reflects transcultural existential, ethical, psychological, and linguistic experiences.

I do think culture helps constitute distinct inner worlds of mind, self, and emotion. To paraphrase Edward Sapir (1929), the psychological worlds of persons of different cultures are different worlds, "not merely the same world with different labels attached."[15] The Newar mind is not a generic mind with an ethnic label attached. Rather, Newars possess customized psyches, culturally different minds, cultural selves—up to a point.

"Everything is symbol," wrote Søren Kierkegaard in this book *Either/Or*: "I myself am a myth about myself, for is it not as a myth that I hasten to this meeting? Who I am has nothing to do with it." This could serve as the motto of a psychocultural relativism that I find compelling in many ways—not, however, to the point of becoming an absolute relativist. Consciousness is, in part, symbolically constituted; cultural models may shape not just what people think, but how they think. Self-concept is part cultural myth, woven out of cultural meaning; in some ways, we do meet each other as myths about ourselves, with self-images and emotional worlds compounded out of different symbols and meanings, the product of different histories, cultures, and lives. And yet—I also think "Who I am" has something to do it; who we are as biological beings must also matter. Mind is embodied in a brain, in neural networks, in a body of flesh. Surely, nature's mind makes culture's mind possible—and must leave traces even in our cultural consciousness.

The challenge facing us is to find ways of recognizing significant cultural differences in mind, emotion, and self, without obscuring the role and significance of their more universal aspects. In sorting this out, the positions of absolute relativists and absolute universalists seem less interesting and useful than the emerging biocultural and cultural psychology paradigms (Shweder 1990).

Thus, while I have adopted a cultural perspective here, I do not advocate a one-sided cultural approach. It is all too easy to slip into a cultural determinism that is as one-dimensional and limiting as psychological reductionism. The fact that emotions are socially and culturally constituted does not necessarily entail the view that social actors are simply programmed by culture to have certain emotions. Social actors are not merely passive receivers of emotional discourse, incapable of acting on and restructuring that discourse in any way. They are agents and subjects of cultural life, biographical, biological, and cultural selves, at the same time—thinking, feeling, and cultural beings all at once. The social and cultural structuring of emotion does not rule out the psychological and biographical structuring of emotion anymore than the importance of culture in emotional life means biology plays no role. Rather, these are complementary perspectives.

For example, the feeling of virtue—or the feeling of moral failure—associated with lajya is felt by actual persons in actual life-situations. This interfusing of culture, feeling, and life moves people to evaluate themselves and their world, preparing them to be moral agents. Lajya is a virtue, generated within the moral order, as well as a feeling, generated within the human body. It is a moral state embodied in emotional knowing, bringing biological potential and cultural meaning together.

Thus, to point out that models found in different cultures make similar assumptions about the categories or organization of mental experience is not to say that the ways in which these assumptions are fleshed out, represented, and reconstructed in particular cultures do not make a difference. They do. The Newar model of mind, emotion, and self takes forms of experience and knowing that may be universal, fuses them with culture, develops and shapes them into local forms of experience and knowing. Newar concepts of a psychologically active and morally sensitive "heart," their vision of a moral god animating and inhabiting this heart-self, and their cultural experience of moral emotions, all help articulate a concept of the person. These ideas build on, and elaborate, the notion that self can passively experience, and yet actively evaluate, thoughts and feelings originated by other parts of self. This culturally envisioned and experienced Newar self integrates a capacity for self-knowledge and self-control (however problematic) with sensitivity to moral emotions.

Newar ethnopsychology thus articulates a concept of a person as at once an agent and a passive experiencer within a complex internal world, and places this concept of the person in a religious and ethical context. Newar concepts of mind, emotion, and self help Newars know that persons are constituted as moral beings, with an "inner" life that participates in the moral and the sacred. Mind, self, and experience are part of the moral order.

CHAPTER FIVE

Creating Moral Selves

In a popular Newari short story,[1] a young boy eagerly anticipates a rite of passage being planned for him. The rite will initiate him into adulthood and integrate him into his caste; but the boy, Jagat, looks forward to it in part because he does not know what it means. He does not know what he is going to lose—a whole way of being and relating to others. He does not anticipate the loss of freedom, the fundamental changes to occur in his relationships, that will flow from the way the rites give new meaning to, and redefine the terms for, relatedness. He is excited, envisioning his initiation as a special day with himself as the center of attention. He does not really see that he will be transformed into another kind of person. His mother, a widow, struggles to make it possible for him to undergo the rite, which is called *kaeta puja*. Brahman priests are expensive, and she is poor. But to conduct the rite for her son is a matter of dharma and of ijjat; she is under pressure from relatives to have the rite performed, and to invite her kin to the convivial feast that goes with religious rites. Worried and sad, she manages to cope—she overcomes the obstacles to performing the rite, and smiles at her child's excitement. At the end of the story, her son finds out the rite of passage is a passage away from what he was. He goes to his best friend's place to tell him that he will be initiated, and finds him at home eating fried meat and dried rice. When Jagat tells his friend this news, his friend bursts into tears, and explains how it will be. "Jagat, now you must give up eating with me and eating food I have touched. Now that it's fixed that you will [be initiated], you can't eat things touched by me anymore. You are *Seyɔya* [high caste], and I'm a farmer. It is said, if you eat what I've touched, you will lose your caste." Jagat wipes the tears from his friend's eyes, eats his friend's cipa (food that contains the substance of the person who first tasted it, and which will be polluting for Jagat after the rite of kaeta puja) and says, "I won't have my kaeta puja." In this way he expresses his closeness to his friend, who now breaks into tears of joy, and hugs Jagat with both arms.

There the story ends. What the story does not say, but what the reader knows, is that Jagat will undergo the rite, will assume his caste, and will lose the intimacy he had with people from lower castes. In the Newar traditional world, the person who has not undergone the basic life-cycle rites, the samskara, is radically incomplete. For the rites place self in society. They signify a moral world, and it is the duty of parents to ensure that their children "see" the rites that mark and evoke this world.

The Educational Samskara

The Newar samskara, like the idea of dharma, have roots deep in the South Asian tradition. The samskara to be explored here consist of a set of life-cycle rites performed during childhood. This set is preceded by others performed during infancy, and followed by marriage, old age, and death rites. All samskara cultivate certain values, and encourage certain turns of mind in those who participate or observe them as well as seek to achieve ritual ends. The rites I will discuss here focus on the awakening consciousness of the child—they supply values and ways of viewing self, society, and the world. These childhood rites bring the child into the moral world as an actor who is expected to have an awareness—not full awareness, but an emergent awareness—of what cultural life requires of social actors. It is for this reason that I term them educational samskara.

In this chapter, I will explore the personal and moral meaning of these rites, and suggest how they may shape a sense of self. I will neglect many aspects of the structure and symbolism of the rituals.[2] My concern is not with the meaning of any ritual per se, but with meanings that relate persons to cultural forms and life. I seek not to interpret the rituals, but to see how Newars interpret the rituals in relationship to a "self" imagined as a moral being. My focus is thus not on ritual structure and symbolism, but on rituals as extensions of self, as "mediating devices" (Holland and Valsiner 1988) for self-making. The experience of the rites, I will argue, creates personal meanings and emotional resonances that are important for the psychological and cultural work of fashioning a moral identity. They generate a moral context for self-knowing.

For Newars, the samskara are a set of obligatory rites, and as such they have a meaningful ritual structure; this can properly be studied as a semiotic system, without addressing the way the rites relate culture and self—but the samskara do relate culture and self. Talk of the samskara is often at least implicitly self-referential; these rites declare what and who Newars are, and where they are going in life, thus providing Newars with one kind of answer to Gauguin's existential questions. This process has both sociological and psychological significance, since it flows from the way the rites coordinate culture and self, social structure and mental structure, giving these crucial coordinates tangible form in ritual practice.

What the Hindu Samskara Are

The range of meanings assigned to the term samskara in classical Sanskrit texts is instructive. Pandey (1969:16) enumerates the use of the term

> in the sense of education, cultivation, training; refinement, perfection and grammatic purity; making perfect, refining, polishing; embellishment, decoration and ornament; impression, form, mould, operation, inbuence; the faculty of recollection, impression on the memory; . . . a sacred rite or ceremony; consecration, sanctification and hallowing; idea, notion and conception; effect of work, merit of action.

He notes a text that views the samskara as proceeding by "the removal of taints (sins) or by the generation of fresh qualities" (1969:16). Inden and Nicholas (1977:37) offer a similar list: "The word samskara means to 'complete,' 'prepare,' 'make over,' 'fully form,' and, above all, to 'purify' (*suddhi*)."

The notion of acting upon something to change it into something more valued in appearance or form is suggested by these glosses. The samskara are a process that removes, adds, or transforms qualities to create a person with certain ritual, social, and moral characteristics. It is ritual work that brings out the values or qualities desired. As a near equivalent for samskara, Pandey suggests the word "sacrament" as used in Catholicism to refer to such rites as baptism, confirmation, or marriage. This may be a dangerous analogy, but captures the ritual aspect—the sense of samskara as a numinous religious rite.

As Inden and Nicholas (1977:38) point out, the analogy breaks down because the cultural meanings of the respective rites differ in some fundamental ways: roughly speaking, the Hindu rites are more concerned with the total, socially embodied, person and not just his spiritual essence. The Newars are concerned not so much with visible signs of an "inner grace," as with the religiously marked boundaries of moral lives in society. The rites mark the passage of individuals through the moral career of the householder—a passage that is sacred, permanent, and ends with death and salvation.

The notion that a person is being "cultivated," "refined," and "trained" is relevant for the Hindu Newar conception of samskara. The samskara are, like the sacraments Pandey mentions as analogous forms, associated with key life-cycle events: birth, maturation, menarche, marriage, and death.

In Newar culture, the innate, unrefined "mind" or "individual" is not viewed as sufficient for life in society or for transcendence. Empirical individuals are not born complete, but incomplete, needing qualities that must be established through rituals. They cannot give themselves these qualities; the moral community must organize the performances of the samskara that ritually transform the person, altering their being or nature. A Newar farmer explicitly linked "nature" or "self-being" (*swabhav*) and the rite of kaeta puja:

> Wherever he is, his nature (swabhav) won't be lost. A child's nature comes out. As long as kaeta puja has not been done, a child's nature comes out. After kaeta puja, a youth's nature comes out. After kaeta puja, when he is married, then maturity will come out. [Ganesh Lal]

I think this posits a principle of conservation: without ritual, people will not change or develop; their "nature won't be lost." Only the performance of ritual has the power to transform—as long as the rite of kaeta puja has not been done, a child remains a child, and no other "state of being" can emerge. Only a child's nature "comes out."

This emphasis on ritual transformation contrasts sharply with Western conceptions of child development as a natural, endogenous process, in which modes of thought, feeling, and moral judgment unfold in "natural" stages given a minimum of appropriate experience. The locus of such "development" is in the individual; the locus of the samskara is a web of relatedness, in which social actors are mutually responsible for each other's "states of being." The samskara stress interdependency, since others act on and for the "self." The samskara are devices for cultivating a certain kind of mind and person—polished and perfected ritually, freed from the taints and limits of natural "being."

For Newars, creating a moral self is not a natural process, but a ritual process. While many in Western cultures take "nature" as the ultimate reality, and attempt to validate themselves and cultural practices by appealing to "nature," traditional Newars attempt to construct and validate "reality" in terms of ritual. Ritual transformation is more important than natural development for Newars, since, in their worldview, "rites" are more real than "nature." I believe this attitude sensitizes them to ritual form, and makes them receptive to the process of fashioning self in ritual terms.

Thus, as we shall see, the samskara do not promote individualism, or individual self-expression outside the contours of traditional social life. The individual has value and reality for Newars, but the ritual transformation of the person is a necessary process: the "self" does not lack cultural recognition, but is valued as embedded in relationships. Individuals are given ways of reflexively knowing and valuing themselves within this matrix of social relationships. The "natural" mind and unsocialized individual that might develop without cultural guidance are viewed as problematic, as not fully social and moral. The educational samskara sanctify and dramatize a person's capture by the moral system.

This process has a particular and complex organization among Newars. The samskara consist of a developmental *sequence* of life cycle rites. The purpose of these rites is to produce a certain kind of finished person, but they do so by established increments. A person is never entirely finished; no final version of the self exists, for a person needs to change at certain thresholds in life. The educational samskara help prepare Newars for life in society, the samskara of marriage makes them full participants in kuldharma, and other samskara mark a withdrawal from society, preparation for death, death itself, and certain post-death transformations.

The major Newar rites of passage are:

1. *Jhivasodhana*: "writing a mantra on the tongue" and *Namakarana*: "namegiving." Rites associated with birth.
2. *Maca janko*: the first rice feeding (*ja cipa(n) thiyekegu*). In this rite, the infant is fed boiled rice, symbolizing movement away from total dependency on its mother and toward greater involvement with others.[3]
3. *Busakha*: the hair-shaving ceremony. A rite for boys, marking developments in social identity that separate them from females and members of other castes.
4. *Kaeta puja*: "rite of the loincloth." A rite for boys marking full membership in their social group and caste. The rite may include giving the sacred thread for certain high castes, such as Brahmans.
5. *Ihi*: the symbolic "marriage" of Newar girls to a deity, Vishnu/Narayana. This rite dramatizes the developing social identity of girls, as females and members of their social group.
6. *Barha* ceremonies: confinement at menarche (*barha cwa(n)gu*) or in preparation for menarche (*barha taegu*).
7. *Byaha*: primary marriage (a marriage with rites, as opposed to "marriage" not formalized ritually).
8. *Budhabudhi janko*: a rite of old age, celebrating survivorship as a victory over death.
9. *Cremation, Dasa Kriya, and Sraddha*: death rites.

Here I have organized the samskara according to a provisional analytic scheme, with brief explanations.

1. Orienting samskara: birth to eight months. The rites "protect" and "nurture" the child. The rites orient adults to children by signifying the child's potentiality as a social actor and moral being, and

by marking the child's place in the web of relatedness. The children who are the focus of the rites are precultural, at least in terms of their capacity to decode the kind of cultural symbols found in the rites, and so are not affected by the "messages" of the rites. Hence the rites are not educational for them, although they may be for older children who observe them as spectators.

2. Educational samskara: For boys, the rite of busakha takes place between ages three to eleven years; the rite of kaeta puja takes place after busakha, usually between ages five to eleven. The two rites may be blended together in a single sequence, or separated by a number of years.

For girls, the rite of ihi takes place between five and eleven years of age, while bara is associated with menarche. It may take place at or before a girl's first menstruation. (The premenstrual version is called barha taegu, while the rite at menarche is termed barha cwa(n)gu).

As educational forms, busakha and ihi are perhaps marginal; they may be done before the child's cognitive development enables him or her to appreciate something of the form or significance of the event.[4] Kaeta puja (for boys) and barha (for girls) repeat the basic themes of the boy's earlier busakha and the girl's earlier ihi. Each gender specific pair (busakha and kaeta puja, ihi and barha) share something of the same basic themes; the system is redundant. The rites stress self-restraint, the importance of duties, and social embeddedness. Although these samskara affect children, they of course also orient adults to the children, and may reinforce an adult's understanding of the moral system. An important and distinctive characteristic of this group of rites, however, is the play of the ritual's meaning on the child's mind—the rites can capture the child's growing self-awareness for the moral system. The child and adults are "coordinated" via reflexivity and mutually meaningful interaction.

In terms of the cultural order, ihi, the mock-marriage to a god, legitimizes the relative freedom of Newar women, without being too overtly subversive of Hindu orthodoxy (Allen 1982). The form of the rite is a Hindu marriage ceremony; but the marriage to a god—who can never die—is sometimes offered as a justification for allowing women to remarry when their human husbands die, which would be prohibited under orthodox Hinduism as practiced by some powerful segments of the wider society. Myth has it that the goddess Parvati, daughter of the god of the Himalayas, came across an old woman crying because her husband had died. The old woman told Parvati that the life of a widow was terrible. Moved to pity by the women's plight, Parvati asked Shiva to prevent women from ever becoming widows in the Himalayas, her home. Shiva agreed, making Narayana the immortal groom of all women so they could never become widows, which is interpreted by some to mean women can take a series of human mates. Others may contest this interpretation, and remarriage in fact often carries some stigma; but the rite and myth do offer some grounds for evading the requirements of strict orthodoxy, for muting disapproval, and reflect the nonorthodox values and practices of some segments of Hindu Newar society.

As I explained in the introduction, my material on women's experience and thought is thinner than my data on men, reflecting local conventions regarding gender interaction. In particular, the rites have associations with sexuality that make them more difficult for a male researcher to explore in person-centered terms, although it is of course possible to describe them in some detail, and several accounts have been published (Allen 1982; Vergati 1982; Levy 1990), although none of these fully explore the cultural psychology of the rites. Since the female rites have been described elsewhere, and my data on their personal meanings are thinner, I will not discuss them here.

3. Marriage (age variable): Marriage brings full integration into society as a mature adult with the complete responsibilities of a householder, although a man's father will continue as head of household as long as he is alive (if competent to carry out the role) and the family has not divided.

4. Budhabudhi janko: This rite is first performed when a person becomes seventy-seven years, seven months, and seven days old, and celebrates victory over death. The celebrant sits in a small chariot, and is pulled around a courtyard or neighborhood. This rite treats surviving as a kind of transcendence; the person who undergoes this rite is nominally "like a god." As such, he or she is no longer part of society in the normal sense; this rite marks a graceful withdrawal from ordinary social affairs and a turning toward death and dying.

5. Death rites: A complex set of rites related to dying, mourning, and the salvation of the dead. The samskara are sometimes said to end with cremation, and a transition is made to rites that transform "ghost" into "spirit," and provide maintenance (offerings of food, water, devotion, and respect) for the dead.

Nature of the Educational Samskara

Each samskara performs an action which is intended ideally to bring a person into some part of the moral system; marriage ideally coincides with a full integration, where the mature adult embodies the values of a householder; and, for individuals surviving to that age, budha janko marks a withdrawal from involvement in society.

Take the case of a Newar boy, our primary focus in this chapter. Each successive samskara provides a new grip for the moral system. The moral system is embodied in the expectations of others; as the child passes through the samskara, significant others begin to hold him accountable to new sets of expectations and definitions. The child is perhaps responsive to changed definitions of self because the rites have caught his attention, and stirred his interest and excitement in anticipation. As the focus of the rites, he is made to feel important. The attentions of adults are gratifying. All this, I believe, is conducive to impressing on him a new sense of self, and a new conception of how he ought to behave. The rites also impress him with a sense of the importance of interdependence. The rites are vital for his development as a "self," but they also reveal the depth of embeddedness in the web of relatedness; others must actively organize and perform the rites that transform the self.

The performance of the samskara set into motion changes in self-image. The child undergoing the rite has, by virtue of the performance of that rite, a different place in the social world, a new status. If children do not know this when they undergoes the rite, they soon will, since others will respond to them according to the new definitions. When they behave inappropriately, others will criticize them; they will be ridiculed for lapses, and exhorted to behave in ways appropriate for those who have undergone the rites. This reminds them of their new status and of the expectation that go with it. As new definitions and expectations coalesce around them children are pushed to keep pace with these changes, to come to grips with them emotionally and cognitively. If children do not immediately and fully appreciate the ritually catalyzed changes in their social personhood, they will find their social world decaying around him: they will, willy-nilly, be forced to change in order to cope with the behaviors directed to them by significant others. This is probably typically the case: rites do not change the child's overall sense of self in a second, but through their temporal reach, the way they shape the terms of future social interaction.

In essence, the child is moved to ask questions of culture, to find answers in culture, to search for the meaning of these events and changes. This involves a dialogue with culture. When Newar chil-

dren perceive change in their personal world, they may respond
with questions, perhaps never consciously formulated, concerning
self—What am I now? What do these events mean for me? How
am I related to others? How should I behave?—and will find
answers in culture. A child must find some way to reconcile change
with self. Rites of passage mark changes in social status, but the
rites also pose problems of meaning and identity, of change and
integration, for social actors, who must interpret themselves, culture, and society. The Newar rites sensitize children to changes in
status, and prompt them to reinterpret themselves and their relationship to society and to cultural practices. Adult discourse and
responses provide material for self-interpretation, for redefining
self, and for fashioning a culturally coherent personal identity.

This redefining takes time. It is not enough to shout at a child,
in so many words, or in a single ritual performance, that "You're
an adult now" as if expecting an instant transformation of the sense
of self. The human material is slower, if eager enough in following
leads—into culture. The clear message about a change in self is followed by a long process of working out the meaning of the message and the changes. When the rites work—by provoking and
guiding processes of self-making—the long-term result is a life
lived in terms of culture, because the psychological work of forming an identity takes account of the experiences and meanings that
were part of the life-cycle rites. The rites provide a framework for
self-socialization; a person does not passively "internalize" and
"enact" cultural norms, but rather actively engages in psychological work through which culture may be made part of self, and self
part of society.

The process of education is continuous; throughout a lifetime,
an individual will observe and participate in rites he or she has
already undergone as the focal figure. This may help maintain the
orientations and commitments acquired through experiencing the
rites. Newars also observe rites that they may undergo in the
future. And so a sense of the unity of life is built up. This is evident
in Newar accounts.

The rites help mediate self-making by giving cultural meaning to
self, identity, and relatedness. By stimulating a dialogue between
self and culture, the samskara help crystallize self-awareness. The
dialogue of self and culture makes possible a person who is prepared to find meaning in the Newar way of life, who is committed

to family and caste life, who knows how to be responsible, and who is capable of self-control. I will now turn to the ethnographic accounts on which I base these tentative generalizations. Keep in mind that this discussion focuses on processes of reflexivity and meaning construction associated with the rites, not on their ritual structure or symbolism per se.

I will use two extended accounts—one by Krishna Bahadur, the other by Shiva Bhakta. I will also examine what some other Newars said about the functions and purposes of the rites. My focus is on the moral and personal meaning they find in the rites— what the rites mean to them. I describe only as many details of the rites as is necessary to understand the moral themes and values that are either being discussed or which tacitly organize the discussion, by being presupposed or implied. A full treatment of the rites themselves would require a separate, thick volume.

Kaeta puja: Krishna's Account

In the following account Krishna Bahadur, of the borderline pure Gatha caste, describes the samskara of kaeta puja, the giving of a loincloth. He describes the purification and fasting preceding the rite, the preliminary offering made to the dead (sraddha), the setting of an auspicious time, and the performance of busakha (tonsure) as a subsidiary rite incorporated, for his jat—his caste, or "kind"—within the larger rite of kaeta puja.

> To do kaeta puja, first you fast, eating only one meal. You only eat one meal for the entire day. The father, the head of the family, the old ones, they bathe and then have one meal. And then the next day, you call the Barber to shave [the celebrant's] hair. The Brahman[5] is brought and sraddha is done. . . . And then we call the members of our family and lineage, the women married into the household, our nephews, we call them in order to worship for the spirits of the dead, our grandfathers and grandmothers. While rites are performed for the dwellers in heaven, for the dead, for those who no longer are, the Brahman priest recites a Sanskrit text.

Offerings are then made to the dead, of round balls of flour (*pindas*), powder, sesame seeds, cow milk, Ganges water, "this kind of thing is all offered" respectfully. "All offer [the dead] water."

If you do this for the dead, your misfortunes will be removed. In your mind, too, there will be joy. If the dead give a blessing, then seven generations will have wealth also. You have to do this.

The interweaving of themes here is complex: much that we have touched on is implicit here. Fasting marks this as extraordinary; it separates the rite from the everyday, as does the shaving of the celebrant's head. Notice the emphasis on relatedness: living kin are called to participate in the rites, and the dead of the family are the object of ritual attention and involvement. The audience of the rite gathers around the celebrant, who is the focus of attention, as well as the passive subject of ritual action.

After the rite for the dead is finished, the Astrologer is brought to set the auspicious time, the hour, the minute, the exact time. At the exact time, the Barber comes. Then, the boy's own paju [mother's brother], and his own nini [father's sister], they cut his hair like this [gesturing a cutting action], and put it in a plate.

The mother's brother cuts locks of hair, which are placed on a plate held by the father's sister; the Barber then shaves the child's head, except the *angsa*, a lock of hair at the back of the head that is an important symbolic referent for the householder stage of life. To cut the angsa signifies renunciation. Notice here the interdependencies of caste and kinship; the Astrologer and Barber are needed to perform the rite, and so are mother's brother and father's sister (or substitutes, if the boy should not have one or the other). The mother's brother has additional roles: at one point in the rite, in some Newar groups, the boy will attempt to run away "to the forest," which symbolizes renunciation; his paju will catch him and bring him back. (In some accounts, the paju is said to tell the boy not to make his mother sad.)

The moment of giving the boy the kaeta is a significant one. He stands naked before family, kin, and other invited guests. His paju ties on the loincloth, and then he is dressed in new clothes.

Then everyone comes and the loincloth is tied on him. A hat [actually a turban] is put on him, and he is dressed in new clothes. And then they gather together puja materials, puja

materials for the head of household to take with him, along with a small goat — and then, playing music, the whole group goes to the shrine of the goddess Brahmani.

Trying to define the emotions of another at a particular moment, when it is inappropriate to ask — and even if you could ask, you would likely get a conventional response, not what a person is actually feeling — is fraught with difficulties. For what it is worth, let me say that when I observed this rite performed for Krishna's son, the boy was not agitated or outwardly excited; he did not laugh or cry. He did not assert himself in any way I could see. I would say he felt rather anxious and uncertain about the attention. He was less animated than the adults. I assume that children will experience the rites in different ways, but in the few cases I observed, the children were rather quiet, their mood subdued.

A sacrifice at one of the protective goddess shrines surrounding the city is the next step. (This is a feature of most samskara.) When I observed a kaeta puja for this man's son, no music was played on the way to the shrine. The family could not afford to pay musicians, and so we walked, without fanfare, out of the city, and across the river to the shrine. There a goat was sacrificed, and blood was sprayed on the unworked stones that embody the goddess. The body of the goat was then taken some little distance away, and the put on a fire, to burn off the hair; the animal was butchered, and roasted, and some of it was offered to the goddess, and to the elephant-headed god Ganesh. Krishna's descriptions followed what actually happened quite closely.

After the offering, the head of the household gives prasad to everyone. He distributes it to those doing kaeta puja, and then gives them sacred marks. He gives them flowers. Then they eat [a small amount at the shrine]. After eating, the puja is finished. Then they circumambulate the deity and return to the house.

At the feast given in celebration of the kaeta puja in some castes or thars the boy will sit at or near the head of the line of diners ranked by seniority. Krishna explains the purpose of the rite in terms of the assumption of ritual and social responsibilities.

(Why is kaeta puja done, then?)

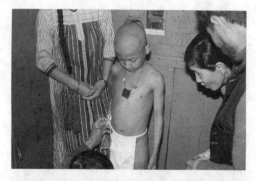

FIGURE 24 A boy receives his loincloth during his *kaeta puja.*

FIGURE 25 Dressed in new clothes, signifying a new state of personhood, the boy is the center of ritual attention during *kaeta puja.*

FIGURE 26 The boy receives a coin from a relative. Note how other children watch closely.

Before doing kaeta puja, you should not marry. The main reason kaeta puja is necessary is—before it, you should not marry. Only if you have finished kaeta puja, are you ready to marry.

(And if you marry without doing kaeta puja, what happens?)

In the world, in front of people, it will be bad. You should not. It can't be done [said with emphasis].

(If you give a loincloth before kaeta puja, what will happen?)

You should not. If the priest has not been brought to do all the regular rites, then you should not.

(Before the loincloth is given, what is it all right to do?)

They are only children. They should play. They should study.
They can do anything. But they must not marry.
(And then after kaeta puja, what should one do?)
After kaeta puja, you must begin to live the life of a householder. You must carry your own house, your own burdens, your
own responsibility. You must feed your woman. And children
will come. You must organize everything. All your own kin will
come to see you—you have to feed them. If you have a mother
and father, they will feed them. But if you do not, then, you must
earn yourself. You must earn money, and put clothes on your
children.

The ritual of kaeta puja thus marks the transition to responsibility
and adult status. In his answer here, Krishna skips the years immediately after kaeta puja, in which a child will be groomed for adult
roles. Instead, Krishna brings into view the entire expanse of
Newar adulthood, and the career of the householder. Krishna, like
many Newars, thinks of kaeta puja in terms of the moral contours
of adult life. But children do not, of course, at once bear the full
"burdens" of adult life.[6] They spend some years in a kind of cultural apprenticeship in adulthood, during which certain behaviors
are targeted and sanctioned as no longer fitting or proper. The rites
evoke a personhood that must be developed, sculpted, and polished over time.

After kaeta puja, a Newar must do dharma, and is responsible
for his successors in the kul, his children.

(After kaeta puja, what should you do?)
After kaeta puja, you yourself must think good thoughts. You
must do dharma. If you do dharma, your sons and daughters will
be better off. Understanding [buddhi] will develop.[7] If you do
whatever you like, then your sons will do like that too. They will
go bad. You have to make a great name for yourself. What to do?
[you think,] so you have to worry.

Much is implied here. After the rite, Krishna feels a person
should engage in reflexive, psychological work, and strive to
have "good thoughts." A person also becomes a moral agent, and
must conform to the moral order by doing dharma. In essence,
what Krishna proposes is that self-making is a sequel to the
rite—a person must strive to create a moral self. This has a spe-

cial context: you make yourself a moral person for your sons and daughters, anticipating their need for a moral model. If you wish to have good children, and to be able to provide them with guidance, you must become good yourself—you exist as a moral being for your children, and alter self to shape their development as moral beings. Self-development is linked to the moral development of others. Tempering this altruism, Krishna adds that self-assertion is another sequel to the rites; the performance of the rites marks an entrance into the public world, where people feel they must make a name for themselves. Since their efforts to do so may result in painful failure, the prospect provokes doubts and anxiety.

The farmer Ganesh Lal gives the following account of kaeta puja:

(Do you have to do kaeta puja?)
We must.
(How do you perform kaeta puja?)
When we do kaeta puja first we must call a member of the Barber caste [to help with the purification process]. We must shave our hair. Then we bathe, purify, and do puja. We perform the rites for the dead. After the rites for the dead are finished, we feed all the guests. After that, the next morning, the hair of the one who is having kaeta puja is cut, his head is shaved. We perform puja then, too. Then we go to the god. We worship, we sacrifice a goat, and then we bring it back to the house. The syu [piece of the head of the sacrificed goat] is given to the one who is doing kaeta puja. Then all the relatives eat on leaf plates— they feast on beaten rice, beer, liquor, meat, goat meat, yogurt, all this part of the feast. It is good!

(Why do you do kaeta puja?)
We have always done so, from long ago. Everyone keeps this tradition.
(What happens if kaeta puja is not done?)
If this is not done, then when we die, we cannot be taken to the cremation grounds to burn.

For Ganesh, the relationship of the rite with death is salient. His discussion of the period before with the period after kaeta puja emphasizes the contrasts of dirtiness and impurity versus cleanliness and purity. He also raises the issue of ijjat, "honor, reputation, prestige."

> (Before being given a loincloth, what is permitted?)
> Before the loincloth is given, it does not matter if a child eats without cleaning himself after defecation, it does not matter if he eats without washing his face. It does not matter what he eats. After he has been given a kaeta, he cannot eat without cleaning [himself after defecating], he cannot eat unless he has washed his face. In the morning, he cannot eat without first worshiping god. So that is why we must go on giving the kaeta. Before he has received the kaeta, he is not yet pure. If he has been given the kaeta, then he has become pure.
> He will have ijjat too. If you do not give your son his kaeta until he is big, you will be told, "you don't care enough to give your son the kaeta." And children will say to your son, "Oh ho, your father won't give you the knowledge of karma" [lit., will not "show karma." Karma here has the meaning of "ritual action"]. You must see karma. You must tell your father to give you a kaeta right away." For this reason, and for our ijjat, we must keep on giving the kaeta. If we do not give the kaeta, our ijjat will vanish. There is no honor in money alone. These days, what does ijjat mean—whoever can feed the poor, whoever can feed their relatives, has ijjat. If someone eats only at other people's houses, then we are obliged to say that he has no honor.

Individuals who eat the food others offer, but never feed others are objects of contempt, since they do not engage either in altruism or reciprocity. Not only does the child come to know ijjat as a result of the rites, but after having undergone them, he can, through his actions, damage or enhance the ijjat of the family. The rites also establish and delineate ritual states of purity and impurity.

> It is a matter of making your own purity. Being pure means that wherever a person goes, his acts will be clean for him. Before the kaeta has been given, his actions are not yet clean. . . . What ever he might do, it is not all right for him to make the offerings [to the dead], it is not all right for him to do any ritual work. . . . Without being given the kaeta, he should not light the funeral fire of his mother and father.

There is a clear moral structure here: roles in the death rites of one's parents presuppose that one has been initiated. Certain duties in life can be fulfilled only if one has been initiated. One has to be "pure" for ritual purposes, and to maintain the purity of the house, the hearth, and the family.

Caste, Purity, and Shame as Samskaric Themes

The childhood educational samskara confirm caste status; while a person is born into a caste, the rites make caste an effective social and psychological fact. (Several Newars noted that an infant of an untouchable caste who still has the umbilical cord attached can be adopted by a Brahman.) Socially, the rites trigger a reorganization of patterns of interaction with others, bringing about a more active integration with the caste system; symbolically and psychologically, they align the "inner world" with the social reality of caste, making caste standing an attribute of self-identity. Govinda Raj observes:

> Kaeta puja is one of the most important of our ritual acts. It is important because, whatever caste a person is, he is not yet pure in that caste until this rite has been completed for him.
> (Not pure yet?)
> Not pure yet. He becomes a person of that jat [caste, kind] for certain only after kaeta puja . . . It becomes final only with the completion of the rite. Until then, his caste is not certain yet. Only after doing kaeta puja does his jat becomes stable and fixed. And only after kaeta puja do moral concerns, issues of what you should and should not do, matter very much. Before kaeta puja it does not matter much. A little bit, but not very much. Before the rite, he does not yet have caste. He does not yet have a sense of shame [lajya], he does not yet have knowledge [gyan]. Only after kaeta puja, does he become a person with knowledge [gyani]. While tying on the loincloth, you also bind him with the dharma. Moral prohibitions and prescriptions are a kind of rope. So when you tie him with these, he does not have the freedom he had before.

From this account, we can see how the rite pulls together many of the central elements of Newar moral experience—the rites evoke these in persons. Ganesh Lal echoes some of these themes:

(What happens if you do not do kaeta puja?)
If you don't do kaeta puja you don't have a place [*pakṣha*]. You would have no place in your own home, you would not be included. Not included—meaning, what would happen, suppose someone dies, for someone who is excluded—when he dies, we can't make the bamboo litter of the dead and take him to his cremation. If he has been give the kaeta, and he dies, we would have to make the stretcher and take him to the burning grounds.
(After kaeta has been given, what is it all right to do?)
After kaeta puja, what is necessary for us is kulacar [the code of conduct of the family line or caste]. Meaning that, just as the Brahmans have ritual initiations [dekha], so do we have this. . . Before kaeta puja, a person does not have a group.

At this point in the interview I ask Ganesh what children are like before doing kaeta puja and he gives the answer I quoted earlier, suggesting that a child's nature "comes out" before the rite, while a youth's nature emerges once the ritual has been performed. He goes on to say that before the rite has been performed for a child "whoever offers him food, he must eat"—regardless of their caste standing. "He can go ahead and eat." The rites declare—with ritual force—the activation of the rules against sharing food with others of lower status.

Ganesh Lal goes on to note that as a youth, after kaeta puja, a boy will feel lajya. A high-caste Newar speaks of the purpose of kaeta puja in this way:

Kaeta puja is one of the very most important rites. . . . Ideas of right and wrong do not count much for children for as long as they have not had kaeta puja. A boy is not a full member of his jat yet. Only right after kaeta puja is it made known, "I am of this caste." Even if a child who has not finished kaeta puja eats boiled rice cooked by low-caste people, it does not matter. Only after kaeta puja does our system of "should, should not" apply. As long as he has not finished his kaeta puja, if he should expose himself [that is, appear naked in public, exposing his genitals and buttocks], it is not yet a bad sign. But if the rule is left, and the kaeta is given when they are big, the above discussion does not apply. You must do kaeta puja while they are still children.

He goes on to note that there are minimal and maximal rites. Wealthier Newars elect to have more elaborate rites, while poorer ones perform the minimal set. One option for poorer (or, some said, stingy) Newars is to perform kaeta puja during the autumn festival of Mohani. Then he continues listing the duties and restrictions that apply to a child after kaeta puja.

> If his mother or father should become ill, and lie close to death before the rite of kaeta puja has been performed for him, then a child will get his loincloth immediately, so that he can perform their funeral rites. One who has not had kaeta puja should not light the funeral fire. They should not perform the role of *kriya putra* [the son as chief mourner or ritual agent at funeral rites]. So if there is the possibility of a death in the family, a simplified, quick version of the rite will be performed. After his kaeta puja, the boy has seen karma [been shown karma]. A person who has seen karma has the authority to light the funeral fire. All Newars, of all castes, big or small, must do kaeta puja.

A Pancthariya, Ratna Bahadur, confirms that the rites of busakha and kaeta puja mark the beginning of the obligation to observe caste rules.

> Until the birth hair is shaved, it is all right to eat anyplace, even if you eat with members of other castes. Because you do not count as an adult yet. When a child has his busakha, after his kaeta puja, he cannot eat just anyplace, he can't do whatever he likes. This is the way the Newar samskara are.

The emphasis on food is striking: the implication is that caste status, marked and constituted as it is by food transactions, is not in effect before these rites are performed. You can eat with members of other castes, and it does not make a difference; only after the educational samskara have been performed would eating with members of other castes be a moral offense. In my view, the samskara provide one of the key links between family and caste. These rites, as central family duties, done with love and care, also project the awareness of children into the realm of caste, since observing caste rules are among their new responsibilities. If they did not think much or care about caste before, the rites introduce the possibility that caste is central to a life and an identity, since that is what the samskara are about, the fundamental moral core of a life in society, the essential goals and duties of a life.

As with most Newars, for Ratna Bahadur the idea of not performing the childhood rites of passage is alien. He reacts to the suggestion by affirming in very emphatic terms that they must be done.

> (If kaeta puja is not done, what would happen?)
> It must be done. The samskara [themselves] keep making us do it [*samskara(n) yakahe tagu da:*]. It must be done. If it is not done, then according to the Newar samskara, he does not yet count as an adult. When his mother and father are dead, when they are taken to the burning grounds, their fires must be lit. So kaeta puja must be done. It is absolutely necessary.

Notice the phrasing. The samskara are not a set of discrete, external rites, but the internal and external motive for it all: from one point of view, the samskara make Newars what they are, and compel them to act as moral beings. To show how necessary these rites are, Ratna Bahadur, like Ganesh, cites an essential duty, lighting the funeral pyre of the parents. The total ritual structure of life has ends that are imperative. This is part of the context of the particular rites. Life thus has the unity of a structure of goals and ends. Newars seem to understand this, since they readily link earlier with later rites in the samskaric series: the educational samskara are means to a set of ends, marriage, lighting the funeral fire of one's parents, having rites at one's own death.

Ratna Bahadur goes on to link busakha and kaeta puja as stages (*taha*) of the same process. Busakha begins, and kaeta puja completes absorption into jat and adulthood. Other Newars, such as Govinda Raj and Shiva Bhakta, make the same point: at busakha, caste is about to begin; at kaeta puja, it is complete. Ratna Bahadur sees kaeta puja as marking the beginning of a period in which habits (*bani*) are cultivated by adults. These habits have to do with the purity of the hearth and of the body.

> After kaeta puja, training begins, practice. Before kaeta puja you could go straight into the *bhutu* [the hearth area, which is kept ritually pure] without doing *nisala* [by sprinkling water at the mouth as purification]. But after kaeta puja, you do nisala [with]

pure water, you wash your hands—only then can you go [near the hearth]. His mother and father tell a boy, "You must take nisala" and the boy says, "All right." As this continues, it becomes a habit. The home is like a school. Before you eat, your mother and father will say, "You must wash your hands, wash your buttocks," and then as these [directives] continue one after another, the habit develops. And then you do not have to tell them.

Mahila the sweeper also sees kaeta puja as setting rules that govern contact between castes and as a device for confirming or fashioning the ritual actor.

> (Do you have to do kaeta puja?)
> It is necessary.
> (Why do you do it?)
> We do it carefully and properly, for we must make the children see karma. Women-children do the mock marriage [*ihi*], and we give the kaeta to men-children to make them see karma.
>
> (Until the kaeta has been given, what is it all right to do?)
> Until the kaeta is given, you can go anywhere, and do anything. You can eat, you can drink—even if you eat from just anyone's hand, it is all right. After the kaeta has been given, you should not eat from anyone's hand.
> (Tell me all about this.)
> A child who has not done kaeta puja is called a god-child. He can eat anything. He can go anywhere and eat anything—and still be pure. But after his birth hair has been cut, as soon as he receives the loincloth—after that he can't eat just anything or just anywhere. Then he can only eat at home. . . . If he has had his kaeta puja, then he should not eat from just anyone's hand . . . there are low castes. We should not eat from the hand of the Jugi, we should not eat with the Damai, with the Sarki, with that kind. After kaeta puja we should not eat [indiscriminately with people of other castes]. If kaeta puja has not been done, it is all right, we can go anywhere and eat with anyone.

With kaeta puja, the transactions that constitute and express the caste hierarchy come into effect.[8] There is some irony in low-caste people performing these rites, since one of the things the rites do is mark the activation of caste rules for children, rules that stigmatize low-caste people. The hierarchical opposition of pure and impure, of high and low, is only an abstract possibility until translated into concrete practices, such as members of different castes refusing to eat together. Children have to learn what this means, and adults need ways of teaching it. These samskara help; Newars use them to construct social reality. The rites declare that the system of hierarchical oppositions (of hierarchy-constituting transactions) is in effect, and that the hierarchical rules apply to a person. The performance of the rites announces that a person has been established in this system of hierarchical relations. Hierarchy might not be understood or taken seriously, if the rites did not mark a transition into a new realm of relatedness and self-identity. The rites thus help organize the socialization of children into caste relations; the "habitus" of caste inequality is learned and reproduced in the household. The rites are a symbolic resource: they supply the scaffolding for the cognitive construction of hierarchy, help mediate social integration into the caste system, and help ensure the psychocultural reproduction of hierarchy.

Shame and Sexuality

Human beings must feel "shame" (lajya). A person without lajya is like an animal. We dislike the person who does not feel lajya. We will rebuke such a person: "You do not have lajya; you are without shame; don't you need to feel lajya? Don't you have even a little bit of lajya? You shameless person." In the same way, to show your nakedness is also a matter for great lajya. So here you cannot expose yourself. Someone who does not cover his nakedness is an animal. Such a person is just the same as an animal. From the moment when people develop knowledge of lajya, from then on, even if they don't cover up their whole body, they must at least cover the perineum (anal and genital region). [A Brahman]

The expression I am glossing, "to expose," could be translated literally as "see the pelvic and anal areas" (the perineum), *pya(n) khanegu*. Since, as one Newar Brahman stated, you cannot even mention genitals in ordinary discourse, the injunction against having the anus and buttocks seen includes the notion of genital exposure. "To cover yourself, you need a kaeta; the kaeta, the loincloth, is what you cover yourself with. A man must always tie on a kaeta. So it is, in this rite [of kaeta puja]." Kaeta puja defines sexuality as a force that must be controlled. The kaeta symbolizes sexual restraint.

In the following passage, a Newar Brahman makes a connection between kaeta puja and sexuality. He links the development of sexual restraint with a traditional Hindu stage of life, the *bramhacarya* stage, which required long-term celibacy and study. Some Newars symbolically enact this stage within the samskara.

> This [bramhacarya stage] involves sexual and mental restraint. For those who live in conformity with the austerities of the bramhacarya, the *linga* [penis] does not rise due to sexual desires. To prevent erections, you have to tie on the kaeta. We give the kaeta during kaeta puja because the kaeta makes for good control.

Shiva Bhakta also noted the association of "shame" with the samskara: "If you have been given a kaeta, you cannot go without a kaeta. Lajya happens. You have become grown-up."

A Newar commentator interpreted the phrase "lajya happens [jui]" as meaning both that a person will feel lajya and that he will find himself evaluated in terms of lajya, suggesting again the unity of body and moral order for the Newars. Lajya, you will recall, is at once feeling and a moral state; moreover, lajya virtually unfolds its own context, since it is felt within the institution, the practices, of social judgment that lajya as a concept, as a code of conduct, helps constitute. The samskaric rites help crystallize the experience (of being judged by self and others) and the practice (of making judgments in accord with standards keyed to the moral state of being that lajya defines). In a way, lajya is self-referential; lajya as a code of conduct defines a context, and lajya as emotional experience embodies a judgment about the relation of self to that context. This recursiveness draws people into engagements with all that lajya means, which in turn helps project people into social life as moral actors. The feeling body becomes an intimate sign of the moral order, since lapses and transgressions are felt with the body, in flashes of feeling and sensation that signify, for Newars, the reality of moral standards. Lajya happens; you will feel it, and it will coalesce around you as a code of conduct, defining you from within and from without as a person who ought to be moral, good, sensitive to the imperatives of social life.

For Shiva Bhakta and others, it is kaeta puja that launches this compelling, self-defining project. The performance of kaeta puja triggers the first systematic implementation of a continuing project of moral socialization; the inevitable rebuke of a child for some lapse after the rite has been performed—being scolded as shameless, asked if he does not have lajya—elicits feelings of anxiety and embarrassment. These in turn prompt learning about standards of conduct, and ground a concern with the proper integration of self with society, propelling a continuing dialogue with the definitions of self and standards of behavior that Newar culture offers as a vision of life as it ought to be.

Shiva goes on to say that this linkage of kaeta puja and shame is problematic in the modern setting. Some modernizing Newars no longer link the rites and the moral emotion of shame in the way they did in the past. They have decoupled rite and emotion, not because they have abandoned tradition altogether, but because they have priorities for what they wish to preserve. The coupling of kaeta puja with caste is more important than the linkage with shame. The development of a sense of shame is linked to the earlier rite of busakha instead of to kaeta puja.

These days, some give the kaeta to youth who are as old as fifteen, even nineteen years old. What has happened is, children now go to boarding school. At boarding school, there are [children of] many castes. At school, they must eat boiled rice together. If they must eat rice [with members of other castes], then they should not receive the kaeta. If the kaeta is given [and they eat boiled rice at boarding school], they will lose their caste [that is, be degraded to a lower caste status], so they are not given the kaeta. After they return here [to Bhaktapur], only then do they get their kaeta, when they are fifteen, sixteen years old.

He endorses this strategy. He notes that, while caste rules are not as strict as they used to be, they are still of great significance in Bhaktapur.

Ratna Bahadur notes that boys will be subject to teasing before kaeta puja and scolding afterwards: "Before they have been given the kaeta, boys go naked. Then the grown-ups say, 'Your bird [penis] is going to fly, it's going to fly. You don't feel lajya.' For children it does not matter—but then after the kaeta has been tied on, it matters."

The connection of shame with sexuality is explicit here; as children develop a sense of shame, they learn to avoid behavior suggestive of sexuality, or else face criticism and teasing. Though I have only meager data on this, the penis of young boys is apparently an object of considerable, if informal, attention before this rite; women will sometimes stroke the penis of a young boy, and they will tease him about it. Siblings and other children sometimes pull or play with the penis of young boys. At kaeta puja, this attention ends. The boy stands, naked, in front of an audience, and then has a kaeta tied on him. He is now bound by sexual shame.

The emphasis on shame, and on developing a mastery of basic cultural practices to protect the self from shame, are central to the Newar sense of being responsible selves. Newar accounts of these rites typically offer a litany of the responsibilities a person assumes with the performance of the rites. Ratna Bahadur: "To eat rice, too, they must purify themselves. Responsibility is handed over to them [when they have received the kaeta]. A boy is made to work, to take on tasks one by one. From then on, we don't show the secret parts of our bodies, either. If a person is grown up, he won't show them."

The emphasis on purifying and cleaning, on having shame and covering one's nakedness, requires a new integration into social life. This presupposes a transformation of actors' selves. The self, left to itself, is problematic—a mass of potential. Persons can develop in many ways: they can absorb impurity (which can transform their self-nature, and thus threaten the purity and moral nature of others), they can be sexual and shameless, and they can be "like animals," adrift in a normless world, moved by impulse and desire, not by habits of restraint. Thus, the willful "self" has to be made to give way, and moral dispositions forged, thereby generating commitment to the moral order. This is a problem in integration: the actor's involvement in the ongoing flow of society has become an issue, a focus for work by self and by others. Cultural discipline is imposed—not just to correct behavior and force conformity, although this is one motive, but also to create a moral (and cultural) turn of mind that will affirm the patterns enforced and the discipline itself, making them part of self.

Children's Conception of the Samskara

During an interview about the impure castes, Kumar, a twelve-year-old Hindu farmer boy of Bhaktapur, describes the break in relations with members of other castes after the performance of kaeta puja:

> (Can you eat what they touch then?)
> No. You can eat before kaeta puja. After kaeta puja it is not all right.
> (Before being given the loincloth [kaeta] it is all right?)
> Yes. After the kaeta has been given, [not only must you refrain from eating with the untouchable Sweepers] you cannot eat anything with the [impure] Jugis either. You cannot eat food touched by anyone.
> (Why can't you eat food touched by them, then?)
> The kaeta is given so that you won't eat the food touched by them.

The link he makes is crucial. He recognizes that the rite declares the separation of castes — it is performed so people will not share food. He knows that the giving of the kaeta marks his obligation to observe these rules against the intermingling of castes. He phrases the point rather more strongly than I would, but has, I think, cogently interpreted the rite, identifying one of the key, strategic declarations the ritual makes. He had his kaeta puja at age nine. The boy goes on to make a connection with wider notions of purity and cleanliness:

> (Why can you eat food they touch before kaeta puja?)
> It does not matter before kaeta puja. You can eat and enter the hearth. After kaeta puja you have to purify yourself before going into the kitchen. You have to wash your hands and mouth [even if you just ate boiled rice or beaten rice (?)] Before kaeta puja, even if you eat boiled rice and then go into the hearth area, it does not matter. But after kaeta puja if you do that it is neces-

sary to paint the hearth room floor with a mixture of red mud
and cow dung. And so you cannot go inside.

The mixture purifies. Direct questioning of children about these
rites often did not elicit this kind of answer. I think that here
Kumar is able to articulate a pattern because he has a context—the
question of eating with those of other castes—that triggers the
associations. He knows that with the performance of the rites some
of the "godlike" freedom a child has (to disregard norms enjoining
purity and cleanliness) is brought to a definitive end, thus pro-
foundly altering the relations of self and other. The rites neutralize
many aspects of self as it has up to now experienced itself, constructing instead a caste-bound, moral person.

Children may not only grasp what behaviors are now transgressions, but possess also a sense of the positive import of the rite.
Kumar, asked if kaeta puja must be done, replied: "Yes, and if you
don't do kaeta puja, then you cannot marry."

The Samskara and the Need for Good Company

If the performance of the samskara encourages Newar children to
interpret their world in new ways—to make the samskara central
to the way they know the world—the rites also cue adults, encouraging them to reinterpret children as potential social actors, as no
longer quite children, at least not in the modern, middle-class
Western sense, but as apprentice adults. The performance of the
rites justify a more active, directive approach to shaping a child.
According to Ratna Bahadur:

> If you provide a child with an education, he won't become bad
> . . . "Don't do that. Study with your father. Associate with good
> people." If you do like this, he won't become bad.

Mostly, he adds; there are exceptions. To prevent "bad"
tendencies, parents must give the child "knowledge" (*gyan*) and
"knowledge-intellect" (*gyan-buddhi*).

> Parents must give good gyan.
> (How do they do that?)
> They say, "You should do this, you must study. You must
> associate with good people." If parents give him a good
> education, then he won't be bad.

Notice that this emphasis on guided learning and shaping places the burden of responsibility on adults—children cannot be left on their own to "develop naturally," as they are in some cultures, nor put on a psychological fast track, as some Americans attempt to do. In fact, there seems to be a rather sharp contrast with certain American concepts regarding child development, education, and socialization (all categories imbued with cultural meaning [Tobin, Wu, and Davidson 1989]). Where Americans see a "developing child," Newars envision "making a person." Americans believe the process of "development" can be retarded, accelerated, or distorted, but they regard it as basically a psychological and educational process, as a matter of nurturing, cultivating, and directing developments that occur naturally, springing from innate psychological sources. The basic concept of the child is as a psychological individual. Society, in the form of parents, teachers, and peers, is an important influence on development, even a partner in the development process, but not an absolute prerequisite of development. For some Americans, at least, the child is a natural individual, before it is a social construction.[9]

In contrast, Newars see "child development" as a process of social construction, and as the ritual fashioning of a person. While Newars recognize individuality, the ideology of child-rearing stresses the way that children are social beings and social products. "Development" is precisely the social production of characteristics and dispositions; it involves the addition and subtraction of qualities. Newars envision "making a person" as a religious process that includes repeated ritual forgings as well as continual social shaping within the "web of relatedness." So while Americans seek to encourage, enhance, and modify "nature," Newars aim to purify persons and endow them with moral qualities, with social *being*. In the samskara, for example, a person is given a social "self," endowed with the sacred and moral reality embodied in social and ritual practices. Ritual and relatedness, not nature and self, are the primary terms of Newar concepts of development, of becoming.

This does not mean the "self" disappears from the experienced world of the Newars. Newars do not stop knowing and experiencing themselves because the formal ideology of development and becoming stresses relatedness and ritual—as the story I began this chapter with suggests, they may experience the process of coming into social being as a poignant, complex, personal moment in their

lives. Thus, I would contend that, although the structure and ideology of the rites stress social embeddedness, the experience of the
rites may bring individual existence into focus in intense, significant ways. We should be balanced in our interpretation, giving
holism its due weight—the rites presuppose, celebrate, make tangible, and assert the far-reaching, fundamental, necessary reality
of relatedness—while recognizing also that Newars know and
experience "self" in terms of the samskara. It is one key to their
self-experience and self-definition.

Of course, the ways of knowing, experiencing, and becoming
"self" that are encompassed in the samskara, while powerful, are
neither exhaustive nor exclusive. Nor do Newars view the samskara alone as enough to make a child into a mature, moral person.
Rather, they view the rites as necessary, but not as sufficient, conditions for fashioning a child into a social and moral being: the rites
induct a child into key practices, define the child as a moral agent,
and signal others that a new phase in the child's socialization has
begun, but the cultural process of "making" a person is open-
ended, requiring continual adult monitoring and inputs.

Kaeta Puja: Shiva Bhakta's Account

In this section, I examine an account of busakha and kaeta puja
given by Shiva Bhakta. Busakha is for Shiva Bhakta's status group
the most important male childhood rite of passage; kaeta puja is
secondary. This is reversed in some other lower castes, where
busakha is a less important preliminary to kaeta puja. Asked if he
needs to do busakha, Shiva bobs his head affirmatively, and then
sets out to explain the rites:

> Busakha is this, to shave the birth hair. When you are born, your
> hair grows. This birth hair is shaved in this rite. You must do
> this. It is done at three, four, five, seven, nine, eleven years. Up
> to eleven years. As early as you can, you should do it, during odd
> years.
>
> It is a religious rite. Before busakha, if for some reason some-
> one dies, when he dies, one does not observe the full rites of
> mourning. . . . One will mourn only for three or four days. But
> after busakha, you must sit in mourning for ten days.

With the performance of this rite of tonsure, the child becomes susceptible to the death pollution and mourning rites that mark lineage boundaries. Observing mourning becomes a duty. The relationship to death rites is crucial; a "person" mourns, and performs funeral rites for socially significant others, and is, in turn, mourned, and has rites done for him to further transform him. Mourning, like food, is an almost primordial medium of relatedness.

> (How do you do busakha?)
> A Brahman is necessary, an Astrologer and a Tantric priest are needed. *Jagya* [sacrifice] is necessary, a fire place is built and a fire lit. An offering to fire is made. A *kalaj* [a copper water pot used in rituals] must be established—this is in order to call the deities. The deities are called and placed there so they can bless and protect [the subject of the rite].

The sacred fire and rites for which a Brahman is necessary are performed as part of the samskaric process of purifying, altering, or transforming the qualities of persons. The act is consecrated by the use of the Brahmanical key set of symbols.

> After this, the paju [mother's brother] cuts the hair. He does not cut all of it, only this is cut [demonstrating], like that—he only pretends to shave it. Like this, he shaves, he touches. With a silver blade. The blade to cut, a gold blade is all right, or a silver blade is made. He only pretends to cut it.

The child's hair was previously tied into five locks. The child's paju cuts four of these locks, which are placed in a special plate the child's nini (father's sister) holds. A Nau (Barber) will then shave the child's head. What he means by saying the paju only pretends to cut the hair is that the mother's brother does not shave the head, but only removes a few locks with a special blade, which has the symbolic significance of shaving the head. The gold or silver blade marks the event as special, as elevated above the routine; the paraphernalia of the ritual are symbols of the extraordinary status of the rite. That haircutting symbolically marks a separation or transition seems a reasonable inference. In my terminology, part of the self is canceled. New horizons are invoked.

And then the Barber shaves the head. At whatever auspicious time has been fixed by the Astrologer, at exactly that time, the paju will cut the hair. Before busakha the child has no angsa. Now the paju makes this "ring hair"—like this [he gestures], the paju takes the hair and ties it up with a ring with nine jewels. This ring is round, and studded with jewels, with diamond, pearl, emerald, ruby, yellow topaz, nine kinds in all. Nine shining gems. This gold ring of nine gems is tied exactly around the angsa. One night before busakha. There is an auspicious time for this too—the Astrologer gives it. The ring is tied, the Brahman comes. It is tied on at the auspicious moment. All night they keep it on so.

The angsa is a critical marker of adult status for Hindu Newars. According to Brahmans, if a person has the angsa, he will not have moksha, "liberation" or release from the suffering of a cycle of rebirths. The angsa marks a person as a householder, a follower of kuldharma. Ascetics shave off the angsa. By doing so, and becoming world-renouncers, under the traditional system they lost the right to a share in the estate of their family.[10]

The next morning the paju shaves the hair. Like this. [Then] they take him downstairs to the Nau-ca [the Barber]. But first of all, they bathe. After they bathe, they cut the hair. After the head is shaved, whatever he is wearing is given to the Nau. They wear old, torn clothes. This they give to the Nau. After that, they toss sweets at the Nau.

(Why?)

The Barber made those involved in the rite pure . . . and so it is theirs to take—the clothes, and the sweets.

The rites typically involve a series of purifications; both bathing and having the Barber complete shaving the head and take the old clothes, are purifying. The child is given new clothes.

(How old were you when you had your busakha?)

I was five years old.

(Do you remember anything about this?)

I know a little, not everything. I have a memory of throwing the sweets during my busakha. Throwing the sweets at the Barber. After busakha, after it was finished, my paju brought me clothes. Clothes, pants, coat, a hat, he gave me everything. This is called *swaga(n)*. Swaga(n) means to do good karma. My paju brought these things for me, as a blessing, and then I put them on.

(After you had busakha, what happened to you?)
It was very different. When I was five, when my birth hair was not shaved, nothing was said if I would eat without washing my face. When you defecate, you must wash—although I did not wash before busakha, it was all right, nothing was said to me. [After defecation, adults wash with water, using the left hand; young children are wiped off, but are not required to observe the stricter rules of using water and the left hand.]
(Before busakha. . . .)
Although you don't do that, it is all right. After busakha you must wash your face, too. You cannot urinate wherever you like. You cannot let this be seen [pointing to his penis]. While a child, if you are naked, it is all right. Although you are without a kaeta [loincloth], it is all right. After that, after busakha, one cannot— he knows how to be good.

With the performance of these rites, being dirty, being impure, or being naked become violations of the standards for the presentation of self. The "self" is required increasingly to present itself as the clean, pure, and properly dressed (and repressed) "person" that others direct a child to be. Even the giving of new clothes suggests making a new person.

Now when I had my busakha I got two, three pairs of clothes. My paju brought and gave me clothes. At home, too, I was given clothes: pants, a new coat, a hat, all these were given to me.
Before this, the birth hair had not been cut. It came down this long [gesturing down his back]. It was long, like a woman's. The hair was kept combed.

A Brahman noted that long hair was "like an animal," and that shaving the hair was a purification. The transition is from being "like an animal" to being a responsible, human person. Shiva Bhakta says it was "long, like a woman's." This association may not be merely descriptive: younger children are part of the domestic domain of women, but boys, after these rites are performed, move into the domain of males. After the childhood samskara, the boy can take on ritual and social responsibilities associated with males. Identifications with females may need to be suppressed. Tonsure may resonate with this.

> When I was a child my hair was kept tied up—it was braided. After busakha, I did not need to keep it tied up. After busakha, you could cut your hair. Before busakha, you shouldn't do that. That was a big change. And I learned how to speak. First, the birth hair was shaved and I learned that I should not do this, should not do that.

Here we have the encounter with moral norms: after tonsure, he says, he learned what he should and should not do. The one line is highly significant: "I learned how to speak." Speech is an essential attribute of the person. The power of speech brings the self into the public, social world. Shiva Bhakta views himself as someone who uses language forcefully; he acknowledges that others sometimes give way to him because of the way he uses language—self-assertively—and is probably not totally averse to imposing his will on his world in this way.

I ask Shiva Bhakta to summarize:

> From the time I had my busakha I learned that I couldn't eat without washing my face, I could not eat without washing [after defecation], I could not go without wearing clothes. I grew up, my body became big. That much changed. And I became better as I changed. I learned well.
>
> (Did the rules of jat also come?)
>
> Until busakha, caste does not count.
>
> (So as soon as busakha is finished, what rules come into effect? [I am trying to get him to talk about the period immediately after the performance of the rite.]
>
> Caste happened. My jat is Chathariya—this happened. That I should not go here, there, that place to eat, mattered. But in relation to busakha, too, it was all right. Mainly, it is only after you have been given your kaeta that it is not all right [to do these things]—then you cannot do such things, for the most part. During busakha, you get up to karma [come into contact with the realm of right action]. Even so, if some one should go just anyplace, and even if he should eat with a caste lower than his own, there is no obstacle for him yet. It won't be said that "Your caste is gone." After the kaeta is given, if we went to eat with low-caste

people, then our caste is gone. Your caste will be the same as the caste of whoever's house you eat at. It is said: If you eat with a Jyapu [farmer], you will be a Jyapu.

Busakha and kaeta puja are often thought of as a single sequence. Here, I think, although my question about the relationship of caste rules was phrased in terms of busakha, Shiva Bhakta first responded in terms of this total sequence. Then he singles out kaeta puja as the more exact marker of when the norms of jat behavior come into effect. As discussed above, with sons in school, he has a reason other than fidelity to the exact ritual code for wanting to make this distinction. His reminiscences also show that he is very conscious that caste rules regarding commensality do not wholly apply before these rites. Children would not, however, be allowed to eat with untouchables even before these rites.

These memories of freely interacting with members of lower castes are not rejected—he does not here express any disapproval of this intimate contact. He may, in fact, feel almost wistful about this period of life—he may experience adult roles as restrictive and limiting. As he says, before these rites,

You can go anywhere. You are permitted to visit the home of a member of the farming caste, to eat with them. I used to go and eat with them. I remember. When I was a child, they let me go— it was all right to go there, to be fed by a farmer. They came and got me, they liked me, when I was a child. In my neighborhood, many people liked me, when I was a child. They said I was a good child, a nice child, and they took me with them. I remember . . . I went to their place to eat. I remember, I went to eat. When I was five, I remember. There is the memory—I still think, I went to that place to eat. Meaning before I was five. This thing happened forty-eight years ago. Now I am fifty-three. I am still remembering what happened forty-eight years ago. I remember that I went to the farmer's place to eat.

The "canceled "self" that I see as implicit in this passage differs from the repressed "ego-alien" of psychoanalytic theory in that much is retained in consciousness. This allows for other values to be "recovered" or "focused" through contrast. Shiva Bhakta goes on to note that he did not "understand" at the time of tonsure, but came to "understand" once he had undergone kaeta puja. He did not "understand" that caste is "real."

Before busakha I really didn't understand. What would I understand? Such a little child can't really understand yet. At five I had busakha; at five one really does not understand, does not understand much. That is so, but this is so, also—I have memories of when I was that little. "We're going to marry you," they said, my parents teased me that they would marry me. "Ay, babu [term of endearment for child], we're going to marry you now, to that man's daughter." I said, "Now I will marry." I did not know what marriage was, I didn't know then—what does a little child know? What they said to me, about me, only for me, was "blow a bamboo flute, and marry you to someone's daughter." They said they would marry me to little Ram Das's daughter. Ram Das was a Nae [Butcher]. They teased me they would marry me to his daughter. . . . they said they would marry me to the daughter of little Ram Das who was water unacceptable [impure]. I said, all right. I didn't know. Because I was a child, I did not know, so I said all right and was happy. I remember this.

This teasing plays with pregnant, not yet fully realized intimations of self (what I am, a high-caste Chathariya) and other (the daughter of a impure butcher); the teasing is an example of discourse which has a role in the acquisition of caste status as an attribute, a felt predicate, of self. Shiva Bhakta may not have understood "at the time"; but he manifestly does now, as he teaches his children—by teasing, reprimanding, instructing, and exhorting—that they are Chathariya. He knows *now* what he did not know *then*; and this perception is conveyed in the above scene from his childhood memory. This and similar episodes may, we can speculate, be key constructs in his awareness of his caste identity. In these narrative fragments of memory, he holds up a possible self; this possible self is at the same time canceled. He did not become a Jyapu; his commensality and enjoyment of them did not establish a social or personal identity. He did not— and could never—marry the butcher's daughter. Neutralizing and distancing this possible self—ceasing to be this innocent, foolish child who had warm relations with the lower castes, who could have married one—marks the separation of castes, expresses the distance that divides him from the low castes, and powerfully asserts their otherness as low-caste. They symbolize—not what he is—but what he is not. Just as he is not a child, he is not low-caste. Innocence and rapport have been abolished—with regrets, but with finality.

High-caste adults find the idea of a high-caste boy marrying a butcher's daughter amusing because they appreciate that it cannot happen. Should a high-caste young man propose to do so, the idea would be violently rejected.

They knew that the little Nae was water unacceptable. This Nae brought us milk. He was our cowherder, he took care of our buffalo.

The samskara ritually declare the canceling of certain areas of freedom, and, by extension, of the possible self that could live that freedom, a possible self that could, in principle, follow through on the lines of development implicit in other social arrangements. The rites help make possible the development of a "hierarchical self." By disposing of the egalitarian, free, "open" self of the child—that is, by rejecting the way the child has known himself and the possibilities for development implicit in the child's previous experience—the rites help establish social and personal boundaries and help constitute the "closed" self of the caste hierarchy. The ritual act of self-canceling reciprocally defines other castes as alien, as not self. Solidarity with them is then not possible. The educational samskara have, then, a role in invoking commitment to hierarchy. They have no power to give rise to a system of social stratification, but they may help integrate actors into that system. In any event, the divide is clear:

Before busakha, it's all right to do anything. After busakha, you cannot do as much. After the kaeta is given, you cannot do anything [you want]—you cannot do anything except keep your own rules, the rules that were set long ago. So you cannot do anything when you go outside [your house and caste]. You cannot eat rice with others. You should not eat feasts with castes lower than your own.

In the samskara, the possibilities of "self" are captured by a ritual structure and captured for the social structure. A child is "like a god" or "like an animal" in its freedom, but a grown person, cultivated by the samskara, is constrained by the "rules" set by tradition, the "long ago," and by dharma as a moral code. But the "rules" are, significantly, "your own rules." In the rites, Newars can grasp the meaning of tradition; what they learn is subsequently extended and grounded in interactions with significant others. Individual rites have significance in terms of the entire set of rites; the structure of the entire set of samskara supply Newars with an outline of the obligations of a life. Through the rites, Newars gain a vision of the unity of life.

Models for Self

For Newars, the samskara are obligatory religious rites. While they could be studied for their religious meaning alone, Newars experience the rites as saying something about themselves, about the meaning of their lives. In fact, the rites are a model for self. As such the rites declare what and who Newars are, and where they are going in life, offering Newars one answer to Gauguin's questions. The rites coordinate culture and self, social meaning and personal existence, offering the self a moral world. Out of such ritual experience with moral meaning Newars can develop a moral vision of self and society, if they follow through on what the rites mean—as I believe they often do.

In this chapter, I have only touched on aspects of the process of forging moral consciousness in Newar rites of passage. In essence, the Newar Hindu samskara constitute a ritual field that organizes an encounter between the creative, self-defining powers of interpreting agents and symbolic structures that represent the social world. In the Newar view, the rites ideally create in the individual a certain moral "turn of mind." The rites are in part moral rhetoric—they advance a vision of reality. Looked at in another way, the rites are paradigms to be learned and mastered; the rites allow individuals to correct their tendency to construct their own personal versions of themselves and the social world, and allow them to formulate themselves as socially embedded in a web of relatedness. From another perspective, the rites embody an ethnopsychology: Newars speak of the samskara not only as rituals, as actions performed, but also as part of the mind or self. They take on personal meaning—they shape self-knowing, and give it a moral context.

As moral rhetoric, as paradigm of the way things ought to be, as ethnopsychology, as moral context for self-knowing, in all these ways the samskara play a crucial role in moral socialization. Something is learned from the samskara: cultural meaning is internalized as part of the mind and self; this does not, I suspect, constitute motives or knowing in any simple sense, but instead sets up a dialogue in the mind, by providing an interpretive system — a source of thoughts, feelings, motives, and evaluations — that is hierarchically and interactively related to other cognitive structures of meaning (D'Andrade 1990).

The creativity of social actors, their ability to construct understandings, is captured and directed by the moral and dramatic structure of the samskara. In a sense, the rites do become mind; they become part of what interpreting agents think and experience with.

Perhaps I can clarify this by comparing the samskara with a very simple "mediating structure" — the checklist. Drawing on unpublished work by Edward Hutchins, D'Andrade says this about the role of a checklist in learning to perform a task: "In using a checklist, the user does not coordinate his or her behavior directly with the task environment, but rather coordinates with a mediating object that has a structure that is like the task environment in some important way" (1990:107).

The checklist acts as a mediating device for learning; the user must "construct a representation of the world" from the list of actions indicated "that maps onto" the world at hand — the relevant, actual world — in ways that allow users to engage and manipulate the actual world, telling them what and when and how to do things by coordinating representations (the checklist), actions (based on the checklist), and the actual world (where actions have consequences). The samskara are more complex mediating structures, but they too coordinate different systems. In using the samskara as mental models of social and moral reality, Newars do not coordinate their behavior (or sense of self) directly with the social world, but rather coordinate themselves with the symbolic representations of the samskara that have a structure like the social world, conceived in religious and moral terms. People base actions (and self-concepts) on the samskara, from which they have constructed a representation of the world, and map this onto their actual social world. They can continually question the samskara about what life means and about their place in it, which they can (if they want or need to) translate into intentions and actions. They can use the samskara to formulate goals. The difference is that samskara, unlike simpler mediating structures, do not just represent the relevant world; they help constitute the social and moral world for Newars. They are more than representations of the social environment, and do more than just provide a "map" of the real world: they help construct reality for Newars.

Viewed in this way, the rites are mental models that have what D'Andrade (1984) has termed "constructive," "evocative," and "directive force." They help define reality, create moral objects, and animate convictions about what people should do, should feel, and should want, providing models and goals in terms of which social actors understand themselves and others, have intentions and act. Thus, when Newars speak of the samskara as causing them to do or feel things, they are quite right: the samskara mediate between their actions and experience and the cultural world of their lives, bringing self and world into significant alignment, so that intending, doing, and feeling have some significance and effect, rather than being meaningless and powerless, futile, autistic gestures, as they might well be if the world, mind, and self were not coordinated, not connected by mediating structures of cultural meaning.

In the rites, individuals discover images and ideas with which they can create an idea of self and a view of the world; a vision of the unity of life is evoked, a unity in terms of which self can be a coherent whole. A coherent, normative relatedness is defined (kuldharma) — which means, among other things, not eating with people of lower castes. The rites are part of a discourse that cancels relatedness with those of other castes; the rites neutralize solidarity with them. Relatedness, expressed by eating with them, is annulled. Eating with them is not longer innocent and transparently moral; it is wrong, and by eating with them, you may lose your self, and corrupt your family. These rites, looked at from one perspective, seem to problematize what seems self-evidently moral and good — a human connection.

Some of the evocative and dramatic qualities of the rites can be understood as ways in which the rites play on minds to get people to subscribe to the values expressed. These evocative and dramatic moments may then play a continuing role in the psychological work of self-knowing, making it truly cultural work, as in Shiva Bhakta's memories.

The vision of the unity of life found in the samskara consists of establishing goals for, and landmarks in, a lived life, within a tradition that connects self to others, living and dead. Having this vision makes it possible for a Newar to have a unified moral identity that can be expressed in an account of the wholeness of a life, its purpose, duties, and meaning.[11] The samskara help, I suppose, to make possible a coherent moral self. But this moral self, tightly constrained by the rigid structure of duties that the samskara have helped it "valorize," retains an image of another possible self, as we saw in Shiva Bhakta's account. The tension here is between the view of self and others found in the ideology of the caste hierarchy—a view that turns people into radically different and separate kinds of human beings—and lingering memories of a time when the individual experienced freedom and relatedness outside the scope of the structure of duties, goods, purposes, and relationships given by the samskara. This contrast may have its uses. It may contribute to the psychological efficacy of the rites, and may play a role in the psychological work of self-fashioning involved in assuming adult roles and identity.

Before these rites, a child is "like a god," unencumbered by the many moral restraints that are part of adult life. After the rites, children are seen, and treated, in a different way; they begin to see themselves in new ways, too—as moral actors. The web of relatedness of the family takes on new meaning and moral force. The rites declare the beginnings of responsibility: after the rites, persons must maintain the purity of the hearth, know shame, and conform to the rules of their caste. The rites mark the assumption of obligations, the taking up of the burden of being a householder.

The rites help Newars place themselves within the moral tradition of the family line—a tradition the samskara express and help constitute. The tradition is moral since it supplies a structure of obligations and ends within which a life is lived. Conversely, moral ideas derive some of their force from tradition, because they are embedded in what came from "long ago," are identified with the family line, and are experienced within the web of relatedness organized by this patriline.

The rites communicate cultural understandings and establish moral contexts, but more is involved than "cultural transmission," conceptualized as the internalization and enactment of cultural norms by passive social actors. For these rites mediate self-knowing and self-making. They prompt people to come to grips with culture. They play on self-awareness, provoking people to ask questions of culture and self, stimulating them to work through their experience and find its meaning in culture. The rites lay down patterns through which persons can come to know themselves, and so help organize the dialectical encounter of culture and self that constitutes the core of an identity.

The rites give salience to some ways of being a person, but mute other possibilities. They provide symbolic grounds for self-awareness, for knowing self in terms of particular cultural values, making it possible for persons to interpret themselves and their lives in certain defined ways; the rites construct and animate a moral view of the world and self. This vision of moral life links individuals to the caste hierarchy, and positions them within their social world as members of particular castes. The rites mediate their views of themselves, and predispose them to commit themselves to the hierarchical social system symbolized and valorized in the rituals.

This is a significant outcome. But it is not the only possible one. We cannot understand men and women in terms of the "official" values of a culture alone, for as we have seen, people do not simply "internalize" and "enact" cultural norms. People evaluate and interpret culture. They interpret culture in terms of self, and self in terms of culture. Thus, just as people shape their lives to culture, by using "mediating structures" to integrate themselves into a social and cultural world, so too they may work at reconstructing culture, seeking to make culture more consistent with their experience, with visions of themselves and their lives based on altered circumstances or efforts to reposition themselves in society.

History, in the form of social and economic transformations, can shuffle the deck, generating new sets of opportunities and constraints, which may require a reformulation of cultural reality and restructure the horizons of self—possibly leading to further change. Self-making can lead to culture-making, as people seek to reimagine society in ways that do justice to their aspirations and experience. "Mediating structures" can be redeployed or restructured, as people develop and invoke other models of the world and self. Moreover, people may do so even while they continue to make use of conflicting models their culture offers in traditional myth, rite, and symbol. Cultural experience is intrinsically diverse, dynamic, and interactive, a moving object that produces, not a single moral consciousness, but varieties of moral consciousness. This fact prompts efforts to prune this growth, to domesticate and tame some species of "wild" consciousness, to weed the cultural garden of others. Confronted with the creative human potential for self-making and culture-making, moral communities fashion trellises, mediating structures such as the samskara, to guide the cultural development of the moral self.

Postscript: Culture and
Moral Knowing

A book, as a device for describing and interpreting culture, and culture itself, as the flow of meaning in human life, are radically incommensurate. A book has a finality—it says what it says—which cultural life ultimately does not. With this in mind, my final words here should be read as a postscript—not as a conclusion. Rather than inviting closure, I hope merely to "stir things up" a little bit more—gently, so that I do not contribute too much to the general murkiness. My question is this: What is culture?—that it should generate moral consciousness?

Regarding culture, I believe with Raymond Williams (1977: 132) that we "must go beyond formally held and systematic beliefs," in defining culture and interpreting cultures, "though of course we have always to include them." As Williams suggests, some academic habits of mind, and especially the impulse to define our job as the "conversion of experience" into "finished products," into satisfyingly coherent and final accounts of "culture," constitute a barrier to seeing cultural life as a historical and lived process.[1] Our constructions of culture should never be mistaken for reality, as the unwary, the innocent, and the incorrigible sometimes do.

In reality, culture is lived—it is embodied in experience, action, and life. It emerges in lives, not as a static, finished product, compelling people to think, feel, and act in predetermined ways, but as a "forming and formative process" (Williams 1977:128). This process involves people as concrete actors, as the agents of cultural lives, not just as passive receivers of cultural knowledge. People do receive much passively, but they also work *with* culture, with the meanings and values, practices and structures that generate the possibilities of, and impose limits on, action and experience. They work as agents with the culture that shapes them as subjects—surely a key paradox of culture. As agents/subjects, they produce cultural lives within the flow of culture within the flow of history. In crucial ways, actors and their lives embody culture. For them, culture is a lived process, and it is within actors and their lives that culture continues to form. My goal has been to offer glimpses of this "forming and formative process"—not to present Newar culture as a final, finished product.

As a lived process, Newar culture does not absolutely predetermine how people act and think, but it does shape what they do and know. This apparent contradiction poses questions about the nature of culture, which I, like many others, have long struggled with, and arrived at no very satisfactory conclusions. People receive culture, yes—it exists before they were born, it exists outside of them, and it acts on them, powerfully. People are shaped by culture, certainly. But—women and men also seek to *author* their lives. They are, and must be, actively engaged in processes of meaning-construction that are relevant to their lives and experience. They get much from culture, but culture as a body of received tradition, knowledge, and practice never supplies everything people need to live their lives and know their world. The world changes around people, making particular cultural formations less relevant to their lives. The economy changes, people grow up and grow older, their associates in life die or fail to do what is expected, political realities shift. All these changes must be absorbed into a life that draws on culture.

What do you do if your brothers, living with you in an extended family, do not want to do their share of the work? What if you do not have enough money to perform a samskara for your child? Simple, real-life situations—but "knowledge" does not apply itself to these situations. People do. They activate cultural meanings and understandings, bringing cultural knowledge to life as they experience it. Moreover, since deciding how to apply norms or values to cases requires social actors to query the meaning of those norms or values, they have an opportunity to construct and reconstruct the meaning of key cultural concepts. Do dharma, Newars tell themselves. But what does this mean? Culture cannot be "known" except in active processes of meaning-construction and social action. That is where culture "lives."

If culture is a forming and formative process, then so are people; cultural selves are not the mechanical product of culture, but living processes within culture. People recreate themselves through their engagements with the bodies of meaning and ranges of possibility a cultural tradition offers, but they never become cultural automatons, simply programmed by culture.

People use cultural meaning to know themselves and to interpret, monitor, and evaluate their engagement with life, making culture part of self in the process, and self part of culture. The process of relating life, self, and culture is dynamic and dialectical, organized, in my view, in terms of "mediating structures" of meaning and emotion, and monitored on an ongoing basis. The mediating structures—for example, lajya as a moral emotion, dharma as a moral concept, the samskara as rites of passage and self-fashioning—link the moral order and the experiencing self, and sustain self-making and culture-making, thus producing and shaping what I have termed moral knowing.

Looked at one way, culture is the flow of meaning in social life, but it is meaning constructed and animated in a community of diverse selves, who voice culture in different ways, not meaning passively received in symbols. These voices, or selves—always social actors—take up culture (from others and experience) and constitute themselves in cultural ways, but as active agents of cultural lives, not simply as passive receivers of cultural tradition. Bound within a social and political structure, people form a community of cultural agents, at times working in concert, but at other moments set discordantly against each other, as they construct lives, and relationships, and aspects of what they know and experience as "reality," by activating and animating shared cultural models in different ways, for different purposes.

I do not want to give the impression that this means there is no cultural structure, no organization, to what such a community of voices (selves, actors) does. Quite the contrary. Without structure, there would be only silence (or an ocean of noise) carrying no meaning. My point, rather, is that persons can vary and alter cultural meanings, and introduce new themes and configurations, giv-

ing rise eventually to new bodies of meaning, new ways of thinking and feeling, of organizing life and behavior.

Perhaps an analogy will help make this point clear. In certain
ways, I envision cultural dynamics as having the qualities of structure and improvisation associated with "raising a hymn" in black
country churches in the American South, as described by Shirley
Brice Heath (1983). After a hymn is introduced, she writes, a congregation "begins singing and may continue through the first verse
before a member of the choir or congregation breaks in with new
words."

> The congregation is quiet while the new self-appointed leader rais-
> es a set of phrases, and they then join in repeating it, then pause for
> another leader to offer another set. This pattern of alternation con-
> tinues until the hymn ends. . . . A variation on this pattern may
> occur when someone begins a testimony or prayer instead of rais-
> ing a new set of sung phrases; on these occasions, the music usual-
> ly subsides into background humming until someone in the con-
> gregation picks up a phrase either given or related to the new theme
> of the testimony or prayer, and the congregation raises a new
> hymn. . . .
>
> The phrases offered by the leader who raises a hymn may become
> a formula which subsequent sets of phrases modify or play with, or
> the initial sets of phrases may only introduce a theme (e.g., grati-
> tude for salvation) which other leaders comment on and vary
> throughout the raised hymn. Thus what may seem like set formu-
> lae are changed, and new formulae are produced as different indi-
> viduals lead the congregation in expanding a particular theme. . . .
> Every performance of a raised hymn is different . . . each interac-
> tion between leader and congregation is unique. . . . Indeed, these
> unique combinations . . . make it possible for each member of the
> congregation to be at once creator and performer. (1983: 203–205)

Living culture is more like "raising a hymn" than reciting a text or
enacting a fixed script; it involves structure, but leaves room for,
even requires, improvisation and negotiation. The process is structured but dynamic, communal but personal, constituting a "forming and formative process" in which lives are made and voices
found, making it possible for social actors to be at once performers
and creators. Only retrospectively can a fixed form be imputed to

the hymn or cultural life—it has been "raised," not recited, performed, not read.

Thus, contrary to what Clifford Geertz declared in his famous
essay "Deep Play," I do not believe "the culture of a people is an
ensemble of texts, themselves ensembles" that the anthropologist
can "read over the shoulders of those to whom they properly
belong" (1973:452). True, shared conceptual structures built out
of meanings are essential to cultural life; but even shared meanings
can be "raised" in a range of different ways, in different contexts,
by different actors—or contested, as Sapir (1985 [1938]) long ago
pointed out. What develops in the course of social and cultural life
must ultimately be negotiated and determined in action itself; it is
not fixed in some absolute way by the cognitive cultural elements
used, since they are "raised," not passively enacted, even though
culture in the form of knowledge, meanings, and norms of interaction and communication does shape the general flow of events, and
may mediate every step of complex sequences of social action
without absolutely determining them.

Rather than reading culture as text, we need to see culture in
motion, as fluid and emergent. Cultural life incorporates a degree
of unpredictability, even an element of randomness, of creative
chaos. H. H. Mitchell writes that the variations and unique com-
binations that arise while "raising hymns" generate what he calls "a
blessed unpredictability that keeps Black preachers at least a little
humble and keeps their audiences in a state of expectancy, always
wondering which way the truth will unfold and which direction
the wind of the spirit will blow."[2] Much the same might be said
about the flow of cultural life. Culture orders life, but not in an
absolute sense; there are many times when actors and anthropologists cannot know how cultural scripts will unfold, or in what
directions the winds of life will blow.

In particular, negotiating practical moral dilemmas may keep
actors wondering, even in a state of disequilibrium, even when
well-known structures of life and feeling are involved. Recall how,
when Bhimsen Lal's extended family was breaking up, various values came into play, but his narrative makes clear that this was a
process negotiated uncertainly and reluctantly, involving a number of false starts and misadventures. As it developed, family members redefined themselves and their relationships, exposed and
probed each others' weaknesses and strengths, attacked each other

and then made peace, only to have the reconciliations fall apart, as relationships unraveled further. The actors advanced claims, attacked each other, expressed their needs and desires, made compromises and compromised themselves, and finally hardened themselves to the almost inevitable outcome. Actions and reactions unfolded problematically, ultimately yielding a harvest of pain and moral failure.

The process was generated in terms of social structure and interpreted in terms of shared meanings, but the twists and turns of events and actions were not simply "given"—not to the people involved, who knew as much about the structure of their plight as anyone. As actors, they had to "raise culture" to negotiate a process set in motion by the structural realities of life in Newar patrilineal extended families.

Actors may not be able to assert their knowledge of moral codes with as much certainty and conviction in such real-life situations as they can when they engage in the kind of hypothetical reasoning so many moral studies have been based on, or are otherwise expected to display their knowledge of the "official" moral code. "Knowledge of" a moral code is not "moral knowing."

In fact, the socially generated quandaries of life may expose the limits of shared meaning (Linger 1992), calling into question "official" moral knowledge. Meaningful relationships may dissolve, meaninglessly, as a family separates. People may feel betrayed by intimates in intimate ways. They may witness brutality and violence on the streets. What people know and do thus reflects the actual conditions of life under which they make use of cultural knowledge; it is not just that they have cultural knowledge in their heads, but that they have lives to go along with their knowledge—and life often outruns their knowledge, their expectations, and their hopes, leaving them vulnerable, bruised, uncertain, resentful, forcing them to adapt and create. Knowing reflects this, even if shared culture does not account for it.

If this is culture, what is the moral? Why do we sometimes attach the label "moral" to some social, cultural, and psychological phenomena? Can we separate "the moral" out of cultural life, and set it in analytic opposition to something else—the "nonmoral"?

Let me begin with the last question first, since I have a more definite answer for it. I do not think we can usefully define a separate moral domain, apart from cultural life, as an object of study—not ultimately. I do believe, however, that we can learn much by examining moral phenomena in the context of cultural life. Moreover, I think we lose something when we ignore such phenomena; after all, people often identify concerns with justice, caring, and duty as centrally significant to their lives and experience.

With these caveats in mind, let me try very briefly to discuss "the moral" in relation to culture. I have ruled out simply treating culture as a moral text that people read knowledge of values and norms from. People do take values and meanings from their cultural tradition, of course, but they must also relate these to circumstances and contingencies; any robust interpretive perspective on the relationship of culture and moral consciousness will ultimately have to be sensitive to culture as *a body of meanings* that help constitute a lifeworld and to culture *as practice* in which these meanings are raised and reconstituted in a dynamic fashion in ongoing social life. Both perspectives seem essential.

The Moral as Meaning

Looked at in one way, human action reflect judgments about what the world should be, as well as about the way it is; moral meanings declare and define key commitments. As a Newar might say: dharma is what you must do. As we saw, however, this is not left hanging in abstraction; what one must do is defined by concrete social reality.

If we adopt this perspective, we commit ourselves to seeing moral meaning as a special class of meaning, with different characteristics and effects than other classes of meaning. It is not representational meaning, although it relies on such meaning; without representations of "what is," declarations of "what should be" lack sense, and so lack significance. Of course, we do not always take note of the way we shift from descriptive to prescriptive or normative formulations of experience, and may hardly ever attempt to disentangle them, but in principle they can be distinguished.

I think people intuitively recognize that some things lack the life-relevance, "the stakes," asserted by framing something as moral. A description of a tree—that is has branches, bark, certain kinds of leaves—is not necessarily moral discourse. Of course, some people may make it so, perhaps by listing the parts of a tree with a tone or attitude of reverence, transforming a recitation of features into prayer or supplication, and certainly this talent for lending moral significance to diverse aspects of reality is an important human capacity, directed and shaped by cultures in various ways. But people can describe, and experience, the world without transforming all they perceive into a sacred and moral mode.

Nor does constitutive or constructive meaning—meaning that defines a cultural object, practice, or institution (D'Andrade 1984)—necessarily give the moral meaning of what it brings into imaginative being, although it may set the stage for the determination of moral meaning in discourse. We can agree on what counts as a strike in baseball without attaching a special quality of obligation and commitment to the game. Of course, some may, but risk being told "It's just a game." Those too earnest about, too committed to, something ultimately unworthy of such attention tempt us to say, "Get a life"—conveying a precise sense of one of the prerequisites for granting a practice or commitment moral standing. More has to be at stake that what is involved in "a game." The moral involves deeper play.

Of course, *some* quality of obligation and commitment must attach to any institution that humans enact with any seriousness of purpose, but this can still lack the emotional and social force expected of what people accord full moral standing. By attaching the label "moral" to an action, state, or practice, we raise expectations about the force and scope of commitment; typically, I think, we mean something closer to ultimate commitments than not— "the moral" identifies the core commitments that define who we are and what we must do, overriding other considerations, at least in our rhetoric of the ideal.

Moral values thus are presumably values people will defend, values they cherish above other values and interests. Of course, what different actors define as their moral values will vary, even within a culture. For example, baseball—although "just a game"— may be self-defining to some who make a living playing it and, more importantly, have made a life in the game. They may have developed an identity within the sport (it defines who they are, what their world is) and identify with the game in ways that shape a moral sensibility. For such persons, perhaps, showing up to play a game of baseball may indeed seem more important—more imperative—than (say) being present at the birth of a child. This would account for the baseball team that fined a player who chose to miss a game in order to be with his wife at the birth of their child. Speaking in justification of the fine imposed on him, some claimed he had "let the team down." The job comes first, a few suggested, and he had an obligation to the team; moreover, in a revealing metaphor that seems to implicitly connect war and work, someone asserted that soldiers on the front lines do not get to "be there" at the birth of their children — so why should a professional baseball player? Many found these quite dubious propositions, but I do not doubt that a moral attitude was being expressed. For some, baseball is a life, not just a game, and family comes second. Others find this backwards, and sad.

What people define as overriding obligations, however, reveals much about their identities, their life-worlds, and the lives they have made. What seems most important is not moral doctrine cut off from cultural life, but the quality and states of self-involvement and engagement with others, plus the perception of having something at stake, a way of life, self.

Not having much at stake, I can describe the institution of witchcraft in a society without recourse to judgments of right and wrong. No doubt some element of evaluation, of interest, must come into play if I am to take note of the phenomena at all, but the mild interest with which I take note of it can be distinguished from the intensity of interest of those who condemn it as an evil or heresy. Where I describe, they judge, building a moral context, insisting that witches are evil, harm the innocent, must be punished and eliminated. For them, witchcraft has value and meaning, even if negative. This may occur even if witchcraft exists only in their imaginations. Imaginatively, they may see witchcraft as a threat to their children or their "values"; this raises the stakes for them. Even if self-professed witches are harmless eccentrics, the impression of a threat might be enough to generate an attitude and a orientation to action that the people involved might themselves identify as moral — or as a matter of morality against immorality, a high-stakes definition of the issue. (Similarly, the dangerous forces "outside" Bhaktapur help evoke commitments to the social order of the city.)

The same general distinctions apply to other institutions. Establishing a common residence, or performing a certain ritual, may count as a "getting married" in a culture. So constituted, marriage may also be understood and experienced as a kind of culturally defined moral project; husband and wife should love, cherish, and protect each other, respect their commitment, and so on—a set of judgments about the way things should be reflect people's efforts to live lives together. They invoke a moral code as part of this, articulating cultural concepts (perhaps) of commitment, fairness, shared responsibility—framing what people should do, and saying why. Newars do this with the concept of dharma; husbands and wives have their respective dharmas. Thus marriage (something many people approve of) and witchcraft (something many people find suspect) are not only culturally constituted social states, given actuality by cultural models, but also moral objects, known and engaged in terms of obligations, imperatives, commitments, and a host of relevant evaluative and reality-defining concepts that evoke strong emotion.

It seems to me, then, that whatever "the moral" is for people, it is the product of the interweaving of different kinds of meaning into a known, felt, and lived reality. It arises from people's engagement with life, it does not develop without a context and a cultural organization. Moral judgment is not a matter of the development of reasoning abilities apart from our engagement with the actualities of life, and moral consciousness does not merely reflect the use of cognitive and analytic skills applied to knowledge that is not life-relevant for social action. Meanings that describe and create institutions—like marriage and baseball—mingle with meanings that are directive and evaluative (D'Andrade 1984), combining in contexts of general, life-relevant significance to produce the kind of meaning and knowing people experience in their lives .

Of course, the actual world of human experience may or may not correspond to the moral order implicit in "should" talk. Tensions between the world "as it is" and the world "as it must be" or "should be" are inevitable. In the gap between them, evaluations come into play, and these may move people to action. While moral concepts may declare a moral order, this order may not be achieved in social life, making disenchantment with the actual world possible. If so, a moral discourse may propose a world that is better, safer, happier than the world as it is, pointing to what should be. Alternatively, moral discourse may stipulate that the way things are has a moral basis (the world is the way it "must" be, from which it follows that people "must not" violate this received pattern for society and life). In either case, moral concepts do not

represent what is, but declare an ideal and a standard for evaluation, giving scope to ambitions and aspirations, generating commitments and orientations to action. Obviously, actors' perceptions of whether the social order is moral or not will depend on
their position in that order, and this will determine the thrust of
their moral discourse.

This may sound simple, but the reality is complex, and difficult
to capture in words. As Bourdieu (1977:166) says, "It is not easy
to evoke the subjective experience associated with this world of the
realized ought-to-be, in which things that could scarcely be otherwise nonetheless are what they are only because they are what
they ought to be, in which an agent can have at one and the same
time the feeling that there is nothing to do except what he is doing
and also that he is only doing what he ought." Indeed, this is not
easy, but I agree with the point, up to a point. I would add that it
is not easy to capture a sense of the subjective experience of the
unrealized ought-to-be, either, in which actors have the feeling the
world is receding away from morality, that life as it is lived propels
themselves and society farther and farther from what they envision
to be moral. Living in terms of an unrealized ought-to-be can be
painful and disquieting.

Put more simply, visions of world, order, and self, framed in
terms of "should" and "must," provide crucial contexts within
which human experience, identity, and action take shape. Events,
actions, practices acquire moral force because people live in an
actual world, but partly in terms of a possible world—dreamed of
in the moral imagination. People may act on the "real" world and
themselves to "do something" about realizing such visions. Moral
values grip the mind by creating a sense of obligation, an urge to
act, either to change the actually experienced world to bring it into
conformity with the way things should or must be, or to resist a
falling away from the "realized ought-to-be," from the actual world
that is taken as embodying what should be and must be.

I do not think that talk of what "should be" or "must be" will
identify everything everyone—Newar and American—would
want to identify as moral, and only those things they want to identify as moral, even if you ignore directives clearly having to do with
technical standards or aesthetic preference; but concepts and practices that have no directive force whatsoever are probably not

going to be defined as moral by natives or observers. Traditional Newars are quite clear that dharma is what they "must" do.

Obviously, the sense of what "should be" and what people "must do" varies wildly across cultures, as does what people may experience as being "at stake." Nonetheless, there may be universals as well as culture-specific beliefs.[3] Let me indicate some concepts that are possible candidates for inclusion in the moral realm for many, if not all, cultures and persons, based on Newar culture: a notion of objective morality (natural law); concepts of justice, of good and duty, love and relatedness; benevolence and protection of the vulnerable. The abstract kernel of the concepts seem less important, however, than the total world of practice and meaning that encompasses them.

Other concepts seem less universal, more part of a distinct cultural tradition. Newars' concepts of society, hierarchy, and holism have moral force, for them, but seem culture-specific. More culture-specific yet, but central to Hindu Bhaktapur, is the way "ordinary" and "dangerous" divinities symbolize and "protect" the human moral order. The "god who dwells in the heart" may grow out of the transcultural experience of self-knowing, but is elaborated in distinctive cultural terms.

In Newar talk, these concepts are often the objects of moral verbs: people must do their duties, must follow the dharma, must worship the deities, must care for their children and should help their neighbors. Universal or culture-specific, Newar moral concepts relate people to each other in an obligatory way, in terms of commitments, but only within a cultural world, within practical consciousness. For example, I think "duty" in the abstract has little meaning for Shiva or Mahila; what infuses them with a sense of commitment is the practical need to care for others; empathic love (maya) in the abstract is affirmed, but it has the most significance and the greatest force, generating feeling and a pressure to act, in the context of relationships with concrete others, in a family world where lives are joined together in an encompassing kinship structure and samskaric project. There, their own lives are "at stake," and so are the people they know, love, and need.

Moral Knowing as Practical Consciousness

Without rejecting the limited perspective on meaning and "the moral" that I have just set out above (the analysis of meaning is an essential, a necessary, preliminary), I would point out that witchcraft, marriage, patriotism, religion, defending civil liberties, and so on, are *also* cultural practices, and not free-floating meaning systems that somehow constitute themselves. The "must" and "should" meanings attached to them do not attach themselves — people do. Moral values and meanings are *active* within life; if not, they are just "known about," not compelling, commitment-generating aspects of relationships and action. We cannot detach "the moral" from cultural life, which is where people have something "at stake," and expect to understand moral consciousness; nor can we ignore cultural concepts of duty, justice, love, empathy as modes of relationship and expect to understand life fully, since people use these concepts, putting them to work in their lives.

If, looked at one way, cultural meaning systems shape what people think, feel, and do, looked at another way they give people ways to shape what they think, feel, and do. Ultimately, I think, it is the practical circumstances and consciousness of lived life that generates processes of moral meaning construction, by driving people to find value and significance in their cultural repertoire. Life-experience, refracted through culture, but not mechanically determined by culture, either prepares people to find sense and significance in cultural models and practices, or renders them incapable or unwilling to do so.

This is why, in an important sense, there can be no discrete field of study that focuses on moral consciousness apart from the rest of consciousness, apart from cultural life. The moral domain is not a separate domain, a territory that exists in isolation, a kind of pristine reserve set aside for a special species of consciousness, a place that can exist untouched by, apart from, the rest of human life and experience. Arguably, the carving out of "the moral" from the rest of life and isolating it for study is a Western academic or folk practice, not something all people in all cultures do — and not something they have to do because of the ways their minds work.

If it is arbitrary to isolate "the moral" from cultural life, however, it may also be arbitrary to ignore "the moral" as part of life. Taken as integral to cultural life, I think the study of moral phenomena is vital. I doubt that we can have either a systematic sociology of order and practice or a powerful cultural psychology of mind, self, and emotion without a basic understanding of those aspects of cultural life that have been given the label "moral" from time to time. This holds even if you question (as I do) the ways a certain range of human action, thought, and feeling has been labeled "moral," made an object of study, and detached from life and practice in much research on "moral" thought and development.

If the moral domain corresponds to what people treat as the ultimate terms of their existence, of their lives together, of their fates, then moral concerns are concerns with the integrity of cultural life, with the nature, significance, potential, and viability of the life that culture makes possible and makes necessary. If the ultimate terms of existence are necessarily cultural terms, then moral discourse stands at the heart of culture.

As an anthropologist, I find "the moral" significant because it embraces phenomena, like the multiple transformations of the sense of justice in caste society or the "connecting" sense of empathy in the web of relatedness of a Newar extended family, that are life-relevant and embedded in cultural practice. Focusing on "the moral" enlarges my sense of "what's going on" in cultural life. It allows me to hear the voices of social actors more clearly; they have things to say about these matters.

Culture and Agency

What are the implications for culture theory? In my view, what I term moral knowing arises out of an interplay of thought, feeling, and action in the lives of social actors who "work" to know themselves and their world. It reflects the working and reworking, imagining and reimagining, of cultural knowledge and experience in action and speech, in emotion and thought. People relate themselves to, and find personal meaning—a sense of what they "must do"—in cultural symbols or schema (Obeyesekere 1981; Ortner 1989). This makes a difference in terms of how they live their lives in culture; they do not simply enact or execute "culture." Thus, in my view, agency and experience are ultimately as important as codes and symbols for understanding moral life.

"Knowing" is a work of culture, but not simply a matter of absorbing cultural knowledge. Rather, people relate themselves to a cultural repertoire, finding meaning in it for themselves, reshaping it to fit their lives, generating new practices in the process. Out of this work of relating themselves to culture, people generate (not merely extract) moral meanings and motives, reasons to act. These are not enacted in a mechanical fashion. They are invoked in life, actively and constructively—as much "raised" as "read." Moral meanings may infuse persons with a felt need to act, because something is "at stake" in a way that engages them as agents of a cultural life; they act because "life is sacred," because "it was the right thing to do," or because "it is dharma."

Ortner (1984) has pointed out that any theory of practice, indeed, any theory of human action, requires a theory of motivation.

> At the moment, the dominant theory of motivation in practice anthropology is derived from interest theory. The model is that of an essentially individualistic, and somewhat aggressive, actor, self-interested, rational, pragmatic, and perhaps with a maximizing orientation as well. What actors do, it is assumed, is rationally go after what they want, and what they want is what is materially and politically useful for them within the context of their cultural and historical situations. (1984: 151)

Do Newars see themselves in these terms? The answer is yes and no. Newars recognize self-interest as a powerful motive, but they do not view it as the only motive. They know how to manipulate cultural and social forms in pursuit of their (culturally defined) goals (see Rosser 1978). But culturally organized self-interest is not everything for them. They recognize other motives in themselves. As Ortner (1984:151) remarks, "although pragmatic rationality is certainly one aspect of motivation, it is never the only one, and not always even the dominant one. To accord it the status of exclusive motivating force is to exclude from the analytic discourse a whole range of emotional terms—need, fear, suffering, desire, and others—that must surely be part of motivation." For Newars, need, fear, suffering, and desire, but also love and duty as they experience them, are important motives.

If emotion terms such as need, suffering, desire need to be included in analytic discourse, then so should terms having to do with commitment and relatedness—a sense of justice, of duty, of empathic responsiveness. As aspects of cultural life and practice, emotions and moral motives complement each other; one acts out of fear or desire, but also out of a sense of duty, or because one cares, or wants "to do the right thing." One person seeks release from suffering; another is moved to act out of a sense of injustice, or empathy, at seeing someone else suffer.

Moral terms thus enlarge the language of motives, in cultural life as well as analytic discourse. A deeper analysis of the nature, and moral force, of human commitments, will be needed if we are to understand fully people's motives and actions from their own perspective. The ways social actors may experience empathy for another, and act out of felt concern, or be moved to act by a powerfully felt sense of duty, or idea of justice, need to be clearly recognized and analyzed. As I have shown, these motives, as they take shape within culture and life, are of central significance for Newars.

As Ortner (1989:127, 198) points out, many culture theorists, from Ruth Benedict to Clifford Geertz and Michel Foucault, have either seen in persons almost nothing but reflections of culture, or at least left the impression that this is their view. To identify person and culture, however, poses difficulties. Yes, culture constructs and constrains, shaping inner worlds—powerfully; but individual existence, which contains an irreducible randomness, a portion of which flows from what we call history, may compel a re-relating of self to culture, and move a person to bring his or her life to culture in new ways, generating new meaning for cultural life (Obeyesekere 1981). Moreover, having abandoned the idea that culture is nothing but a reflection of the human psyche, it does not, as M. Rosaldo (1984:141) remarked, "make sense to claim that individuals—with their different histories, different bodies, and different ways of being more or less emotionally involved—are cultural systems cast in miniature."

Ortner's reflections on the choice we make as culture theorists and ethnographers, either to conflate selves and culture, or to separate them, are worth quoting:

It seems important to articulate a position that recognizes the ways in which actors are indeed cultural products, and yet that does not conflate actors' intentions and cultural forms. Correspondingly, it seems important to articulate a position in which there is some distance between actor and culture, and yet which does not postulate a culturally unconstrained actor. . . . My solution to this problem is to propose an actor who is "loosely structured," who is prepared — but no more than that — to find most of his or her culture intelligible and meaningful, but who does not necessarily find all parts of it equally meaningful in all times and places. The distance between culture and actor is there, but so is the capacity to find meaning, in more than a manipulative way, in one's own cultural repertoire. (1989:198)

Having recognized the need to recognize some "distance between actor and culture," the next step is to think through the relationship of culture and the human subject — the actor, self, agent. If people do not simply "internalize and enact" their culture, if they do not passively receive their emotions and intentions from cultural forms, symbols, or meanings, and if we cannot conceive of people exclusively as pragmatic actors who manipulate their culture to achieve their goals, then what does connect culture and the human subject? What intermediates? What sort of theoretical perspectives will help us see how actors are not so "embedded" in culture that they disappear, but equally are not fixed at such a "distance" from culture that culture cannot affect how they think, feel, and act at all?

These are questions I have struggled with, and I think you can see the signs of this struggle in the ethnographic chapters of this book, which represent one possible kind of answer — a cultural perspective tempered by a concern with self, life, and practice. Others will prefer a different balance, and will place self and culture closer together or farther apart.

I want to stress, however, that all anthropologists make judgments about this, and ultimately psychologists must, too. Different theoretical traditions suggest different "distances" for culture and self or mind — from mutual exclusion ("they basically don't have anything to do with each other") to identity ("they're virtually the same thing"). I find most interesting theoretical traditions that maintain a certain distance, but put them in significant relationship. For example, Wertsch and Stone (1985:162) examine the concept of "internalization" in the work of the Russian psychologist Vygotsky and his school. In this tradition, internalization is not a process that replicates culture within individuals, but one that transforms social and cultural material ("external activity").

> . . . the Vygotskian approach begins by rejecting both the assumption that the structures of external and internal activity are identical and the assumption that they are unrelated. . . . The first position makes the very notion of internalization uninteresting and trivial, whereas the second makes it unresolvable. Vygotsky argued that there is an inherent relationship between external and internal activity, but that it is a *genetic* or *developmental* relationship in which the major issue is how external processes are *transformed* to *create* internal processes. (1985:163; emphasis in original)

The mind here does not—mindlessly—duplicate external cultural forms. What was external, part of culture and society, becomes internal, part of mind and self, but is transformed. This transformation creates distance between culture and self, but links them in a dynamic, dialectical relationship. This cultural self is not "programmed" by culture, but is primed to find meaning in culture. Although generated in culture, the self is psychologically active and autonomous; even while seizing meaning from culture, persons bring meaning to culture, by tapping other sources of meaning, for example, elements of biographical and historical experience that are poorly represented in culture. Persons synthesize such personal meaning with cultural perspectives, so that self-making and culture-making are dynamic, reciprocal processes.

Cultural meanings, in any domain, do not just define ways of thinking, feeling, and doing; they have a deeper, two-way mediatory structure, giving shape to minds, but also giving minds the means of reshaping themselves, ultimately making it possible for minds to reshape culture or reconnect themselves with culture in new ways. Cultural meanings do not just produce consciousness in some mechanical fashion; by shaping minds up to a point, they provide actors with the means of grasping, producing, and transforming consciousness and life. People use some of the cognitive structures of culture to act on themselves and culture. The samskaric rites of passage are an example of how culture can be grasped as a reflexive tool, used to shape self, to generate commitments to key practices, and to reproduce cultural patterns, offering people one possible means of giving coherence and purpose to life, identity to self, moral meaning to social existence.

What wind
Serves to advance an honest mind.
— John Donne

To invoke Edward Sapir (1929) again, the moral worlds of other cultures are "distinct worlds, not merely the same world with different labels attached." Culture makes a difference; it makes different worlds, and we will not fully understand people unless we understand how they live their lives in these different worlds. At the same time, we need to recognize that many of these worlds also bear distinct family resemblance to each other. To reduce different moral worlds to an identity or to perceive them as wholly incommensurate seems equally false.

People everywhere do not think a god dwells in the heart, and not every moral order is protected by dangerous goddesses. Not everyone thinks of society as a god. These are real differences, and they make a difference in how people know themselves and their world. On the other hand, there may be moral universals that are part of every culture and near-universals that are embedded in many different cultural worlds. I do not know if every culture has a conception of justice (whether embedded in social actuality or nurtured in moral fantasy and in resistance to injustices), but Newars do, and their concepts resemble those found in some other cultures, without being identical—the karma doctrine encompasses the intuition that people (should) get what they deserve.

Extreme universalism and radical relativism seem limited perspectives, and adhering too strongly to either one may threaten our capacity to understand how people relate themselves to the values and self-images of their culture. We may need to tack between them—but not run aground on them—if we wish to get anywhere at all.

If the challenge we face is not to find what wind advances an honest mind, but to explore how culture nurtures the development of a moral self, I think the outline of a partial answer for Newars is clear from the ethnographic material. No doubt psychological developments advance a mind to moral consciousness, but cultur-

al experience propels the development of a moral self, completing
the process and completing the person. In part, it does so by defining what is real, what is valued, and what is self (offering self a
moral identity). In the Newar case, culture advances consciousness to moral states by enhancing empathy in the web of relatedness, by instilling a sense of kuldharma, by giving the self an identity in the samskara, by constituting a dialogue between self and
divinity, and so on.

What Newars as cultural actors know about dharma, their intuitions about what ultimately is at stake in their lives, their powerful sense of what must be, of what they must do, their concept of
the way their lives are joined together—all these flow from
Newars' engagement with specific cultural concepts and practices.
Their experience of myth, ritual, and symbol, their identifications
with others who are identified with cultural practices, the way
emotions relate them to the social world, their self-defining psychological work based on cultural self-images, the continual ritual
forging of the self—all these help Newars instill Newar moral consciousness in Newars. A moral ethos develops within the Newar
psyche, a mode of self-understanding, a mode of relatedness, as
Newars interact with cultured others, who help them know themselves. Quite simply, Newars work at knowing themselves in culture, work at making themselves out of what culture offers them,
and work to make themselves part of culture—often successfully.

This work—and I believe work is the best word to express the
idea of agency within culture—makes it possible for Bhaktapur
Newars to know the world and the self in the ways they do, as
Bhaktapurian Newar Hindu householders. When in the course of
the autumn festival, they join the celebrating crowds going with
drums and cymbals, with paper lanterns and offerings, to worship
at the Goddess shrines just beyond the city, Newars enact and live
the dharma-world of their own moral imagination.

NOTES

Introduction

1. See Shweder (1990); Stigler, Shweder, and Herdt (1990); Shweder and LeVine (1984); White and Kirkpatrick (1985); and Holland and Quinn (1987), among others.

2. Anthropological studies of morality include Ladd (1957); Read (1955); Beidelman (1986); Fiske (1990). Some of the most significant contemporary work has been undertaken by Richard Shweder and his colleagues, based on research in an Indian temple town (Shweder, Mahapatra, and Miller 1987). T. N. Madan (1987) has written on the moral values of the Hindu householder.

3. For a range of Western academic views, see the philosophers Gerwirth (1978); MacIntyre (1981); Rawls (1971); Wuthnow (1987). The tradition of cognitive-psychological studies of moral development that originated with Jean Piaget is associated most closely with Lawrence Kohlberg, but has been developed in new directions by Elliot Turiel and his associates.

4. Other studies of the Newars include: Allen (1975, 1976, 1982); Greenwold (1978, 1981); Gellner (1992); Gutschow and Kolver (1975); Gutschow and Michaels (1987); Iltis (1985); Lewis (1984); Nepali (1965); Slusser (1982).

1. Learning to See a Sacred City

1. Williams (1977: 132) coined the term "structure of feeling." It denotes "meanings and value as they are actively lived and felt," whether part of a formal belief system or not.

2. The title of this chapter is adapted from Anthony Forge's (1970) article "Learning to see in New Guinea."

3. Levy (1990: 56) calculates that 39,061 people lived as permanent residents in 6,484 households in Bhaktapur; 60 households were non-Newar (Levy 1990: 59). In the 1971 census, 8% identified themselves as Buddhist, 92% as Hindu.

4. See Slusser (1982) and Levy (1990) on Taleju.

5. See Levy (1990: 153–156, 158–159, 228–231) on these goddesses and Bhaktapur as mandala. Some of the perimeter shrines are enclosed in structures.

6. The line dividing city from surrounding paddy fields was still fairly sharply defined in the early 1980s, although new construction was beginning to blur it. The process of secondary urbanization invading agricultural lands had proceeded much farther in Kathmandu.

7. This symbolism is part of a general South Asian tradition, but only two of Bhaktapur's three cremations grounds are on the far side of the river. Infants are not cremated, but buried in a special area. Lower, "impure" castes may be cremated in fields around the city, not at the cremations grounds.

8. This passage from the Devi Mahatmya accords well with verbal accounts offered by Newars and other Nepalese; it is taken here from Agrawala's (1963) translation, quoted in Levy (1990: 246) and Bennett (1983: 264–265).

9. From the Devi Mahatyma, quoted in Levy (1990: 560).

10. Cutting the animals throat is seen as Newar, while sacrifice by decapitation, as done in the government-sponsored sacrifices, is more characteristic of other ethnic groups.

11. Levy (1990); Gutschow and Basukala (1987).

12. On Tantrism in general, see Gupta, Hoens, and Goudriaan (1979); on Tantrism in Bhaktapur, Levy (1990); and on Newar Buddhist Tantrism, Gellner (1992) .

13. As Levy (1990: 208) points out, Newars identify different deities as the all-encompassing, creative source of the divine, such as Shiva or the Goddess; more impersonally and abstractly, the principle of divinity may be called *brahma* or paramatman, while others speak of Bhagavan or Isvara. Harper (1959), Babb (1975), and Wadley (1975) discuss the pantheons of other South Asian communities.

14. See Levy (1990: 282–283) on divinities as "persons," or "person-like" in Bhaktapur and in comparative perspective.

15. A different approach to death and salvation is available to upper-caste males with Tantric initiations. They must also meditate on Vishnu (a non-Tantric deity) but Tantric discipline can also help the dying person quiet his mind, eliminating bad thoughts that might lead to a bad rebirth (Levy 1990: 318).

16. On the Bhaktapur Kumari, see Levy (1990); on Kumari worship in the Kathmandu Valley, see Allen (1975, 1976).

17. On myth models, see Obeyesekere (1981).

18. Members of a thar may see themselves as sharing an ancestor in some cases, but in other thars, thar membership and the shared surname has to do with a common historical origin in an occupation or group (Levy 1990: 138). Gellner (1992: 64–65) links thars to the caste system, and says thar names identify what he calls caste subgroups, which have a social and religious identity within the status system, but are not themselves exogamous like kin units or endogamous like more inclusive caste units. Thar names locate people in the caste system, without thars, strictly speaking, being "castes" or "subcastes" themselves.

19. The idea that a dying person should be close to the earth is a Hindu idea (Kane 1953) found in other South Asian communities (Gold 1988).

20. A household may include others beyond this core, such as a deceased brother's children. In a survey of a farming group in Bhaktapur, I found that 43% of 66 households were extended at the time of the survey; 40% could be categorized as nuclear family households, and 17% did not fit into either category. Clearly the joint family is frequently both an ideal and an empirical reality. Average household size was 7.3; this is close to the figure given by Acharya and Ansari (1980) for Bhaktapur as a whole (based on their survey of 327 households). These farming families ranged in size from 2 to 16 members.

21. Compare Bourdieu (1977): Rosaldo (1989), and Sapir (1985) [1934].

22. Theodore Schwartz's (1978) concept of the distributive locus of culture and of "idioverses" as the subjective segment of a larger cultural universe is relevant here.

2. Society, Person, and Moral Order

1. We cannot totally free ourselves of culture in our reflections on culture or self; most thought is thought-in-culture, even when it is culture-transforming thought.

2. South Asian cultural ideology recognizes agency, of course—that actors are what they are because of what they do is incorporated in South Asian thought alongside the notion that actors do what they do because of what they are (E. V. Daniel 1984: 213). The power of actors to "make"

themselves and society is often treated as very limited, however, and their substance—their material or biomoral, action-determining, essence—viewed as mutable only in quite limited ways. See Marriott (1976, 1990); Inden and Nichols (1977); E. V. Daniel (1984) on code and substance, actor and action.

3. The translation here glosses—imperfectly—the key word *samskara*, which means training, education, sacrament; here used in the sense of a culturally cultivated "being," or "nature." The term also refer to key rituals.

4. Govinda is alluding here not only to the role of kin, but to the death societies (*si-guthi*) that every Newar belongs to, which see to the cremation of the corpse.

5. Dangerous forms of the Goddess may represent the problematics of women's place in society from the perspective of men (Bennett 1983). Perhaps the dangerous goddesses also resonate with suppressed rage women experience in a male-dominant culture; see Menon and Shweder (n.d.) on women's anger as an element in the interpretation of the mythology and iconography of the dangerous goddess Kali in Orissa, India. Iltis (1985) describes a compilation of stories in which Parvati is involved as a humanlike figure struggling with recognizably human problems that arise in Hindu society; this text is also discussed by Bennett (1983).

6. The woman must be from a "water acceptable" caste, rather than from one of the castes considered more polluting, for example, the Butcher caste, or from an untouchable caste, such as the Pore.

7. Kane (1953) traces the range of meanings given the term *dharma* in Hindu texts. See also Lingat(1973).

8. Wadley and Derr (1990: 139) quote an "elderly Brahman" as saying dharma "has no color nor has anyone seen it."

9. A person's duties to predecessors include performing rites that create a "spiritual body" for those who have died, and the making of offerings (of balls of flour called *pinda*).

10. The differentiation of the moral discourse of Newar informants of different castes could be interpreted in terms of the nondistinction or interchangeability of the physical and the moral, the natural and the social, in South Asian thought: Brahmans say and do what Brahmans say and do because it is the nature of their moral being to do so; high-caste Chathariyas know and act in ways consistent with what they are, with their distinctive biomoral nature; moral views of untouchables reflect their substance, the natural kind of persons they are. I have no objection to applying this interpretation here, as long as we also try to see how this discourse is "positioned," and do not try to reify "coded-substance" as an exclusive explanatory principle. These three Newars might well agree with the proposition that "people do and know what they are"—some-

times. And deny it in another context. To mechanically reconstruct their testimony in terms of cultural theories of coded-substance seems perilous; doing so, we have to make free use of the "privilege of totalization" (Bourdieu 1977), drawing on what we know about South Asian culture as analysts. While doing this is unavoidable and necessary, we should be cautious not to overinterpret. That moral diversity can be glossed in terms of a particular cultural theory only proves it *can be* glossed in those terms, not that the diversity we encounter here was *generated* or *experienced* in those terms, and only those terms.

11. I adopt terms used by linguist Ronald Langacker's here (1986, 1987); see also D'Andrade (1990: 74–77). Meaning derives not from either the base or the profile, but from their combination or relationship. Dharma may designate what Langacker terms a "basic domain" or an "abstract domain." A basic domain is not, at root, an aggregate or a construction. An abstract domain is defined in terms of a basic domain, and then serves as the matrix for other, higher order concepts. Examples of basic domains are "space" and "time." According to Langacker (1987: 149), "basic domains occupy the lowest level in hierarchies of conceptual complexity: they furnish the primitive representational space necessary for the emergence of any specific conception."

12. On dharma and related concepts, see Gellner (1992) on Buddhist Newars; and Srinivas' (1976) account of an Indian village.

13. On the concept of pap/sin in a Hindu village in North India, see Wadley and Derr (1990); Bennett (1983) discusses pap among the Chetris of Nepal as it applies to women.

14. On karma, see Keyes and Daniel (1983); O'Flaherty (1980); Neufeldt (1986); Sharma (1973); Obeyesekere (1968). Newars often use the word "karma" to refer to ritual action, and use phrases such as "the sins of the previous life" to refer to the karmic doctrine that one may suffer in this life for the acts of previous lives.

15. As one informant put it: "Another easy way [of removing sin] is . . . . to wash your face . . . to bathe, to wash your eyes. These are forms of purification. . . . [Bathing] removes the dirt of the body. . . pap is dirt too. It is bad, although the eyes cannot see it." Although associated with pap, the idea of purification is more fully developed in terms of the *relatively* independent concepts of impurity. The equating of "sin" and "impurity" has a venerable history in South Asia (Kane 1953: 37)

16. Dharma Raj is clearly drawing on the tradition of moral and legal texts. Compare Kane (1953: 173). See Kane (1953: 37, 61–65) on intentional and unintentional sins.

17. I asked such questions when I was trying to determine whether there would be any value in using the sort of hypothetical stories that have been a common method of studying "moral reasoning" in research

in the United States and cross-culturally; one of the stories, the (in)famous Heinz dilemma, concerns what a man should do to save his wife, who is dying, and can only be saved by acquiring a treatment he can not afford to pay for. I decided not to use this methodology because the Newars I tried it out on tended to dismiss the stories as transparent or naive—and I agreed. (Of course the man should steal, said one Newar—smiling—what could be clearer?—the story presented no dilemma at all to this informant. Another said—unsmilingly—that the woman would die, and argued that the story proposes possibilities of action and justice lacking in the real world.) The stories are hypothetical, appear culture-bound, and seem to tap how people read and gloss stories rather than how people make moral arguments based on their own culture in ways relevant to their own lives. Shweder and Much (1987) take advantage of the way the Heinz dilemma is the product of a culture to show how an Indian informant responds to the story in terms of a different, but sophisticated, set of moral assumptions.

18. On theodicies as cultural formations, and on the "ethicization" of religion in general, see Obeyesekere (1968).

19. I suspect Newars might "fail" to achieve the "highest stage" of "post-conventional" moral reasoning proposed by Lawrence Kohlberg (1969, 1971, 1981, 1983) as the end-point of moral development in research based in the same cultural tradition as Western moral philosophy. See Shweder, Mahapatra, and Miller (1987) for a summary of the extensive criticism of the Kohlberg paradigm.

20. Not only may a philosophical holism that takes society as the grounds for speculation about the nature of moral existence be as rational a starting point for discourse as philosophical individualism, it may be just as one-sided. Such discourse may obscure the value of the individual self, just as I suspect the rhetoric, and even the critique, of Western individualism obscures the actual, the felt, the enacted significance of holism in many segments of the not-so-homogeneous Western world.

3. The Web of Relatedness

1. After writing this passage, I discovered that the Millennium series for public television, narrated by anthropologist David Maybury-Lewis, invokes Gauguin's painting and its title, suggesting these questions are indeed "good to think."

2. Dumont (1960, 1980, 1983, 1985, 1986). To say, on the basis of Western concepts of the individual, that Indian or Hindu culture neglects the individual or finds no value in the existence of the individual self seems ethnocentric. Newars and others may simply find different mean-

ings in individual existence and value it in different ways. For a critique of Dumont, see McHugh (1989).

3. The echo of Geertz's famous definition of the "Western" concept of the person is deliberate (1984).

4. Mandelbaum (1970) and Kakar (1981:132) note that the relationships of fathers and sons in the Indian joint family are often marked by a certain reserve and distance. This has some parallel in some Newar households.

5. I suspect this sea change in attitude expresses a degree of guilt about striving for independence in the face of the father's need for continuity.

6. Among Newars, the priority of males and male-based bonds is not as strongly stressed as in some other patrilineal cultures, however, even cognate cultures in Nepal (Bennett 1983).

7. Perhaps an identification with the son's wife also exists. Since the bhau maca is their son's sexual partner, this may be disturbing, and so undermine empathy.

8. The words for "to grow" and "to be born" are close; the ambiguity may be intentional here.

9. Madan (1987: 25–26) notes that Kashmiri Pandits have similar ideas. Following Delaney (1987) we might term this a theory of monogenesis—which recognizes the male contribution to the genesis of the person, but not the female one. The informant defined women as nurturing shapers of persons in other contexts.

10. Madan (1983: 105–106) notes a similar stress on the mother's nuture as source of recognized moral and emotional bonds among Kashmiri Pandits.

11. In Bengal, Fruzzetti, Östör, and Barnett (1983: 18–19) write, husbands and wives "are cultivator and field. Men sow the seed and the field accepts the seed." Compare Inden and Nicholas (1977: 52). Kashmiri Pandits use the same analogy (Madan 1987: 26). The imagery is also found in Turkey, where villagers sometimes point out that the idea of women as field and men as providers of seed is found in the Koran (Delaney 1987: 38)

12. Purity and impurity have been the subject of much attention by anthropologists who have produced a vast literature on the topic. For a fuller discussion of purity and pollution among Newars, and a review of theories, see Levy (1990, ch. 11).

13. Gellner (1992: 242) in his study of Buddhist Newars makes this point in terms of rites associated with the worship of lineage deities. The rite has male lineage members sip beer from a skull bowl offered by the senior unwidowed female. Gellner concludes that "the ritual is clearly one of lineage solidarity since—a point emphasized by informants—all share others' pollution (cipa) by sipping from the same bowl. . . . since the bowl

passes from senior to junior it also emphasizes rank: juniors share seniors' pollution but not vice versa."

14. Practices vary: some households have relaxed, others strict, attitudes. On cipa, see Levy (1990: 118–120).

15. Care is taken not to pollute food while cooking; this is enforced by the female head of house.

16. This is my formulation, not a Newar one. It seems to me that some actors—those more central to the domestic group—can potentially minimize substance-sharing transactions, while others are forced to accept substance from a wide range of others. This defines a direction of flow of substance. However, some Newars ignore this potential structure, and allow a freer commingling of substance or essence, perhaps with the goal of enhancing intimacy.

17. Some Newars reported that a woman in this position may resist eating the cipa of brothers' wives. The micropolitics and communicative pragmatics of this deserve further study.

18. Other forms of pollution also mark the "unity" of the family. Death and birth pollution separate a family from others, and mark the internal solidarity (or equivalence) of the family. Hierarchy structures this context as well; for example, when a senior male dies, his eldest son will act as chief ritual mourner.

19. Thus, it is not surprising that the "family resemblance" Newar concepts bear to constructs of relatedness found in other groups extends beyond South Asia. For example, Myers (1986) examines Pintupi concepts of relatedness, showing how fundamental the construction of relatedness is to their cultural life. It is not easy to imagine two cultures more different than the Newars, with their urban caste hierarchy, and the Pintupi, traditionally hunters and gatherers in the Western Desert of Australia, but there appear to be important similarities, as well as fundamental differences. Both groups generate a "nurturing hierarchy," stressing the way people must "look after" others. In both, "autonomy is inseparable from relatedness" (Myers 1986: 239), although in different ways.

20. For important discussions of "love" and "empathic" emotions, see Trawick (1990) on *apnu* in Tamil culture; Gerber (1985) on the Samoan *alofa*; and Myers (1986) on "compassion" and "relatedness" among the Pintupi.

21. The double meaning of the term *maya* suggests the opposition/complementarity of the moral worlds of the renouncer and of the householder in Hindu culture. Madan (1987: 1n1) notes that either their opposition or complementarity may be stressed, either in analysis, or, presumably, in life.

22. See Kakar (1981: 52–112) for a psychoanalytically oriented analysis of the mother-infant relationship in Hindu India.

23. Did this woman and her children face hunger, or did she only feel deprived? Either or both are possible. Hunger, like food, is both an aspect of biological reality and a cultural metaphor for Newars.

24. Particular visions of kin grow out of intimate contact with persons, and absorb something of the unique history of two connected lives. The psychological and cultural organization of relatedness make certain kinds and degrees of conflict probable.

25. That is, empathy seems to me to be a sociocognitive institution in which people work to know themselves and each other—it is a product of the cultural linkage of mental and social structures, not of some innate mental capacity alone. Freud once suggested that "A path leads from identification by way of imitation to empathy" (1959:42). I would amend Freud's statement to say that a path leads from identification by way of cultural symbols or meanings to empathy. Reciprocally, people acquire culture through identification with cultured others.

26. Carol Gilligan (1982) has written of the gender differences in moral style among Americans, arguing that women tend to stress an ethic of care and empathy, while men stress justice perspectives.

27. See Kane (1953).

28. The continuity of the lineage achieved in terms of identification runs not only from successor to predecessor, but from predecessor to successor (see Geertz 1973). Madan (1987) quotes Kashmiri Pandits as saying "As we do for our ancestors so will our sons and grandsons do for us."

29. I have adopted the term "hierarchical love" from Inden and Nicholas' study of Bengali kinship (1977) and modified it to fit the Newar case; Inden and Nicholas also speak of egalitarian love, but I prefer "empathic" love because it suggests emotions that can be experienced in hierarchical relations and contexts as well as egalitarian ones. Roland's (1982, 1988) insights into "emotional structures" of hierarchy and relatedness in the Hindu family are also relevant to the discussion here.

30. McHugh (1989) and Mines (1988) critique the overstressing of holism.

31. "Official" ideology, of course, may construct holism as value or objective reality, or at least the analyst, assuming what Bourdieu (1977) calls "the privilege of totalization" may construct and reify a version of official ideology that constructs and reifies a particular vision of reality— excluding much of actual cultural experience and practice.

32. R. S. Khare (1978) identifies "symbolic formations" in South Asian thought—e.g, "one becomes many," "parts are essentially the same as the whole"—that may help generate webs of relatedness by making it possible for people to be "one" (group) and "many" (selves) at the same time. People can follow such symbolic links "upward," identifying themselves

with the whole, and then follow them back "downward" into plurality and self-identity in a recursive fashion.

4. The Sacred Mind

1. On emotion and culture, see, e.g., Abu-Lughod (1986); Herdt (1987); Levy (1973, 1984); Lindholm (1982); Lutz (1988); Lutz and White (1986); Lutz and Abu-Lughod (1990); Lynch (1990a, 1990b); McHugh (1989); Myers (1979, 1986); Obeyesekere (1981); M. Rosaldo (1980); White and Kirkpatrick (1985).

2. Some mention head and brain as involved in mental processes, especially thinking. This may represent a modern viewpoint influenced by outside conceptions, or simply the notion that speech is analogous to thought. The term *nuga:* refers to the physical organs of the chest cavity as well as to mental entities and processes. In other ways, it is quite close to the Nepali concept of *man* and the Gurung concept of *sae*, which are also located in the chest and are the seat of intention, cognition, memory, and emotion (McHugh 1989). Although nuga: might be glossed "heart-mind" or "heart-self," I have decided to follow English-speaking Newars in glossing it simply as "heart," except where it seems useful to emphasize the way nuga: fuses together what we would distinguish as "mind" and "self."

3. I draw on D'Andrade's (1987) discussion of the American "folk model" of mind, for comparative insights, and here echo his comments on the taken-for-granted quality of the American "folk" model of mind.

4. Notice how what happens inside the mind is mapped out in terms of what happens outside the self, in the public, perceptible world. D'Andrade (1987: 145) notes that cultural understandings of mental life cannot be totally private; if they were, neither children nor ethnographer could learn anything about them.

5. See McHugh (1989) for a discussion of the analogous Gurung concept of *sae*. Sae, like *nuga:*, allows individuals to represent self-experience in cultural terms.

6. I am speaking here of the ethnopsychology of everyday experience. The idea of the "inner" manipulation of mental states is, of course, highly developed as a religious practice in many of the religious traditions of South Asia, including Newar Tantrism. The relationship of Tantrism to the ethnopsychology of everyday life is a subject that merits more research.

7. Much research exists on "shame," dating from early attempts to identify and contrast "shame cultures" and "guilt cultures" (Piers and Singer 1971). In South Asia, Obeyesekere (1984: 499–508) has discussed shame and the socialization of shame in the context of Sinhala culture,

suggesting that the particular cultural emphasis on shame makes the Sinhalese vulnerable to the loss or enhancement of self-esteem, and highly sensitive to status precedence. He conceptualizes shame in terms of sensitivity to the responses of others, as I do for Newars. Obeyesekere associates a desire to humiliate others, and to become enraged at slights, with the sense of shame. Such themes do not seem to be as pronounced in Newar culture. In my view, the relationship of shame and empathy deserves attention. Both seem to involve a dialectical, culturally mediated, relationship of self and other (Sartre 1963; Obeyesekere 1984: 502–503).

8. Menon and Shweder's (n.d.) work in Orissa, India, suggests how lajya may be linked conceptually to the control of female rage as well as sexuality.

9. Compare Abu-Lughod on Bedouin women (1986).

10. Some Newar women view the relationship of lajya and behavior in pragmatic terms. Consider the following bit of an interview (reconstructed from notes): (Did anyone ever say "lajya is a woman's jewel"to you?) Yes. (Who said it to you?) My mother. (What do you think she was trying to tell you by saying that?) She was trying to tell me I shouldn't act like a man. I should be shy and gentle, and serving. (Are you any of those things?) Sometimes. (Why was she telling you to be like that?). So that I can please my husband. (So you would please your husband? Why do you need to please your husband?) So they won't kick you out from the house, as husbands often do. (That is the only reason you should please your husband?) No, not the only reason. (What other reasons?) So that my husband will be happy, and earn money to feed the family.

11. Methodologically, it may often be wisest to begin with culturally explicit ethnopsycholoical theories and discursive constructions of emotion (Lutz and White 1986; Rosaldo 1983) as long as we do not identity the totality of emotional experience with these.

12. *Vrata* are practices, involving worship and austerities of various kinds, including fasts, that Hindus view as means to desired ends. Wadley (1983) terms them "transformers of destiny."

13. Bateson (1972) pointed out that people's models or understandings of self-control might, in some cases, be wrong in such a way that efforts to exercise self-control would produce the opposite results—a loss of control.

14. The language of "transgression" and "retribution" in moral accounts of anger would seen to presuppose the possibility of a "self" who may take a stand. See Lutz (1988) for an illuminating discussion of "justifiable anger" in the context of Ifaluk values and ethnopsychology.

15. Quoted in Shweder (1990).

5. Creating Moral Selves

1. *Kaeta Puja*, by Hridaya Candrasingh Pradhan.

2. See Levy (1990); Nepali (1965); and Toffin (1984) for descriptions. Other kinds of rituals and festivals are also of great importance in Newar life (Levy 1990) but space does not permit discussion here.

3. See Toffin (1975); Levy (1990).

4. Cole and Cole (1989: 411) note that studies from different societies report an increase in time spent without adult supervision between ages five to seven (e.g., Whiting and Whiting 1975). Children tend to be given more independence and responsibility beginning at this age, and to be held more accountable for their actions. Cole and Cole (1989, ch. 13) cite work suggesting that biological developments in the brain during the five- to seven-year-old period may underlie this. They also summarize evidence for suggesting that children during these years may develop a new "quality of mind" based on new "forms of remembering," or on an increased integration of forms of remembering, working in relationship to an increased "knowledge base," a store of information about the world. I would speculate that cognitive and biological developments at about ages five to seven prepare children to learn culture in new ways, as links between what the child knows and cultural knowledge (not only a body of information, but an organization of knowledge) are forged, making possible increased responsibility to networks of cultural norms. Children may enter a period of cultural apprenticeship at this age — adults translate their observations that children can learn more and be more responsible into expectations that children will learn and enact cultural behaviors, and so adults begin to declare and enforce norms for such behavior.

5. He means a Lakhe Brahman, who acts as family priest to lower status groups, not a Rajopadhyaya Brahman.

6. For comparative purposes, I define adulthood as the stage of life during which men and women assume full responsibility for themselves and others, and possess nearly the fullest autonomy their culture grants. This may sound slightly paradoxical, as if people have the most freedom when they are most constrained, but I think the connection is necessary. Responsibilities are entrusted to those with the greatest capacity to carry them out, and this typically requires they have nearly the fullest autonomy their society confers, so that they can use judgment and apply their talents. To deny that South Asians have individual autonomy because they are socially constrained misses this critical link between autonomy and relationship, among others. Only when Newars have married and had children do Newars become full "adults." Even then, they may be subordinate to their father or to senior in-laws within the extended fam-

ily, achieving complete autonomy and responsibility only when this older generation dies, loses, or surrenders authority.

7. It is not clear whether he means "understanding" comes if you do dharma, or generally develops after the performance of kaeta puja.

8. Note that Mahila places his jat above the Jugi, in contrast to the "ideal" consensus which places his lower.

9. In my discussion here, I am making a *relative* judgment. Clearly, Americans also see themselves as shaping children. For example, the anxiety that many American parents experience seems to reflect the concept that they make—or spoil—their children. Thus, if I were contrasting American culture with some other cultures—with Tahitian concepts of child development (Levy 1973), say, or with the practices of the Inuit people (Briggs 1973), or with the concepts of childhood prevalent among the Fulani (Riesman 1992)—I would (as Riesman does for the Fulani) be more inclined to emphasize the way Americans see themselves as shaping or making children. But I think Newars stress the social production of children even more than many Americans, at least more than those influenced by some developmental theories. And I would want to explore the possibility that even American concepts of social shaping are influenced by a concept of nature and by the ideal of an autonomous, developing, individual self. Most Americans, I would speculate, do not think of children's being and becoming primarily in terms of social and ritual transformation, as flowing primarily from relatedness and ritual action. Even concepts of "social development" may reflect a psychological orientation.

10. The Buddhist Bare—the Vajracarya and Shakya—do not have angsa, presumably because at one time they were in fact celibate monks rather than householders, as they are now.

11. Here I am inspired by some remarks in Rawls (1971: 404–415).

Postscript: Culture and Moral Knowing

1. See Sapir (1985 [1934]), who reminds us that it is all too easy to assemble cultural materials into a "culture" that does not in fact correspond to anything in reality. Compare Bourdieu (1977, 1990).

2. Quoted in Heath (1983: 389n9).

3. Compare Shweder, Mahapatra, and Miller (1987: 18), Shore (1990).

GLOSSARY

Note on transliteration: Diacritical marks have been omitted in this volume, except for the use of (n) following a vowel to show the nasalization of that vowel and the use of a colon to indicate the *visarga* of Devanagari script, which the scribes who transcribed my interview tapes used to mark a lengthening of the vowel. Newari is a Tibeto-Burman language that has adopted many words and usages from Indo-European languages, and its moral and intellectual vocabulary is much influenced by Sanskrit. There is no standard system for the transliteration or spelling of Newari, and in some instances I have made arbitrary decisions (e.g., by using a Sanskritized, rather than a colloquial, form of a word). I have based my choices largely on the conventions used by the Bhaktapur scribes who transcribed my interviews into the Devanagari script and, secondarily, on Levy's (1990) system for Bhaktapur Newari.

angsa — a tuft or queue of hair at the back of the head symbolic of the status of a Hindu householder

atma [atman]–soul, the ultimate spiritual essence of each person, the portion of divinity within each person

barha cwa(n)gu/barha taegu – menarche ceremonies, life-cycle rites

bhau maca – daughter-in-law

bhutu – hearth, hearth area

bibek – intelligence, discrimination, used sometimes in the sense of the ability to know what is the right thing to do

buddhi — understanding, intelligence

busakha — a boy's head-shaving ceremony, one of the Newar samskara

cipa — food or objects that have absorbed transferable essences or substances by being tasted or touched by a person; in the idiom of impurity, food or items "polluted" by contact with a source of impurity

dharma — duty, religion, prescribed custom, moral law; the objective and nonarbitary basis of morality and social roles; the moral order that is the foundation of the cosmos and human society

digu dya: — a form of lineage deity

dukha — suffering

gyan — knowledge

guthi — an association established for some purpose, e.g., to help with funeral rites and cremation

iccha — desire

ihi — a girl's symbolic marriage to Vishnu/Narayana, one of the Newar samskara

ijjat — prestige, honor, reputation, social esteem

jat — caste, kind

Jyapu — a farmer, the farmer caste

kaeta puja — the rite of giving the loincloth; one of the samskara

karma — the idea that what happens to an individual—his or her fate or condition—is the result of his or her actions, either in the current life or in previous lives; also used in sense of action, ritual action

kul — lineage, the family line

kuldharma — the dharma of the kul, the duties of the householder and lineage member

lajya — shame, embarrassment, shyness, modesty

maca janko — first rice feeding ceremony, one of the samskara

maya — love, illusion

Mohani — a religious festival celebrating the Goddess Bhagavati, also known as Dasain in Nepali

moksha — liberation from suffering, release from cycle of rebirths

Nae — butcher caste

Nau — barber caste

nini — father's sister

nuga: — heart, heart-self

nyaya — justice

paju — mother's brother

pap — sin, wrong, transgression, a violation of dharma

pastae — remorse, regret, contrition

phuki — a lineage group

Pore [or Po(n)] — an untouchable caste; Sweepers

prasad — items such as food or flowers offered to a divinity that are retrieved by, or distributed to, worshipers at the end of puja, who eat or adorn themselves with these items

puja — worship

samaj — society

samskara — a rite of passage; by extension, the attitudes, mental states, qualities of mind and self that are the product of such rites

shakti — spiritual power

ta(n) — anger

thar — a clanlike surname group that locates people in the caste system

twa: — the ward or neighborhood of a Newar city, with some of the qualities of an "urban village"

BIBLIOGRAPHY

Abu-Lughod, L. 1986. *Veiled Sentiments*. Berkeley: University of California Press.

Acharya, R. and H. Ansari. 1980. *Basic Needs and Government Services: An Area Study of Bhaktapur Town Panchayat, Nepal*. Center for Economic Development and Administration, Tribhuvan University, Kathmandu, Nepal.

Agrawala, V. 1963. *Devi-Mahatmya: The Glorification of the Great Goddess*. Varanasi: All-India Kahiraj Trust.

Allen, M. 1975. *The Cult of Kumari: Virgin Worship in Nepal*. Kathmandu: Institute of Nepal and Asian Studies.

— 1976. "Kumari or `Virgin' Worship in the Kathmandu Valley." *Contributions to Indian Sociology* (n.s.) 10(2): 293–316.

— 1982. "Girl's Pre-Puberty Rites Amongst the Newars of Nepal." In *Women in India and Nepal*, M. Allen and S. N. Mukherjee, eds. Canberra: Australian National University Press.

Babb, L. 1975. *The Divine Hierarchy: Popular Hinduism in Central India*. New York: Columbia University Press.

— 1983. "Destiny and Responsibility: Karma in Popular Hinduism." In *Karma: An Anthropological Inquiry*, C. Keyes and E. V. Daniel, eds. Berkeley: University of California Press.

Bailey, F. G. 1983. *The Tactical Uses of Passion*. Ithaca: Cornell University Press.

Bateson, G. 1972. *Steps to an Ecology of Mind*. New York: Ballantine Books.

Beidelmann, T. O. 1986. *Moral Imagination in Kaguru Modes of Thought*. Bloomington: Indiana University Press.

Bennett, L. 1983. *Dangerous Wives and Sacred Sisters: Social and Symbolic Roles of High Caste Women in Nepal*. New York: Columbia University Press.

Blum, L. 1987. "Particularity and Responsiveness." In *The Emergence of Moral Concepts in Young Children*, J. Kagan and S. Lamb, eds. Chicago: University of Chicago Press.

Bourdieu, P. 1977. *Outline of A Theory of Practice*. Cambridge: Cambridge University Press.

— 1990. *The Logic of Practice*. Stanford: Stanford University Press.

Briggs, C. 1986. *Learning How to Ask*. New York: Cambridge University Press.

Carrithers, M., S. Collins, and S. Lukes, eds. 1985. *The Category of the Person*. Cambridge: Cambridge University Press.

Cole, M. and S. Cole. 1989. *The Development of Children*. New York: Scientific American Books.

D'Andrade, R. G. 1984. "Cultural Meaning Systems." In *Culture Theory: Essays on Mind, Self, and Emotion*, R. A. Shweder and R. A. LeVine, eds. New York: Cambridge University Press.

— 1987. "A Folk Model of the Mind." In *Cultural Models in Language and Thought*, D. Holland and N. Quinn, eds. Cambridge: Cambridge University Press.

— 1990. "Some Propositions About the Relations Between Culture and Human Cognition." In *Cultural Psychology*, J. Stigler, R. A. Shweder and G. Herdt, eds. Cambridge: Cambridge University Press.

Daniel, E. V. 1984. *Fluid Signs: Being a Person the Tamil Way*. Berkeley: University of California Press.

Daniel, S. B. 1983. "The Tool Box Approach of the Tamil to the Issues of Moral Responsibility and Human Destiny." In *Karma: An Anthropological Inquiry*, Charles Keyes and E. Valentine, eds. Berkeley: University of California Press.

Delaney, C. 1987. "Seeds of Honor, Fields of Shame." In *Honor and Shame and the Unity of the Mediterranean*. D. Gilmore, ed. Washington, D.C.: American Anthropological Association.

Dumont, L. 1960. "World Renunciation in Indian Religions." *Contributions to Indian Sociology* 4: 3–62. Reprinted as Appendix B in *Homo Hierarchicus*, 1980. Complete revised English edition. Chicago: University of Chicago Press.

— 1965. "The Functional Equivalents of the Individual in Caste Society." *Contributions to Indian Sociology* 7: 85–99.

— 1980. *Homo Hierarchicus: The Caste System and Its Implications*. Complete revised English edition. Chicago: University of Chicago Press.

— 1985. "A Modified View of Our Origins: The Christian Beginnings of Modern Individualism." In *The Category of the Person*, M. Carrithers et al., eds. Cambridge: Cambridge University Press.

— 1986. *Essays on Individualism: Modern Ideology in Anthropological Perspective*. Chicago: University of Chicago Press.

Durkheim, E. 1915. *The Elementary Forms of the Religious Life*. New York: Free Press, 1965.

Fisher, J., ed. 1978. *Himalayan Anthropology*. The Hague: Mouton.

Fiske, A., ed. 1990. *Moral Relativism*. Special issue of *Ethos* 18 (2).

Forge, A. 1970. "Learning to See in New Guinea." In *Socialization*, P. Mayers, ed. London: Tavistock.

Freud, S. 1959. *Group Psychology and the Analysis of the Ego*. New York: Norton.

Fruzzetti, L., A. Östör, and S. Barnett. 1983. "The Cultural Construction of the Person in Bengal and Tamilnadu." In *Concepts of Person: Kinship, Caste and Marriage in India*, A. Östör, L. Fruzzetti, and S. Barnett, eds. Delhi: Oxford University Press.

Fuller, C. J. 1992. *The Camphor Flame: Popular Hinduism and Society in India*. Princeton: Princeton University Press.

Geertz, C. 1973. *The Interpretaion of Cultures*. New York: Basic Books.

— 1983. *Local Knowledge*. New York: Basic Books.

Gellner, D. 1992. *Monk, Householder, and Tantric Priest: Newar Buddhism and Its Hierarchy of Ritual*. Cambridge: Cambridge University Press.

Gerber, E. 1985. "Rage and Obligation: Samoan Emotions in Conflict." In *Person, Self, and Experience: Exploring Pacific Ethnopsychologies*, G. White and J. Kirkpatrick, eds. Berkeley: University of California Press. .

Gerwith, A. 1978. *Reason and Morality*. Chicago: University of Chicago Press.

Gilligan, C. 1982. *In A Different Voice*. Cambridge: Harvard University Press.

Gold, A. G. 1988. *Fruitful Journeys: The Ways of Rajasthani Pilgrims*. Berkeley: University of California Press.

Greenwold, S. M. 1978. "The Role of the Priest in Newar Society." In *Himalayan Anthropology*, J. Fisher, ed. The Hague: Mouton.

— 1981."Caste: A Moral Structure and A Social System of Control." In *Culture and Morality*, A. Mayer, ed. Oxford: Oxford University Press.

Gupta, S., D. J. Hoens, and T. Goudriaan. 1979. *Hindu Tantrism*. Leiden and Cologne: E. J. Brill.

Gutschow, N. and B. Kolver. 1975. *Ordered Space Concepts and Functions in a Town in Nepal*. Kathmandu: University Press.

Gutschow, N. and G. M. Basukala. 1987. "The Navadurga of Bhaktapur: Spatial Implications of an Urban Ritual." *In Heritage of the Kathmandu*

Valley, N. Gutschow and A. Michaels, eds. Sankt Augustin: VGH Wissenschaftsverlag.

Habermas, J. 1990. *Moral Consciousness and Communicative Action*. Cambridge: MIT Press.

Harper, E. B. ed. 1964. *Religion in South Asia*. Seattle: University of Washington Press.

Heath, S. B. 1983. *Ways with Words*. Cambridge: Cambridge University Press.

Herdt, G. 1987. *Guardians of the Flute*. New York: Columbia University Press.

Höfer, A. 1979. *The Caste Hierarchy and the State in Nepal: A Study of the Muluki Ain of 1854*. Innsbruck: Universitatsverlag Wagner.

Holland, D. and N. Quinn, eds. 1987. *Cultural Models in Language and Thought*. Cambridge: Cambridge University Press.

Holland, D. and J. Valsiner. 1988. "Cognition, Symbols, and Vygotsky's Developmental Psychology." *Ethos* 16 (3): 247–272.

Iltis, L. 1985. *The Swasthani Vrata: Newar Women and Ritual Nepal*. Ann Arbor, Mich.: University Microfilms International.

Inden, R. B. and R. W. Nicholas. 1977. *Kinship in Bengali Culture*. Chicago and London: University of Chicago Press.

Kakar, S. 1981. *The Inner World: A Psycho-Analystic Study of Childhood and Society in India*. 2d ed. Delhi: Oxford University Press.

Kane, P. V. 1953. *History of Dharmasastra*. Poona: Bhandarkar Oriental Research Institute.

Keeler, W. 1983. "Shame and Stage Fright in Java." *Ethos* 11: 152–165.

Keesing, R. 1987. "Anthropology as Interpretive Quest." *Current Anthropology* 28(2): 161-

Keyes, C. and E. V. Daniel, eds. 1983. *Karma: An Anthoropological Inquiry*. Berkeley: University of California Press.

Khare, R. S. 1978. "The One and the Many: Varna and Jati as a Symbolic Classification." *American Studies in the Anthropology of India*, S. Vatuk, ed. New Delhi: Manohar.

Kohlberg, L. 1963. "The Development of Children's Orientation Toward a Moral Order. I: Sequence in the Development of Moral Thought." *Vita Humana* 6: 11–33.

— 1969. "Stage and Sequence: The Cognitive-Developmental Approach to Socialization." In *Handbook of Socialization Theory and Research*, D. A. Goslin, ed. New York: Rand McNally.

— 1981. *The Philosophy of Moral Development: Moral Stages and the Idea of Justice*. San Francisco: Harper and Row.

Kolenda, P. 1964. "Religious Anxiety and Hindu Fate." In *Religion in South Asia*, E. Harper, ed. Seattle: University of Washington Press.

Ladd, J. 1957. *The Structure of a Moral Code.* Cambridge: Cambridge University Press.

Lakoff, G. and Z. Kövecses. 1987. "The Cognitive Model of Anger Inherent in American English." In *Cultural Models in Language and Thought,* D. Holland and N. Quinn, eds. Cambridge: Cambridge University Press.

Langacker, R. 1986. "Introduction to Cognitive Grammar." *Cognitive Science* 10: 1–40.

— 1987. *Foundations of Cognitive Grammar.* Stanford: Stanford University Press.

Levy, R. I. 1973. *Tahitians: Mind and Experience in the Society Islands.* Chicago and London: University of Chicago Press.

— 1977. "Tahitian Gentleness and Redundant Controls." In *The Socialization of Aggression,* A. Montague, ed. New York: Oxford University Press.

— 1984. "Emotion, Knowing, and Culture. In *Culture Theory: Essays on Mind, Self, and Emotion,* R. A. Shweder and R. A. LeVine, eds. New York: Cambridge University Press.

— 1990. *Mesocosm.* Berkeley: University of California Press.

Lewis, T. 1984. *The Tuladhars of Kathmandu: A Study of Buddhist Tradition in a Newar Merchant Community.* Ann Arbor: University Microfilms International.

Lindholm, C. 1982. *Generosity and Jealousy.* New York: Columbia University Press.

Lingat, R. 1973. *The Classical Law of India.* Berkeley: University of California Press.

Linger, D. 1992. *Dangerous Encounters.* Stanford: Stanford University Press.

— n.d. "Has Culture Theory Lost Its Minds?" Manuscript.

Lutz, C. 1988. *Unnatural Emotions.* Chicago: University of Chicago Press.

Lutz, C. and G. White. 1986. "The Anthropology of Emotions." *Annual Review of Anthropology* 15: 405–36.

Lutz, C. and L. Abu-Lughod. 1990. *Language and the Politics of Emotion.* Cambridge: Cambridge University Press.

Lynch, O. 1990a. "The Social Construction of Emotions." In *Divine Passions: The Social Construction of Emotion in India,* O. Lynch, ed. Berkeley: University of California Press.

— 1990b. "The Mastram: Emotion and Person Among Mathura's Chaubes." In *Divine Passions: The Social Construction of Emotion in India,* O. Lynch, ed. Berkeley: University of California Press.

McHugh, E. 1989. "Concepts of the Person Among the Gurungs of Nepal." *American Ethnologist* 16: 75–86.

320 * Bibliography

MacIntyre, A. 1984. *After Virtue*. Notre Dame, Ind.: University of Notre Dame Press.

Mackie, J. 1977. *Ethics: Inventing Right and Wrong*. New York: Penguin Books.

Madan, T. N. 1983. "The Ideology of the Householder Among the Kashmiri Pandits." In *Concepts of Person: Kinship, Caste, and Marriage in India*, A. Östör, L. Fruzzetti, and S. Barnett, eds. Delhi: Oxford University Press.

— 1987. *Non-Renunciation: Themes and Interpretations of Hindu Culture*. Delhi: Oxford University Press.

Mandelbaum, D. G. 1970. *Society in India*. 2 vols. Berkeley: University of California Press.

Mandler, G. 1975. *Mind and Emotion*. New York: Wilen.

Marriott, M. 1976a. "Hindu Transactions: Diversity Without Dualism." In *Transactions and Meaning*, B. Kapferer, ed. Philadelphia: Institute for the Study of Human Issues.

— 1976b. "Interpreting Indian Society: Diversity Without Dualism." *Journal of Asian Studies* 36: 189–195.

— 1990. "Constructing an Indian Ethnosociology." In *India Through Hindu Categories*, McKin Marriott, ed. *Contributions to Indian Sociology* (n.s.) 23(1). New Delhi: Sage Publications.

Marriott, M., ed. 1990. *India Through Hindu Categories*. New Delhi: Sage Publications.

Marriott, M. and R. B. Inden. 1974. "Caste Systems." In *Encyclopedia Britannica*, 15th ed., 3: 982–991.

— 1977. "Toward an Ethnosociology of South Asian Caste Systems." In *The New Wind*, Kenneth David, ed. The Hague: Mouton.

Mayer, A. 1981. *Culture and Morality*. Oxford: Oxford University Press.

Menon, U. and R. A. Shweder. n.d. "Kali's Tongue: Cultural Psychology and the Power of `Shame' in Orissa, India." Manuscript.

Mines, M. 1988. "Conceptualizing the Person: Hierarchical Society and Individual Autonomy in India." *American Anthropologist* 90: 568–579.

Myers, F. 1979. "Emotions and the Self: A Theory of Personhood and Political Order Among the Pintupi Aborigines." *Ethos* 7: 343–370.

— 1986. *Pintupi Country, Pintupi Self: Sentiment, Place, and Politics Among Western Desert Aborigines*. Washington, D.C.: Smithsonian Institution Press.

Narayan, K. 1989. *Storytellers, Saints, and Scoundrels: Folk Narrative in Hindu Religious Teaching*. Philadelphia: University of Pennsylvania Press.

Nepali, G. S. 1965. *The Newars: An Ethno-Sociological Study of a Himalayan Community*. Bombay: United Asia Publications.

Neufeldt, R. W., ed. 1986. *Karma and Rebirth: Post Classical Developments*. Albany: State University of New York Press.

Nisbett, R. and T. D. Wilson. 1970."Telling More than We Can Know: Verbal Reports on Mental Processes." *Psychological Review* 84: 231–59.

Obeyesekere, G. 1968. "Theodicy, Sin, and Salvation in a Sociology of Buddhism." In *Dialectic in Practical Religion*, E. R. Leach, ed. Cambridge: Cambridge University Press.

— 1981. *Medusa's Hair: An Essay on Personal Symbols and Religious Experiences*. Chicago: University of Chicago Press.

— 1984. *The Cult of the Goddess Pattini*. Chicago: University of Chicago Press.

O'Flaherty, W. D., ed. 1973. *Asceticism and Eroticism in the Mythology of Siva*. London: Oxford University Press.

— 1975. *The Origins of Evil in Hindu Mythology*. Berkeley: University of California Press.

— 1980. *Karma and Rebirth in Classical Indian Traditions*. Berkeley: University of California Press.

Ortner, S. 1973. "On Key Symbols." *American Anthropologist* 75: 1338–1346.

— 1984. "Theory in Anthropology Since the Sixties." *Comparative Studies in Society and History* 26(1): 126–166.

— 1989. *High Religion: A Cultural and Political History of Sherpa Buddhism*. Princeton: Princeton University Press.

Östör, A., L. Fruzzetti, and S. Barnett, eds. 1983. *Concepts of Person: Kinship, Caste, and Marriage in India*. Delhi: Oxford University Press.

Pandey, R. B. 1969. *Hindu Samskaras: Socio-Religious Study of the Hindu Sacraments*. Delhi: Motilal Banarsidass

Parish, S. 1991."The Sacred Mind: Newar Cultural Representations of Mental Life and the Production of Moral Consciousness." *Ethos* 19(3): 313–351.

— n.d. "Hierarchy and Its Discontents." Manuscript.

Peristiany, J. G., ed. 1966. *Honour and Shame*. Chicago: University of Chicago Press.

Piers, G. and M. Singer. 1971. *Shame and Guilt*. New York: Norton.

Quigley, D. 1986. "Introversion and Isogamy: Marriage Patterns of the Newars of Nepal." *Contributions to Indian Sociology* (n.s.) 20(1): 75–95.

Rawls, J. 1971. *A Theory of Justice*. Cambridge: Harvard University Press.

Read, K. 1955. "Morality and the Concept of the Person Among the Gahuku-Gama." *Oceania* 25: 233–282.

Reddy, M. 1979. "The Conduit Metaphor: A Case of Frame Conflict in Our Language About Language." In *Metaphor and Thought*, A. Ortony, ed. Cambridge: Cambridge University. Press.

Riesman, P. 1992. *First Find Your Child a Good Mother: The Construction of Self in Two African Communities*. New Brunswick, N.J.: Rutgers University Press.

Roland, A. 1982. "Toward a Psychoanalytical Psychology of Hierarchical Relations in Hindu India." *Ethos* 10(3): 232–253.

— 1988. *In Search of Self in India and Japan: Toward a Cross-Cultural Psychology*. Princeton: Princeton University Press.

Rosaldo, M. 1980. *Knowledge and Passion: Ilongot Notions of Self and Social Life*. Cambridge: Cambridge University Press.

— 1983. "The Shame of Headhunters and the Autonomy of the Self." *Ethos* 11: 135–57.

— 1984. "Toward an Anthropology of Self and Feeling." In *Culture Theory: Essays on Mind, Self, and Emotion*, R. A. Shweder and R. A. LeVine, eds. New York: Cambridge University Press.

Rosaldo, R. 1989. *Culture and Truth: The Remaking of Social Analysis*. Boston: Beacon Press.

Rosser, C. 1978. "The Newar Caste System." In *Caste and Kin in Nepal, India, and Ceylon*, C. von Fürer-Haimendorf, ed. New Delhi: Sterling.

Roy, M. 1972. *Bengali Women*. Chicago: University of Chicago Press.

Sabini, J. and M. Silver. 1982. *Moralities of Everyday Life*. Oxford: Oxford University Press.

Sapir, E. *Selected Writings in Language, Culture, and Personality*, D. Mandelbaum, ed. Berkeley: University of California Press, 1985. Includes:

— 1924. "Culture, Genuine and Spurious."

— 1929. "The Status of Linguistics as a Science."

— 1934. "The Emergence of the Concept of Personality in a Study of Culture."

Sartre, J. P. 1952. *Saint Genet: Actor and Martyr*. New York: Pantheon Books, 1963.

Schwartz, T. 1978. "Where Is the Culture? Personality as the Distributive Locus of Culture." In *The Making of Psychological Anthropology*, G. Spinlder, ed. Berkeley: University of California Press.

Sharma, U. 1965. "Theodicy and the Doctrine of Karma." *Man* 8(3): 347–364.

Shore, B. 1990. "Human Ambivalence and the Structuring of Moral Values." In *Moral Relativism*, Alan Page Fiske, ed. Special Issue of *Ethos* 18(2): 165–179.

Shweder, R. A. 1984. "Anthropology's Romantic Rebellion Against the Enlightenment, or There's More to Thinking than Reason and Evidence." In *Culture Theory: Essays on Mind, Self, and Emotion*, R. A. Shweder and R. A. LeVine, eds. Cambridge: Cambridge University Press.

— 1990. "Cultural Psychology—What Is It?" In *Cultural Psychology: Essays on Comparative Human Development*, J. Stigler, R. A. Shweder, and G. Herdt, eds. Cambridge: Cambridge University Press.

— 1992a (in preparation). "The Cultural Psychology of the Emotions." Prepared for *The Handbook of Emotions*, M. Lewis and J. Haviland, eds. New York: Guildford Publications.

— 1992b (in preparation). "You're Not Sick, You're Just in Love: Emotion as an Interpretive System." To appear in *Questions About Emotion*, P. Ekman and R. Davidson, eds.

Shweder, R. A. and E. Bourne. 1984. "Does the Concept of Person Vary Cross-Culturally?" In *Culture Theory: Essays on Mind, Self, and Emotion*, R. A. Shweder and R. A. LeVine, eds. Cambridge: Cambridge University Press.

Shweder, R. A., M. Mahapatra, and J. G. Miller. 1987. "Culture and Moral Development." In *The Emergence of Moral Concepts in Young Children*, J. Kagan and S. Lamb, eds. Chicago: University of Chicago Press.

Shweder, R. A. and J. G. Miller. 1985. "The Social Construction of the Person: How Is It possible?" In *The Social Construction of the Person*, K. J. Gergen and K. E. Davis, eds. New York: Springer-Verlag.

Shweder, R. A. and N. Much. 1987. "Determinations of Meaning: Discourse and Moral Socialization." In *Moral Development Through Social Interaction*, W. M. Kurtines and J. L. Gewirtz, eds. New York: Wiley.

Shweder, R. A., E. Turiel, and N. Much. 1981. "The Moral Intuitions of the Child." In *Social Cognitive Development: Frontiers and Possible Futures*, J. H. Flavell and L. Ross, eds. New York: Cambridge University Press.

Slusser, M. 1982. *Nepal Mandala: A Cultural Study of the Kathmandu Valley*, vol. 1. Princeton: Princeton University Press.

Solomon, R. 1984. "Getting Angry: The Jamesian Theory of Emotion in Anthropology." In *Culture Theory: Essays on Mind, Self, and Emotion*, R. A. Shweder and R. A. LeVine, eds. Berkeley: University of California Press.

Spiro, M. 1984. "Some Reflections on Cultural Determinism and Relativism with Special Reference to Emotion and Reason." In *Culture Theory: Essays on Mind, Self, and Emotion*, R. A. Shweder and R. A. LeVine, eds. Cambridge: Cambridge University Press.

Srinivas, M. N. 1976. *Remembered Village*. Berkeley: University of California Press.

Stigler, J. W., R. A. Shweder, and G. Herdt, eds. 1990. *Cultural Psychology: Essays on Comparative Human Development*. Cambridge: Cambridge University Press.

Strawson, P.F. 1959. *Individuals*. London: Methuen; reprinted 1965.

Tobin, J., D. Wu, and D. Davidson. 1989. *Preschool in Three Cultures*. New Haven: Yale University Press.

Toffin, G. 1975. "Ja(n)ko: A Newar Family Ceremony." *Contributions to Nepalese Studies*, 2(1): 47–56.

— 1978. "Intercaste Relations in a Newar Community." In *Himalayan Anthropology*, J. Fisher, ed. The Hague: Mouton.

— 1984. *Societe et Religion Chez Les Newar du Nepal*. Paris: Editions du Center National de la Recherche Scientifique.

Trawick, M. 1990. *Notes on Love in a Tamil Family*. Berkeley: University of California Press.

Turiel, E. 1983. *The Development of Social Knowledge: Morality and Convention*. New York: Cambridge University Press.

Turiel, E., M. Killen, and C. Helwig. 1987. "Morality: Its Structure, Functions, and Vagaries." In *The Emergence of Moral Concepts in Young Children*, J. Kagan and S. Lamb, eds. Chicago: University of Chicago Press.

Vergati, A. 1982. "Social Consequences of Marrying Visnu-Narayana: Primary Marriage Among the Newars of the Kathmandu Valley." *Contributions to Indian Studies* 16(2): 271–287.

Wadley, S. 1975. *Shakti: Power in the Conceptual Structure of Karimpur Religion*. University of Chicago Studies in Anthropology Series in Social, Cultural, and Linguistic Anthropology. Dept. of Anthropology, University of Chicago.

— 1983. "Vrats: Transformers of Destiny." In *Karma: An Anthropological Inquiry*, C. Keyes and E. V. Daniel, eds. Berkeley: University of California Press.

Wadley, S. and B. Derr. 1990. "Eating Sins in Karimpur." In *India Through Hindu Categories*, M. Marriott, ed. New Delhi: Sage Publications.

Wertsch, J. and C. A. Stone. 1985. "The Concept of Internalization in Vygotsky's Account of the Genesis of Higher Mental Functions. In *Culture, Communication, and Cognition*, J. Wertsch, ed. Cambridge: Cambridge University Press.

White, G. and J. Kirkpatrick, eds. 1985. *Person, Self, and Experience: Exploring Pacific Ethnopsychologies*. Berkeley: University of California Press.

Whiting, B. and J. Whiting. 1975. *Children of Six Cultures*. Cambridge: Harvard University Press.

Wierzbicka, A. 1986. "Human Emotions: Universal or Culture Specific?" *American Anthropologist* 88(3): 584–594.

Wikan, U. 1987. "Public Grace and Private Fears: Gaiety, Offense and Sorcery in Northern Bali." *Ethos* 15(4): 337–365.

Williams, R. 1977. *Marxism and Literature*. New York: Oxford University Press.

Wuthnow, R. 1987. *Meaning and Moral Order*. Berkeley: University of California Press.

INDEX

Designer: Linda Secondari
Text: 11/13 Cochin
Compositor: Columbia University Press
Printer: Edwards Brothers
Binder: Edwards Brothers

DATE DUE

APR 01 2002			
			Printed in USA

HIGHSMITH #45230